The Divorce Coach: How to Prepare and File for Divorce in Arizona

Welcome to learning how to do your own divorce in Arizona. This book is for anyone thinking about divorce or going through a divorce. Become empowered; know the law and the rules so you can make the best decisions for yourself and your family.

Best Law Firm can help you help yourself. We try to solve problems, not add to them. Call us today for a free telephone consultation or call and make an appointment for a legal consultation, document preparation, or mediation.

BEST LAW FIRM
Telephone: (480) 219-2433
14300 N. Northsight Blvd., #127
Scottsdale, AZ 85260
Website: www.bestlawaz.com
Email: thedivorcecoachaz@gmail.com

The Divorce Coach™

DATED MATERIAL: This book was printed in November 2010. Do not use an old Edition of this book. Out-of-date information can cause problems.

DISCLAIMER: Great care has been taken to make sure this information is correct. But the rules changes, the courts change, and sometimes the law changes. We make no warranty or assume any liability. You should always consult with an attorney if you have any questions.

ISBN: 9780615386713

Cover and inside design: Nathan Holaway

This book is dedicated to all our clients and judges who have taught us so much.

Thank you for your assistance and support in the creation and writing of this book: Katie Anderson, Peggy Larson, Lian Enger, Lesa Fritz, Lee C. Best, Eric Enger, Matt Weissner, Gerry LaFountain, Debbie Skopek, Christina Davis, Jan Ayres, Kathy Heasley, Mary Ann Abell, and Nathan Holaway.

"The best things in life are nearest. Breath in your nostrils, light in your eyes, flowers at your feet, duties at your hand, the path of right just before you. Then do not grasp at the stars, but do life's plain, common work as it comes, certain that daily duties and daily bread, are the sweetest things in life."

~ Robert Louis Stevenson

Table of Contents

Chapter One:

OVERVIEW AND INTRODUCTION

CHAPTER 1: OVERVIEW AND INTRODUCTION

OVERVIEW OF ARIZONA LAW, DO IT YOURSELF, AND ELIGIBILITY

Introduction

Divorce is one of the most devastating and life-changing events you will ever experience. You need to know what you are getting into and be involved in the process. There are decisions to make for yourself and your children. We urge you to become educated about this process, so you can make wise decisions. You most likely are reading this in an effort to save money, but even if you choose to retain an attorney, the Divorce Coach will empower you by providing the information necessary to help yourself. You most likely have heard all kinds of wrong information about divorce, custody, child support and alimony. You need to have the playbook, so you know what attorneys and the courts know. The differences between law and equity are both important concepts to understand. It is helpful to understand the decisions that you must make along the way and the possible outcomes. Once you see the full game plan, you might want to avoid this scenario entirely.

Before you decide about the "big game" (your divorce), you have to ask yourself if you are ready and whether you really want to be in the game. Divorce is a big decision; it should be taken seriously and thought through very carefully. We hope that you think carefully through each step of this process, keeping an open mind as you go. You do not want to end up at halftime or when the final whistle blows wishing you had never driven to the stadium. There is quite a bit of work involved in a divorce, but be aware that even though you may be exploring this option for your life, you can decide to stop at any time. It is not like jumping off a cliff; you can take baby steps until you know it is right for you. The beginning of a divorce is a reversible course. If you discover along the way that you would like to reconcile with your spouse, you should feel free to do so. You can actually quit anytime before the court signs the decree.

By reading this book, you are already way ahead of the game. You want to know the rules, the plays, the strategy and what the outcome of divorce will look like for your family. This book will assist you in figuring out what options you have and what decisions you need to make. Some people start and finish this process without any help from an attorney. That might work fine for some people; for others, not so well. Some people begin and then start feeling overwhelmed. This book will take the mystery out of the process. You want to do this right the first time: there are at least an equal number of post-divorce modifications filed in Arizona as there are first-time divorces. (Modifications are changes that are filed to change the original paperwork; often, these modifications are necessitated by mistakes made in the original divorce).

This introductory chapter outlines various aspects of the divorce process that are dealt with in more detail in succeeding chapters. A glossary of family law terms appears at the back of the book, as well as some useful Arizona statutes (laws) and a resource guide for online assistance in Arizona.

Options for Your Divorce

Many people think of only two options when they consider divorce: with an attorney or without an attorney (by yourself, *pro per*). Today, more and more people cannot afford to pay large advanced fees for an attorney. Yet, many people still need legal help short of retaining an attorney, from beginning to end. Family law rules and procedures can be complicated, so there are myriad costly mistakes that can be made, some of which you may not even realize for one or two years after your divorce.

Worst of all, how can you possibly know just *what* you do not know? Maricopa County has some valuable tools to use on their website, but you still may not understand the whole process or procedure. Best Law Firm offers alternatives to help people because we understand the need. Court staff and judges do a great job, but they are often overwhelmed and are not allowed to give you legal advice. So, you need to read this book, become familiar with the process and recognize what additional help you may require. There are many options available to you, depending on your circumstances and finances. Here are some options, from least to most expensive:

1. **Complete Do-It-Yourself:** Get the forms from the self-help desk at the courthouse or from the court website (see Resource Guide at back of book).

2. **Legal Consultation**: Pay an attorney by the hour to give you specific legal advice on your issues and then draft your own documents.

3. **Attorney Document Preparation**: Pay Best Law Firm to draft your documents on a flat fee basis, which includes a free attorney consultation, up to one hour.

4. **Attorney Document Preparation and Legal Consultation**: Combine number 2 and number 3, with flat fees for document preparation and hourly fees for consultation.

5. **Pay for an Attorney Anytime During the Process:** When you need some help, such as for a court hearing or when you need an attorney to be your advocate in mediation.

6. **Hire an Attorney as a Third Party Neutral Mediator:** To get you and your spouse over any impasse in making agreements.

7. **Retain an Attorney**: pay them an advanced fee (used to be called a retainer), and they will bill you by the hour, from beginning to end.

Clearly, the most expensive option is the last, which is to retain an attorney to handle everything for you. Your attorney will charge you an advance fee anywhere from $2,500 to $10,000 or more. Sometimes it seems as if retained counsel are trained to prepare for court and fight every step of the way, rather than sorting things out without going to trial. That is usually not a good idea for you, because it can increase the pain and the cost. The average cost of a divorce can be $18,000 for each side. So, unless you have money to burn, you might consider other options.

Following are two charts that outline the divorce process. The first exemplifies the typical process when both parties have an attorney. The second demonstrates the stages of litigation when the parties work together for their divorce.

Litigation Process When Both Parties Have Attorneys

Stage 1 Preparation

- Retain two attorneys
- Pay substantial advanced fees to each attorney
- Pay attorney to draft and file petition
- Serve documents on other party
- Pay attorney to draft Response to Petition
- Rule 49 disclosures

Stage 2 Litigation

- Each party collects identical documents (as outlined in Rule 49)
- Collect and send discovery to attorney to mail to other party's attorney
- Read costly emails and letters back and forth between the parties
- Motion the court if the other party does not disclose necessary documents
- Draft and file Motion for Temporary Orders
- Resolution Managment Conference with opposing attorney and client
- Engage in depositions
- Attend mediation or settlement conference
- Subpoena records (e.g., medical records, bank records)
- Participate in Parenting Conference or Custody Evaluation
- Endure mental health exams
- Possible drug testing
- Choose and pay additional money to hire experts

Stage 3 Explosion

- Prepare trial exhibits
- Draft a Joint Pretrial statement with opposing party
- Prepare witnesses
- Prepare experts
- Conduct trial (1 hour to 1 day long)

Litigation Process When the Parties Work Together During Their Divorce

Stage 1 Preparation

- Draft and file Petition documents
- Service of Process
- Wait for Response (20, 30 or 40 days depending on the type of service)
- Attend Parent Information Class
- Disclose all assets and debts

Stage 2 Negotiation

- Decide legal custody, physical custody, parenting time schedule, and child support
- Divide real property
- Divide personal property (e.g., cars, furniture)
- Divide bank accounts, investments, retirement and deferred compensation accounts
- Divide debts
- Court sets Early Resolution Conference/ Resolution Management Conference

Stage 3 Finalization

- Mediation or settlement conference
- Draft consent decree, parenting agreement and property settlement agreement (if needed)
- Must wait at least 60 days before filing a stipulated consent decree
- File consent decree

You can see the importance of educating yourself about the process; reading this book is a good first step. You may then want to hire a mediator to help resolve and negotiate your issues. At the end of a mediation, you can hire an attorney by the hour to give you specific legal advice about the negotiated agreement before you sign it.

Another option is to pay for legal consultations by the hour. An experienced attorney will give you specific legal advice about your case. After a legal consultation, you can also have an attorney draft your documents for a flat fee. Best Law offers all of these services and options are explained on our web site at www.*bestlawaz.com*.

The point is that there are various ways to go through this process, with an attorney and with mediation, without losing all your hard-earned money and suffering untold stress. This book will empower you with knowledge to help you with this transition in your life.

Arizona Family Law Courts

Family law courts are courts of equity. This means that the judges are asked to make decisions based on fairness. Arizona family law courts are governed by Arizona statutes (in Section 25, Marriage and Domestic Relations), by the Family Law Rules of Procedure and by the case law that has interpreted these statutes and rules. (Case law is what a court of appeals or the Arizona Supreme Court has determined is the actual meaning of the rules or statutes).

Sometimes, you will read a statute and think you know exactly what it means, but a court has decided another interpretation. Luckily, most cases and most divorces are not that complicated, and the parties do not need an in-depth legal analysis. If you find your case in a grey area and you do not know the answer, that is the time to consider consulting with an experienced attorney. If your question is straightforward, remember that hourly consultations are much cheaper than advance (retainer) fees.

Because family law courts are courts of equity, there are no juries. Although you may find a jury box in your family law courtroom, the judge alone will make all decisions in your case if there are disputed issues that must be litigated (brought to trial). However, there are ways to handle your entire divorce without ever having to set foot into a courtroom. You and your spouse can make all the decisions instead of a judge. That brings up our next point.

The High Road

Divorce is one of the most financially traumatic things you can go through. Money spent on getting mad or getting even is money wasted.

~Richard Wagner

"Always take the high road." You may be wondering why you should take the high road when you sense that your spouse will not. Our answer is that for this process to proceed smoothly, someone has to start out on the high road and ask the other side for good behavior. Remember; "You teach people how to treat you." This is exactly what you are doing to start your divorce.

If you do not display the utmost in courtesy and cooperation, you can be assured that the other side will not do so. Be careful how you begin this procedure, because it sets the tone for the entire process. If you begin in a hateful and hostile manner, you most likely will be met with the same. Even if you feel ill will toward your spouse, it is important to keep those feelings at bay during this time.

A hostile and mean-spirited start makes any retreat or reconciliation much more difficult. Also, a calm, reasoned beginning bodes well for settlement, negotiation and getting what you ultimately want and need. The legal divorce process is the wrong arena to fight your emotional battles; those belong elsewhere. The court system is not equipped to handle these emotional issues and you will find yourself disappointed if you place those expectations on the process, on the court, on your partner, or on your attorney.

Part of your decision-making at this crossroads is whether you need to obtain counsel or whether you and your partner would like to attempt negotiations to work out all your issues in mediation. Again, if you come out swinging, it is hard to reverse course. If, on the other hand, you attempt a gentler, kinder approach from the beginning, you can always change course, should it become necessary in order to protect your interests. If you try the softer approach at the beginning, you will have a better chance at negotiation later.

Often, people think that hard-nosed aggression is the only way to get what they want or need. We believe that you both can get what you deserve in a win-win situation, making the best of the bad situation of a divorce. There can be times when an aggressive approach is a necessary evil, but this book is written for people who want to get what they want in a fair, professional, kind and gentle manner.

You can break the stalemate and start off on the right foot. However, taking the high road is not enough. You must also understand Arizona law and your rights under that law. You must understand the legal process, its abilities and its limitations. Once you have that basic knowledge, you can continue collecting data and making sure that divorce is a step that you need to take; indeed, whether you even want to enter the arena.

Jurisdiction: Are you Eligible for the "Big Game"?

What are the Requirements to File for a Divorce in Arizona?

There are three requirements to file for divorce in Arizona.[i]

1. One party must have domiciled[ii] (lived) in Arizona for at least 90 days at the time the divorce was filed. If one party was stationed here in the military, that party must have been stationed in Arizona for 90 days.

2. Conciliation has been attempted and not worked or has not been attempted and will not work.

3: The marriage is irretrievably broken. The marriage is not a covenant marriage, as designated on your marriage certificate, or if it is a covenant marriage, the requirements have been met. Very few marriages are covenant and you would know if yours was. See questions at the end of Chapter 1.

What to Expect During the Game and an Overview of Arizona Law

Arizona is one of ten community property states in the U.S. All property acquired during marriage until the time one party is served with the divorce paperwork is presumed to be community property. All property acquired before marriage or after service of the dissolution paperwork is presumed to be separate property. All property acquired by gift, devise or will during marriage is also presumed to be separate property.

It is important that you familiarize yourself with Arizona community property law as you start this process. Knowledge of the law will take out the guesswork as to what each spouse is entitled. Most, if not all, of your property obtained during your marriage will be considered community.

The "petition" is what is filed to start the divorce and "service" is the official way that the other side is notified that the petition has been filed. The other side is called the "respondent." Service is discussed more fully in Chapter 4 and terms are defined in the glossary.

Community Property

Once property is considered community property, it must be divided equitably between the spouses. That is why it is important to determine the characterization of the property at the beginning of the divorce. There may be arguments about whether property is community or not, but most property is fairly easy to characterize. Property includes real property, which is land or a house. Property also includes your furniture, bank accounts, savings account, investments and deferred compensation plans, such as 401ks or IRAs.

Property for division, however, does not include Social Security benefits. Social Security law governs your Social Security account and it cannot be changed in a divorce decree. If you want to know specific information about your Social Security benefits, you might want to contact the Social Security Administration to find out about your specific income. Most property disputes revolve around houses. For some reason, many couples maintain complicated information regarding when and how a house was purchased and whose name is on the deed. It is important that you know if your name is on your house deed. You can check that on the Internet, courtesy of the Maricopa County Recorder's Office at *recorder.maricopa.gov/.*

Commingling

Another problem area is the commingling (mixing) of funds. For instance, if you received an inheritance during the marriage, the question becomes whether it is your sole and separate property. What if you put it in the bank and added your spouse's name to it; is it automatically community property? The short answer is probably not, but these kinds of complications are beyond the scope of this book and can be better answered with more facts and an attorney's advice.

Just remember, parties are always free to make their own decisions, without regard to what a judge would decide. For example, if you and your spouse decide that the money was and should be yours, you can make that agreement and the court will not disturb it. The exception to that rule is if there are children.

Even if there are agreements about the children, especially with regard to child support, the court will look very carefully at any agreement and proposed child support for the children to make sure that it is fair for the kids. Do not let this scare you; most agreements are approved by the court, because most negotiated agreements do prove to be fair for the children and the family.

Separation or Divorce?

A common question spouses have is whether they should get a legal separation instead of a divorce. The answer depends on what you are trying to achieve. If you want some financial protection, or you want to continue your health insurance, a legal separation will accomplish both. If you want to get remarried, you need to get divorced. A legal separation is almost identical to a divorce, except that in the end you are separated, not divorced. The procedures are identical in terms of filing, costs and the final agreements. Financial agreements in a legal separation will become the same financial agreements in a divorce. In other words, you cannot make a decision regarding finances in a legal separation and then change your mind about the same issues in a divorce. So, the financial agreements (or court decisions) *cannot be changed in a subsequent divorce action.*

Again, children are an exception to this general rule. You and your spouse can make certain decisions and agreements for a legal separation concerning children and then be free to renegotiate or litigate those decisions in a subsequent divorce. Be advised that there is some duplication if a legal separation turns into a divorce.

If the person who initially filed for a legal separation changes his or her mind and decides that he or she prefers a divorce, then that spouse may file an amended petition and request the dissolution of marriage. A new filing fee does not need to be paid. On the other hand, if one spouse files for a legal separation, the responsive party can convert the legal separation into a divorce by their responsive pleading (answer), without the consent of the party who filed first and without paying additional filing fees. They must still pay the answer fee, which is currently $256.00 in Maricopa County.

Do not be lulled into thinking you are getting legally separated when, in fact, your action may cause your partner to convert your separation filing into a divorce. If either party wants a divorce, there is nothing the other person can legally do to stop it.

Children and Custody

Here is a brief overview of custody, with more to come in later chapters. Custody might be easier to understand if you think of two kinds of custody for children: legal and physical. "Legal" refers to who makes decisions and "physical" refers to where the kids live and how they "visit" their parents. Do not be confused by some of the court forms; "joint legal custody" has nothing to do with where the kids live and how they visit. You will need to determine how you and your spouse share decision-making, where the kids live at what times, how to split holidays, and who pays what for the children.

These details are in Chapter 4, but rest assured, they can be worked out with parenting plans and honest discussions between the parents, always keeping the needs of your children paramount in your negotiations. There are as many parenting plans as there are families; you can be creative about what works for your family, remembering that a good spirit and flexibility will ensure that your children do not become the collateral damage of your divorce.

In 2001, Maricopa County drafted Model Parenting Guidelines that are very useful (See www.superiorcourt.gov/sscdocs/pdf/drv10h/pdf).

The court re-drafted new parenting guidelines, but they are not quite as helpful, because they omit all information about the developmental stages of children and how that interplays with their parenting schedules (see Chapter 4 and Resource Guide).

Joint Legal Custody

First, who makes major decisions for the children regarding their health, religion and education? Arizona law reads: "Joint legal custody means the condition under which both parents share legal custody and neither parent's rights are superior, except with respect to specified decisions as set forth by the court or the parents in the final judgment or order."

Sole Legal Custody

Sole legal custody means that one parent can make all the legal decisions for the child without the consent of the other parent. Some legal custody arrangements require the sole legal parent to consult with the other parent before decisions are made, but the sole legal parent can ultimately do what he or she thinks is in the best interest of the children.

Courts generally will consider awarding sole physical custody to one parent if the other parent is deemed unfit – for example, because of alcohol or drug dependency, a new partner who is unfit, or charges of child abuse or neglect. If this is your situation, you should consider seeking the advice of an attorney.

Joint Physical Custody and Primary Physical Custody

Joint physical custody means that the physical residence of the child is shared by the parents in a manner that assures that the child has substantially equal contact with both parents. The actual schedules that carry out this plan can vary with each family. Primary physical custody means that a parent has the child more than 50 percent of the time.

When the child already lives primarily with one parent and has parenting time with the other, generally the parent with whom the child primarily lives will have primary physical custody, with parenting time for the other parent. Joint physical custody is not always a good idea, especially when the child is an infant or toddler. You can also decide to have a graduated parenting schedule if you have very small children at the time of your divorce. That allows the schedule to take into consideration a growing child's changing needs.

Joint physical custody works best if parents live near each other, as it lessens the stress on children and allows them to maintain a somewhat normal routine. Joint custody has the advantages of assuring the children continuing contact and involvement with both parents and it alleviates some of the burdens of parenting for each parent.

There are, of course, disadvantages, which include shuttling children around; serious negative effects on children if there is parental non-cooperation or ill will; and the expense of maintaining two homes for the children. Nonetheless, joint physical custody might be the best option for children when both parents are in agreement and want to parent cooperatively.

Parenting Time

Parenting time is the scheduled time the parents are with their child. A variety of parenting time schedules can be set up by a family, and the schedules can be as different as the families who use them. Some popular parenting time schedules include alternating weeks or spending weekends and holidays with one parent and weekdays with the other.

Custody Thoughts

Do not let your children become your personal battleground! If you and your spouse are good parents, everything can be worked out. These admonishments do not apply to the parents who find themselves in the ugly predicament of dealing with domestic violence, child abuse, drug abuse or mental disorders. Those parents may need to fight to protect their children. This book and these comments are not directed to those tragic situations. Contact Best Law Firm or other experienced family law attorneys if you have any questions.

Spousal Maintenance

Spousal maintenance was formerly called alimony. There seem to be more misconceptions about spousal maintenance than almost any other area of divorce. You may have heard that you will get spousal maintenance because your spouse makes more money, but it is not that simple. Spousal maintenance can be highly discretionary, depending on the judge. In fact, it is often a mystery as to how spousal maintenance has been determined, seemingly very dependent on the court.

There is a statute to follow, but it is very factual and case-specifically dependent. That may be why it is hard to pinpoint rules and outcomes with any certainty. Spousal maintenance is most common in long-term marriages of 20 years or more, where one spouse has been a stay-at-home parent who never worked outside the home and has limited job skills and prospects, compared to the working spouse.

Specifically, the court first determines any one of the following: the spouse lacks sufficient property to provide for reasonable needs; the spouse is unable to be self-sufficient through appropriate employment (that is, "who takes care of whom" if age or condition precludes the spouse from working); the spouse contributed to the education of the other; or the marriage was of long duration and the spouse may be too old to be employed and self-sufficient.

Once the court determines that any of these factors are met, there are 13 other factors that the court may use in order to determine how much and how long maintenance should be paid. Even though there are 13 factors, often the court and the attorneys use a "spousal maintenance guideline" calculation. We share this calculation with you in Chapter 7. While not a set rule, these guidelines are a starting point for negotiations. If you go to court on this issue, the outcome is anyone's guess.

Frequently Asked Questions

How long will it take to get a divorce?
According to Arizona Revised Statute, Section 25-329 and Arizona Rules of Civil Procedure 4.1(c), you must wait at least 60 days from the date your spouse was served before going to court and having the Decree of Dissolution of Marriage entered. This assumes you and your spouse have agreed on the terms or your spouse is in default. When the spouses cannot agree on how to settle issues such as assets and debts, the length of time to get divorced can be longer. If you litigate the issues, it can take up to a year.

How much does it cost to file for divorce in Maricopa County?
The petitioner (initiator of the divorce) must pay Maricopa County $321 as of November, 2010, and the respondent pays $256 for filing an answer.

Who actually divorces me?
The divorce decree will be from the judge or commissioner assigned to your case who works for the Superior Court of Maricopa County, which is a state court.

Where do I file for my divorce?
There are currently four courthouse locations in Maricopa County, which are located Downtown, Northeast, Northwest and Southeast. These include:

Central Court Building	201 W. Jefferson, Phoenix, 85003-2243 Family Court Administration: (602) 506-1561
Old Courthouse	125 W. Washington, Phoenix, 85003-2243 Family Court Administration: (602) 506-1561
Northeast Courthouse	18380 N. 40th Street, Phoenix, 85032 (602) 372-7601
Southwest Regional Center	4264 W. Tierra Buena Lane, Surprise, 85374 (602) 372-9400

Southeast Court	222 E. Javelina Ave., Mesa, 85210 (602) 506-2020

You can file your documents at any courthouse, but the judge assigned to your case will most likely work in the courthouse closest to the home address of the petitioner (the person who files first).

Other courthouses in the state of Arizona are listed in Appendix D.

Can my spouse and I file for divorce together?
No. Arizona does not have a provision for any type of joint filing.

Am I considered the "bad guy" if I file first?
Someone has to be the petitioner and someone has to be the respondent. There is no advantage or disadvantage to either, other than perhaps assignment of the courthouse nearest to the petitioner.

What if my spouse filed and I do not want to get divorced?
You cannot stop your spouse from divorcing you, but you can file a request with the court to order a one-hour conciliation meeting to try and reconcile. These rules change; depending on the budget, there may be a fee associated with reconciliation. During this "time out" for 60 days, there can be no "discovery" (see glossary) taking place.

Do I need an attorney for my divorce?
Arizona law allows you to do this yourself. You are considered *pro se* or *pro per;* you must follow all the same rules as parties with attorneys. You may have to go into a courtroom, but you are held to the standard of an attorney. Maricopa County has a self-help web site at:
http://www.superiorcourt.maricopa.gov/SuperiorCourt/Self-ServiceCenter/index.asp.
Even if you do this yourself, it is always a good idea to have an attorney review your work and give you legal advice.

Does it matter if my spouse was having an affair?
No. Arizona is a "no-fault" state, which means that the court does not require one spouse to prove blame or responsibility in order to end the marriage. However, in Covenant Marriage (see below), a court will not enter a decree of dissolution of marriage unless certain criteria are met. (See Arizona Revised Statute, Section 25-903 for the specific requirements).

What is a Covenant Marriage?
You will most likely know if you have one of these; it is an optional type of marriage created by the state legislature that requires partners to complete marital counseling prior to marrying and to sign a special declaration to obtain a marriage license. In a covenant marriage, a legal separation or divorce may be granted only for certain reasons listed in state law. The law regarding covenant

marriages can be found in Sections 25-901 through 25-906 of the Arizona Revised Statutes.

Is it possible to represent myself in court?

Yes, as it is not a requirement that you have an attorney to represent you in divorce proceedings. However, the same rules and procedures apply whether you have an attorney or not, which means all papers must be correctly completed and filed on time.

What if I change my mind after starting a divorce?

If you and your spouse decide to stay married, the divorce case can be canceled or dismissed by filing a request with the Clerk of Superior Court and signed by both parties.

What is a divorce "decree?"

Arizona Revised Statutes §25-312 and §35-325 provide that a Decree of Dissolution of Marriage is the final order of the court which makes each party a single person again, and includes separate orders concerning child custody and visitation, child support, division of property and debts, spousal maintenance and any other appropriate orders. The decree is the final order of the court, legally ending the marriage. Spouses are not divorced until the court grants the divorce and the decree is signed by the judge. A Decree of Dissolution is a court order and can be enforced just as any other order of the court. A certified or duplicate copy of the decree can be obtained from the Clerk of Superior Court for a small fee.

Where do I get a divorce?

In Arizona, only the Superior Court (a state court) can grant a divorce. To get a divorce, one spouse must start a court case in the Superior Court. Although the Superior Court has at least one facility in each Arizona county, a court case to end a marriage must be started in the county where the person requesting the divorce lives.

Who can start a divorce case?

In Arizona, either spouse can ask the court for a divorce. A divorce is not awarded to either spouse; rather, it simply changes the status of the marriage relationship.

What if I do not have money to pay the filing or response fee?

You may request that the court waive or postpone payment of the filing or response fees. Forms must be completed and signed by you and submitted to the court. The forms are free of charge and are available in the office of the Clerk of Superior Court.

When is my dissolution final? (A.R.S. §25-325)
Your dissolution of marriage is final after the judge or commissioner signs the decree and files it with the Clerk of the Court.

Will I have a jury if my divorce proceeds to trial?
No, even if your case is litigated, you will not have a jury. One judge will make all the decisions that the parties cannot agree on.

When can we start mediation?
You can start this at anytime, even before you file.

I cannot afford health insurance. If I file for divorce, can my husband stop paying for it while we are in the divorce proceedings?
No. After one spouse is served with the dissolution or legal separation documents, no insurance of any kind can be cancelled or modified to the detriment of the other spouse. You must read the paperwork that comes with the divorce filings. There is a preliminary injunction that controls certain actions and behaviors after a divorce is served.

Chapter Two:

PREPARING FOR THE "BIG GAME"

CHAPTER 2: PREPARING FOR THE "BIG GAME"

HOW DO I WANT TO PLAY? (Options of document preparation, mediation, or litigation. How much help do you need or want?)

Let's be blunt: If you hire a divorce lawyer today, there is a good chance you will hire a bankruptcy lawyer within two or three years.[iii]

Your Goals, Our Guidance

You're reading this book to save money; you want what is best for your family, even while recognizing that this divorce is necessary. We are here to help you figure out your rights, your issues, your choices and your solutions. We are experienced family law attorneys who have seen first-hand the devastation and damage caused when people act out their emotional issues in a divorce through the legal system. In this chapter, we explain how to conduct your own divorce and when, if necessary, to seek professional help.

We repeat: "Always take the high road." That is not always easy, and it may seem impossible while going through a divorce. But this book was written to help you do exactly that: save time, money, and stress. Of course, it takes two people to make agreements, resolve issues and negotiate conflict. Emotional issues from a divorce are better handled outside the legal system, not through an expensive adversarial process that is ill equipped to handle the delicate details of a family in turmoil. We often ask a judge to listen to an hour or two of evidence and then make lifelong decisions for people that he or she has never met prior to that day in court. That may not seem right but it is the only system we have. So, if you want more control over your destiny, keep reading.

Do It Yourself

What exactly does it mean to go through your own divorce without an attorney? It means that you will file your paperwork, understand the rules and follow the law; just as if you were an attorney. That may sound a bit daunting at first, but not if you follow these step-by-step procedures. If controversy and arguments arise, do not despair: you may still be able to salvage your ability to go through this without an attorney by understanding and outlining your issues, and perhaps using a mediator. A mediator is a neutral third party who will visit with you and help you and your partner work out any disagreements that you are having as you go through this process.

The court will also hold you to the standard of an attorney, so if you are going to do this without an attorney, learn the rules and procedures of the court so you are educated about what is going on.

Why Would You Want to do Your Own Divorce?

The simplest answer may be money: divorce attorneys are not cheap. Using your attorney as a sword to duel with your partner is very expensive. Actually, it is ridiculously expensive. So, if you and your partner have any inclination to work things out, and you most likely will be able to, you should try to do part, if not all, of your divorce yourselves. You may need help along the way, but that does not preclude you from doing much of it yourself. If you run into bumps, you can always use an attorney for a consultation in a limited scope representation or as a mediator.

For instance, you can pay an attorney at Best Law Firm for one hour of time to give you legal advice and to advocate for you. Or, at our firm, you can hire an experienced mediator to avoid court. A mediator does not give legal advice or take sides, but is a paid neutral party who consults with you and your partner together. Having practiced family law in Arizona courts, we know you are better off if you can avoid a messy courtroom confrontation. (See www.bestlawaz.com).

You can do your divorce yourself or with as much help as you want. You can do it spending as little or as much money as you decide. You can handle it with as much or as little conflict as you allow yourself to participate in. Let's go through all the various options of handling a divorce, which include doing it yourself, using document preparation services, hourly legal consultations, mediation and of course, with lawyers.

Forms and Filing for Doing It Yourself

There are self-help forms at the courthouses and you can find them online at superiorcourt.maricopa.gov/. There are also explanations about these forms on that website. While a do-it-yourself divorce may work for some, it can be dangerous and disastrous for others. At a minimum, you should review the forms and the instructions and review this book. If you have some questions after reading this book, you might want to call Best Law Firm for an attorney consultation or to have someone fill out the forms for you for a flat fee.

Document Preparation by an Attorney

Another option in preparing for divorce is to have Best Law Firm draft your documents for a flat fee (see www.bestlawaz.com). If you are interested in this type of service, we provide potential clients with a Divorce Coach questionnaire and we can complete the necessary documents for filing pertinent to your specific situation, often within 24 hours. Our document preparation is handled by attorneys who understand the legal requirements of your case.

Also, if you have any questions, you can call our office and speak with an attorney specifically about your case and your needs. A free consultation (up to one hour) comes with the flat fee package for your initial document preparation. Another option is to pay for hour long attorney consultations as needed. Note: once you consult with an attorney, that same attorney cannot act as a mediator in your case, because that would be a conflict of interest. Any case can be mediated, even though one or both parties has an attorney.

Why Come to Us?

Individuals often come to us after trying to do it alone or after experiencing a court disaster. But some mistakes cannot be undone.

It is easy to fall into the trap of thinking that you can handle your situation on your own. Do-It-Yourself forms make legal matters seem very simple. Unfortunately, there are many dangers to using these template legal forms. Because of the potential dangers, there are several reasons why people should come to an attorney to have their legal documents prepared:

1. You are held to the standard of an attorney when you deal with the legal system.
2. You simply do not know what you do not know, and not knowing can lead to costly mistakes that can haunt you for years.
3. You may think that you understand the forms, but you may not understand the legal significance of what you are doing and the long-term effects it can have. A form cannot anticipate future problems and provide protection. A form cannot counsel you about additional legal documents you may need.
4. Non-lawyers who prepare documents cannot give you legal advice, suggest strategies, or advise you about your rights.

As experienced attorneys, we are able to provide the guidance you need to avoid problems. Our clients benefit from peace of mind, knowing an experienced attorney is preparing their legal documents and answering their questions, without the high costs associated with a lawyer who does everything.

Mediation

This is a negotiated process where you and your partner/spouse hire a neutral third party mediator, usually an attorney, to negotiate and work through all the issues that need to be resolved to end your marriage or resolve your disputes. Best Law Firm provides this kinder, gentler approach to resolving family disputes.

The parties come to the office, where they meet together or in separate areas. Mediation is conducted in a comfortable office atmosphere. Sometimes parties can make all their agreements in one meeting; sometimes it takes several meetings over one to two months.

Best Law Firm can also provide document preparation services to document the decisions made during the mediation. A Memorandum of Understanding is included in the price of the mediation, so the parties have a signed, legally enforceable settlement outlining their agreements. Parties can choose to mediate *either before or after* they file for the divorce. If you choose mediation prior to the court filing, you can make decisions in your own time frame. Once you file for dissolution, you must follow all the court rules, and you could be required to go to court before you are ready.

The court must set an Early Resolution Management Conference (if neither party has an attorney) or a Resolution Management Conference (if at least one party has an attorney) shortly after you file, so unless you have settled by that date, the court will require you to appear in court and file the required resolution statement before your court hearing. To avoid any rush, you might want to consider mediation before you file. After the mediation, our office can then help you file all the documents required for starting the proceedings and for finalizing your divorce (such as the decree, the property settlement agreement, the parenting agreement, the child support worksheet and the spousal maintenance worksheet as explained in Chapter 8).

Parties can mediate their divorce on their own, but most people find it helpful to have some assistance. A good mediator will make sure that your personal objectives are clear to you so they can be clearly communicated to your partner. It is imperative that you *know what you are legally entitled to, before you can make an educated request* for what you want. There will be some give-and-take and some negotiated points, but there are certain black-and-white issues that are not negotiable, even if you go to court.

For instance, it is black letter law that you are entitled to half of any deferred compensation plan that was earned during the marriage. The negotiations, however, may end up giving one partner all of a retirement plan in exchange for an equal or almost equal asset, such as a car or house. The pie needs to be divided equally when all is said and done, but who gets what piece is what negotiation is all about. Sometimes, neither party wants the pie divided exactly down the middle. *It is important to choose a mediator who knows Arizona law and has courtroom experience.*

Frequently Asked Questions

Can traditional document preparation services help me?
Document preparation services cannot provide you with legal advice. So, unless you know the law and the procedures, you could make some devastating mistakes by filling out forms without understanding your rights. Best Law Firm's document preparation is conducted by an experienced attorney.

How much does document preparation cost?
You may call our law firm to find out our current specials and prices. If you purchased this book, you are entitled to a discount on a package deal. You are also entitled to a free consultation (up to one hour) with an attorney.

How long does it take for document preparation?
We can finalize documents within 24 hours.

How do I get started for a document preparation?
Just call our office at (480) 219-2433 or go to our website, "Start Your Divorce Now," and fill out the Divorce Coach questionnaire. After we receive your completed questionnaire and payment we will finish your documents, usually within 24 hours, and provide them to you online. Or, you can pick them up at our office or we can simply mail them to you.

How do I get a one-hour attorney consultation?
Just call our office at (480) 219-2433. We will meet with you as soon as possible, usually within 48 hours if you are available. We make ourselves available: we know how much stress and anxiety you are feeling. We can also conduct legal consultations over the phone or by SKYPE, as long as a limited scope fee agreement is signed and an hourly fee is paid.

Can I call for a telephone consultation?
We provide free telephone consultations to go over our services and the general legal issues and processes involved in a divorce in Arizona. These phone calls do not give legal advice to you. You can receive legal advice by requesting a "meeting" (this can be in person, or by SKYPE or telephone) with an attorney, who will provide you with a limited-scope fee agreement for specific legal advice billed at an hourly fee. If you have any questions to begin with, please call our office at (480) 219-2433.

What is a mediator?
A mediator is a neutral third party who can help you negotiate and resolve your divorce.

Can a non-lawyer be a mediator?
Yes, but they do not always have the legal experience to know what really happens in a courtroom. Sometimes, parties are more eager to cooperate and negotiate when they recognize how nasty and unpredictable it is to litigate.

Should my mediator be an attorney and practice law?
We think it helps a great deal when we mediate. We know what can and will happen in court with certain issues and with certain judges, but we also know that sometimes there is no predicting what the court will do with particular facts and issues. Because it can be a crapshoot, an attorney understands the risk/reward of going to trial.

Can an attorney help me if I get stuck after trying to fill out the online forms?
Yes, you can make an appointment and meet with an attorney on an hourly basis.

Are there pitfalls that I need to be aware of?
Yes, they are numerous. If you have questions, you should consult an attorney.

Will the judge help me?
Judges are very good, but they are not allowed to give you legal advice. They do the best they can within their own limitations imposed by the court.

Can I have an attorney and a mediator?
Yes, you can mediate with or without an attorney. You can mediate all your issues and then have the agreement reviewed by an attorney before signing it.

Can a paralegal draft my documents?
Yes, but this can be dangerous. There are paralegals who offer this service, but they cannot give you legal advice, nor are they experienced in litigation to prevent certain mistakes and problems.

How much does a mediator cost?
Most mediators charge by the hour, anywhere from $200 to $400. Most mediators do not ask for retainers.

How much does it cost to have someone draft my documents?
This is a flat fee and you will know and agree to the price before the work is started. At Best Law Firm, our prices vary, depending on the documents. You can find this information on our website, along with a price list and questionnaire.

You can complete the questionnaire and return it, and we will provide you with your documents within 24 hours. Also, we offer an attorney consultation with every initial filing package or decree package. Best Law Firm offers a Limited Scope Fee Agreement for these services.

Chapter Three:

SHOULD I GET A DIVORCE OR LEGAL SEPARATION?

CHAPTER 3: SHOULD I GET A DIVORCE OR LEGAL SEPARATION?

The most difficult thing is the decision to act, the rest is merely tenacity. The fears are paper tigers. You can do anything you decide to do. You can act to change and control your life; and the procedure, the process is its own reward.

~Amelia Earhart

A common question spouses have is whether they should get a legal separation instead of a divorce. The answer depends on what you are trying to achieve. If you want some financial protection or you want to continue your health insurance, a legal separation will likely accomplish both. If you want to get remarried, you need to get divorced. It is also common for a spouse to file for a legal separation to stop the debts incurred by the other spouse from becoming a community debt. When a petition for a legal separation is filed and served, each party is then responsible for any debt incurred after that service date.

A legal separation is almost identical to a divorce, except at the end, you are separated and not divorced. The procedures are identical in terms of filing, costs, and the final agreements regarding finances. Financial agreements in a legal separation will become the same financial agreements in a divorce. In other words, you cannot make a decision regarding finances in a legal separation and then change your mind about the same issues in a divorce, unless both parties agree. The financial agreements in a legal separation cannot be changed in a subsequent divorce action, except by agreement of the parties.

Children and Legal Separation

If, regarding children, you want to have different decisions in a divorce than were made in a legal separation, you can do so. Children are an exception to the general rule that decisions in a legal separation are final in a divorce. You and your spouse can make certain decisions and agreements for a legal separation concerning children, and you are then free to renegotiate or litigate those decisions in a subsequent divorce. Please recognize that there is some duplication of documents, times and litigation expense if a legal separation turns into subsequent divorce.

If the person who filed for a legal separation decides that he or she prefers a divorce, then that spouse may file a petition to modify the original petition and request a dissolution instead. If one spouse files for a legal separation, however, and the other party wants a divorce, that responsive party can convert the legal separation into a divorce without the consent of the party who filed first, and without paying additional filing fees.

Do not be lulled into thinking you are just getting separated, when your initiating separation may, in fact, cause your partner to respond with a divorce. You may find yourself trying to stop a runaway train if you file for a legal separation, falsely believing that a divorce cannot result from your initial filing. Use caution in filing any papers, and never use it as an attention-getting device, because it may go further than you wanted. Remember, if either party wants a divorce, there is nothing you can legally do to stop it.

Frequently Asked Questions

What is the difference between a legal separation and a divorce in Arizona?
An Arizona legal separation and an Arizona divorce are almost identical. In fact, there are more similarities than differences. In both cases, the court will issue final orders dividing the spouses' debts and assets, enter custody and parenting time orders regarding the parties' children and enter child support and spousal maintenance orders. Additionally, the community property rights and obligations previously existing between the spouses are terminated. The only significant difference between a divorce and legal separation in Arizona is that the parties are not legally restored to the status of single persons and may not, therefore, remarry.

Why would someone choose a legal separation over a divorce in Arizona?
Although there are many personal reasons a person may seek a legal separation, as opposed to a divorce, some of those reasons may be: religion, health insurance and debts, such as gambling. Also, circumstances may exist in which a spouse has a significant physical ailment that would not be covered by his or her health insurance plan or by some other plan if the parties were divorced. In some circumstances, a legal separation may provide a more suitable alternative to a divorce.

How do I obtain a legal separation in Arizona?
A legal separation in Arizona is obtained in the same manner as a divorce. In both cases, an initial petition is filed with the Superior Court. The petition is served on the other spouse, and the parties either submit a settlement agreement resolving all of the issues in the case, or the issues are presented to the court at a trial, after which, the judge issues final orders resolving the issues in the case. The procedural steps in an Arizona legal separation case are identical to the steps necessary to complete a divorce.

May I stop an Arizona legal separation proceeding?
You may only stop a legal separation proceeding if the other party has not been served with the petition or the other person has been served with that petition,

but he or she agrees for the case to be dismissed. In either case, the dismissal of the legal separation must occur before the court enters a final Decree of Legal Separation.

May I later convert an Arizona legal separation to a divorce?
You may always convert an Arizona legal separation to a divorce at any time. In fact, you may convert the legal separation to a divorce before or after the final Decree of Legal Separation is issued by the court.

What does the court do if one spouse seeks a legal separation and the other spouse seeks a divorce?
The court has no discretion when one spouse seeks a legal separation and the other spouse asks the court to enter a divorce. The court must allow the divorce to proceed if either spouse requests a divorce.

How do I start a legal separation?
To start a legal separation, one party needs to file a petition for legal separation. There are two different petitions; one for families with children and one for families without children. The petition must be served on the other party, just as in a dissolution.

Who gets to live in the home and how are bills paid during the period the legal separation is being prosecuted?
These issues can be addressed by agreement between the parties, but if you do not have agreements, the court can grant temporary orders to address specifically those and other issues. These temporary orders will govern until the case is finished. This is the same process in a dissolution.

What happens if I get served with separation papers?
Many people simply ignore the papers they receive, or simply take the word of the other spouse that they do not have to do anything. Ignoring the paperwork and failing to file a response can lead to disaster. Despite how much you may want to cooperate with your spouse, or be unable to react due to the emotional stress, you cannot ignore the paperwork. A divorce or separation is like any other civil lawsuit. If you do not respond, you will be in default and can lose many rights that could have protected you.

Does it matter who files first?
In Maricopa County, the party who files first will have his or her case set in the courthouse nearest their address. There are four courthouses in the Valley and you may prefer being in one location rather than another.

Do all separations have to go to trial?
No, in fact the majority of separations in Arizona eventually settle without the need to go to a final trial. However, if you are unhappy with the settlement proposals being made by your spouse or they are refusing to accept your proposals, then you may need to mediate, obtain counsel, or go to trial.

How are property and debts divided in a legal separation?

Arizona is a community property state. This means that any property that was obtained, income acquired or debt incurred during the marriage will most likely be divided evenly. Property that was gifted to or inherited by one spouse or was owned by a spouse prior to the marriage is considered separate property and may be protected from the claims of the other spouse. This is the same law that applies to property in a dissolution. (Please see Chapter 6.)

Chapter Four:

CHILDREN AND CUSTODY

CHAPTER 4: CHILDREN AND CUSTODY

If you bungle raising your children, not much else you do in life really matters. ~*Jackie Onassis*

Shattered

I came home from school and the house was really quiet. I put my backpack on the dining room table. There was a gloom in the air that I did not understand. The house seemed eerie. Then I saw my mom and dad sitting in the living room. My mom sat on the short couch near the window and my dad sat on the big couch by the porch.

"Christopher," my mom said. Her voice sounded odd. "Will you go upstairs and get your sister, please?" I told her that I would, so I started up the stairs to tell my sister to come down to the living room. My sister was reading a book on her bed and I told her that Mom wanted her downstairs. We slowly walked down the steps. It was like there was dread in the air. When we got to the living room, my mom asked us to sit down. We did. My mom started speaking but I could barely hear her. She kept speaking anyway and my head started to spin. "Your father and I are getting a divorce," she told us. My father added that yes, they were getting a divorce. I know they kept talking, but I could not keep listening. I ran from one couch to the other, back and forth, yelling "No, no, no." I think my sister was crying.

I did know one thing. My life as I knew it had ended when I was 5 years old. My life would never be the same again. (By Christopher, age 10)

What About the Children?

Our guess is that you are very concerned about how your divorce will affect your children, which is why you are reading this book, to figure out how to be part of an uncontested divorce. Perhaps all you need to know can be clarified with this story by Cindy Best:

I was a mediator in a case not long ago where the divorced parents were fighting over an issue that, along with many others, had been an ongoing battle for more than 10 years. I thought for days about how to settle this case, but I had no idea really how to help these parents. On the day of the mediation, as I drove to the office, two questions came to mind that I needed to ask these parents:

1. What is the worst thing that ever happened to your children?
2. What is the second-worst thing that ever happened to your children?

I spoke with the father in a separate conference room and I asked him these two questions. He replied, "the worst thing that ever happened to our children is our divorce. The second-worst thing that ever happened is the constant conflict after the divorce." Then he added, "I have those two things reversed."

When I spoke with the mother, she answered, "the worst thing that ever happened to our children has been the conflict since the divorce. The second worst thing was the divorce."

These two wise parents knew what they had been doing to their children for more than 10 years! But they could not stop. However, on this day, they did. Once they both recognized and admitted what they had been doing to their children, they settled their ongoing issue. They knew that nothing was more important than their children, but I fear that it was too late for their kids, the damage had been done. Children who grow up in constant conflict may turn to drugs, drop out of school, become abusers or victims of abuse. Their lives may be adversely affected forever; they have been robbed of their childhood. Maybe this story will help you and your children. For the sake of your children and their future happiness, please avoid the conflict. Your interests are not the most important issue in your divorce, your children's interests are. It really is all about them.

Who Will Take Care of the Children and Where Will They Live?

Where will your children live and who will make decisions about them? These are the two major issues that you and the other parent must decide. This will depend on how far apart you live from each other, how old your children are, school hours, work hours, the care provider situation, the family support system and to some extent, the desires of the children. You are trying to do what is in your children's best interests. This has been defined by statute in Arizona: A.R.S. 25-403 in the appendix.

This statute is what the judge uses if you have to litigate legal or physical custody. You, as the parents, know this information intuitively if you are honest with yourselves and you place the needs of your children above your needs. You and your spouse can make agreements that are in the best interests of your children without court intervention.

Legal and Physical Custody

The courts do not always explain custody in terms of legal and physical custody, but it is easier to grasp when you understand the two separate concepts. One is legal custody, or who makes the legal decisions for your children. It is either joint or sole custody. In joint custody, you and the other parent will make all decisions together, after consultation. In sole legal custody, one parent has the legal right to make all decisions (see questionnaire at the end of this chapter).

Physical Custody and Parenting Time: Joint Physical Custody or Primary Physical Custody

Physical custody involves where the children live and when they see each parent. Again, it can be joint physical custody, in which the children live with each parent approximately the same amount of time. If one parent has primary legal custody, then the other parent has parenting time. This is a less than 50-50 parenting schedule. So, the two choices are either joint physical custody or primary physical custody, with parenting time for the other parent. Legal and physical custody can be handled in a variety of ways. You can have sole legal and joint physical custody. You can also have joint legal custody and one-parent, primary physical custody (worksheets appear at the end of the chapter).

Specific Issues

You and the other parent will need to determine how you share decision-making, how you decide, what to do when you cannot decide, where the kids live at what times, how to split holidays, who pays for the children, who pays for extra-curricular activities and who picks them up and drops them off. These details can be worked out with parenting plans and honest discussions between the parents, always keeping the needs of your children paramount in your negotiations. There are as many parenting plans as there are families. You can be creative for what works for your family, remembering that a good spirit and flexibility will ensure that your children do not become the collateral damage of your divorce.

Legal Custody Issues

Hypothetically, let's say that your child needs braces. Can you get them, and who pays? What if you want your children to be raised Catholic, but your spouse refuses. What if you want your son to play football, but your spouse objects that it is on "her time." Your son needs medication for ADD, but your spouse refuses to allow it. These problems are almost infinite and can cost a great deal of anguish, anxiety and conflict if they are not dealt with upfront during the divorce. The last thing your child needs is a decade or so of conflict. The divorce is difficult enough, and chronic conflict can have a lifelong, devastating impact. So, how do you resolve these issues?

Legal custody is the right of a parent to make important decisions regarding education, health, recreation and religion. Joint legal custody leaves these decisions up to the parents together. That presents the inevitable problem of who gets to break the tie? You must put in a tiebreaker provision in your parenting agreement. For instance, you could mediate all ties, before going back to court. Your mediator in this situation can be an attorney, pastor, grandparent, social worker, counselor, psychologist or anyone else who can help you. You could decide that one parent can break the tie in two matters and the other parent breaks the tie in the other two areas. You could attempt to negotiate as many of these issues during the divorce as you can anticipate.

If you know your child will need braces, plan for it now and negotiate it now, before anger or other future partners muddy up the water. Let's say that you know your child will play soccer and it will be played on Saturdays. Saturdays are both Mom's and Dad's parenting time on every other weekend. You can write into your agreement that sports that fall on the non-residential parent's parenting time can be made up by agreement of the parties. Soccer that falls on both parents' time alternately, when the parents have 50-50 parenting time, will not be a reason to keep the child out of sports and there will be no make-up time. If you know that one grandparent always takes the kids to the lake in the summer for a week, write that into the agreement now. But do not put your child in the middle. We repeat: do not put your child in the middle. EVER!

Best Law Firm has a joint parenting agreement that will help anticipate these issues. You should attach such an agreement to your decree, because it is required by the court. (Please see the partial example in this book or our website for document drafting services, where we can draft a joint parenting agreement specifically tailored to your family). We can draft a parenting agreement for a flat fee, either implementing what you and your partner have agreed to, or what has been mutually negotiated through mediation with our attorneys.

The more you can decide now and put in writing during the divorce process, the less chance you have of future disagreements. The last thing in the world you want is to argue over every decision about every sport or every activity your child ever participates in. Remember, it is not "your" parenting time, it is your child's time and his or her childhood. You will have a much better relationship with your child if you are not thwarting his or her every move, just because it is inconvenient for you.

Assistance with Parenting Plans and Agreements

Our experienced attorneys at Best Law can help you and your spouse draft a negotiated parenting and custody agreement. We can provide insight and anticipate future problems. We provide this service at an hourly rate and provide you with a court-approved form at the conclusion that can be filed with the court, along with your decree.

Every parenting plan needs:

1. Each parent's rights and responsibilities for the personal care of the child and for decisions in areas such as education, health care and religious training.
2. A schedule of the physical residence of the child, including holidays and school vacations.

3. A procedure by which proposed changes, disputes and alleged breaches may be mediated or resolved, which may include the use of conciliation services or private counseling.
4. A procedure for periodic review of the plan's terms by the parents.
5. A statement that the parties understand that joint custody does not necessarily mean equal parenting time.

Parenting Time

Joint Physical Custody

As described in Chapter 1, joint physical custody means that the physical residence of the child is shared by both parents almost equally. Where the child lives primarily with one parent and has visitation (now called parenting time) with the other, generally, the parent with whom the child primarily lives will have primary physical custody, with visitation to the other parent. Joint physical custody (approximately 50/50) works best if parents live relatively near to each other, as it lessens the stress on children and allows them to maintain a somewhat normal routine.

Joint physical custody has the advantages of assuring that children continue their contact and involvement with both parents, and alleviating some of the burdens of parenting for each parent. There are, of course, disadvantages, which include shuttling children around, negative effects on children in the event of parental non-cooperation or ill-will, and the expense of maintaining two homes for the children. As your child grows, his needs may change as well. It is not beneficial to change the schedule of a baby under 2 years of age often, yet when a child is 9 or 10, the situation is much different.

Courts generally will not hesitate to award sole physical custody to one parent if the other parent is deemed unfit. Parents are often deemed unfit if there is domestic violence, alcohol or drug dependency, a boyfriend or girlfriend who is unfit, or any child abuse, neglect or criminal behavior. It is understandable that there may be animosity between you and your ex-spouse, but it's best not to seek sole custody just because you want your children with you. Always consider what is in the child's best interests. It is perfectly fine to decide whatever you and your partner think is best for your children. Joint physical custody is not always a good idea, especially when the child is an infant or toddler.

Custody Thoughts

Do not let your children become your battleground. If you and your spouse are good parents, everything can be worked out. These admonishments do not apply to the parents who find themselves in the ugly predicament dealing with domestic violence, child abuse, drug abuse or mental disorders. Those parents may need to fight to protect their children. This book and these comments are not directed to those tragic situations. Help can be found at our website, through an attorney, at a domestic violence website or through legal aid for those difficult, contested cases.

Interest Of The Child
© Marsha K. Moore[iv]

What is in the best interest of the child
Parents fighting in the home
When one decides to roam
Parents fighting when they split
When they no longer give a shit
Parents playing the child one against the other
Teaching the child there's no value in being a father or a mother

Or is it simply
Parents being the best that they can be
Speaking to one another cordially
Parents setting aside their differences they feel
To show their child what is truly real
Parents' being what is necessary to be
To make the child's life happy and healthy

The 'best interest' is
That the child grows up to be the best that they can be
Will that be to handle things in a way of hurt or harmony
The bottom line is
We should want them to grow up to be great
Don't let your hurtful ways decide their fate

So when it comes to what is in the best interest of the child
Be the parent that shows them you can make it thru the trials
Being the father or the mother
That puts the needs of the child's before any other[v]

Parenting Time Schedules

Parenting time is the scheduled time a non-custodial parent can spend with a child. There are a variety of parenting time schedules that can be set up by a family, and the schedules can be as different as the families who use them.

Important Factors to Consider When Choosing a Plan

- the child's age, maturity, temperament and strength of attachment to each parent
- any special needs of the child and parents
- the child's relationship with siblings and friends
- the distance between the two households
- the flexibility of both parents' work schedules and the child's schedule to accommodate extended access
- childcare arrangements
- transportation needs
- the ability of the parents to communicate and cooperate
- the child's and parents' cultural and religious practices
- a parent's willingness to provide adequate supervision, even if the parent has not done so in the past
- a parent's ability and willingness to learn basic care-giving skills such as feeding, changing and bathing a young child, preparing a child for daycare or school or taking responsibility for helping a child with homework
- a parent's ability to care for the child's needs

Model Parenting Plans for Birth to Age Three from the 2001 Maricopa County Parenting Guidelines

The following is from the Maricopa County Parenting Guidelines from 2001. These are located online at http://www.azlawhelp.org/documents/ModelParentingTimeGuide.pdf.

Birth to 12 Months

> Infants learn at a rapid rate. They are learning to love and trust familiar caregivers. Infants learn to attach to parents and others through consistent, loving responses such as holding, playing, feeding, soothing, talking gently and lovingly and meeting their needs promptly. They begin to respond to the different (but equally valuable) types of parenting mothers and fathers provide.

Infants cannot retain experiences over time, so it is important that they have frequent contact with both parents and a predictable schedule and routine. But infants can retain "emotional memories" of conflict that can have long-term negative effects, so parents should not argue when children, even infants, can overhear.

By six months, infants can recognize their parents and other caregivers and may become uneasy around strangers. Regular caregivers are able to recognize their signals for food, comfort, and sleep. When away from them, infants may become anxious and may experience eating and sleeping problems.

At this young age, it is important to maintain the infant's basic sleep, feeding and waking cycles. Schedules should be adjusted so that disruption does not occur. For example, in creating access plans for this age group, parents should consider the special needs of breast-feeding infants.

Plan A(1): Three periods of 3-6 hours, spaced throughout each week.
Comment: Frequent contact helps the parent and child bond.

Plan A(2): Two six-hour periods spaced throughout each week.
Comment: This plan is helpful when the parents' work schedules or their levels of conflict make more frequent exchanges difficult. Because there are only two visits each week in this plan, bonding between the parent and child may proceed more slowly and the child may experience some difficulty going from one parent to the other.

Vacation: Time blocks that vary significantly from the above are not recommended.

Holidays: When holidays or special occasions like Father's Day, Mother's Day and birthdays do not fall on a parent's access day, parents should consider dividing them consistent with the time blocks noted above.

Plan B: Two three-hour periods and one eight-hour period spaced throughout each week.
(See Plan A above for Vacation and Holidays)

Plan C: Two periods of three to six hours and one overnight each week.

Vacation: Presuming that Plan C overnights have been ongoing, parents may have three consecutive overnights, weekend or midweek, twice each year. Each parent shall give the other parent thirty days written notice of vacation plans and an itinerary of travel dates, destination and places where the child or parent can be reached.

Holidays: When holidays or special occasions like Father's Day, Mother's Day and birthdays do not fall on a parent's access day, parents should consider dividing them consistent with the time blocks noted above.

12 to 24- Months

One- to two-year-olds are becoming more aware of the world around them and the people who are frequently in contact with them. A baby at this age can be attached to many caregivers including grandparents, other extended family members, daycare providers, babysitters and family friends who are frequently in contact with the child.

One- to two-year-olds are also becoming independent and are developing the ability to comfort themselves by thumb sucking or holding onto favorite blankets or toys. Their sleeping and eating schedules are also becoming regular. They continue to respond to the different (but equally valuable) types of parenting mothers and fathers provide. Two-year-olds commonly test parental limits ("terrible twos") and appropriate parental responses can build the child's self-esteem for years to come.

Transitions between homes may become difficult for some one- to two-year-olds and they may become upset at these times. Some resistance to exchanges is normal for some children. This behavior does not necessarily mean that the other parent is not a good parent or that the child does not want to be with the other parent. Parents can make exchanges easier for the child by following predictable schedules and by supporting the child's relationship with the other parent.

Plan A(1): Three periods of three to six hours spaced throughout the week.
Comment: frequent contact helps the parent and child bond.

Plan A(2): Two six-hour periods spaced throughout each week.
Comment: This plan is helpful when the parents' work schedules or their levels of conflict make more frequent exchanges

difficult. Because there are only two visits each week in this plan, bonding between the parent and child may proceed more slowly and the child may experience some difficulty going from one parent to the other.

Vacation: Time blocks that vary significantly from the above are not recommended.

Holidays: When holidays or special occasions like Father's Day, Mother's Day and birthdays do not fall on a parent's access day, parents should consider dividing them consistent with the time blocks noted above.

Plan B: Two four-hour periods and one eight-hour period spaced throughout each week.
(See Plan A above for Vacation and Holidays).

Plan C: One daytime period of three to six hours and two non-consecutive overnights each week.

Vacation: Presuming that Plan C overnights have been ongoing, parents may have one period of three consecutive overnights, midweek or weekend, with children 12 to 18 months olds. After the age of 18 months, parents may have two one-week periods separated by at least four weeks. Each parent shall give the other parent thirty days' written notice of his/her vacation plans and an itinerary of travel dates, destination and places where the child or parent can be reached.

Holidays: When holidays or special occasions like Father's Day, Mother's Day and birthdays do not fall on a parent's access day, parents should consider dividing them consistent with the time blocks noted above.

24 to 36 Months

Ages two to three are an important time for children to develop independent skills. Although children this age are learning to be independent, they may still cling to their caregiver and resist separation. They may be negative and say "NO!" to parents' requests and demands just to express their independence. They may also be fearful about unfamiliar activities and objects. Predictable, regularly scheduled routines help children manage their fears and help them learn that the world is a safe place. Moving between parent's homes may become difficult for children at this age and they may become upset. This behavior does not necessarily mean that the other parent is not a good parent or that the child does not want to be with the other parent. Parents must ensure that the transitions between the two parents' homes are free of parental arguing and tension.

Plan A(1): Two three- to four-hour periods and one eight-hour period spaced throughout each week.

Vacation: Time blocks that vary significantly from the above are not recommended.

Holidays: When holidays or special occasions like Father's Day, Mother's Day and birthdays do not fall on a parent's access day, parents should consider dividing them consistent with the time blocks noted above.

Plan A(2): Two periods of three to six hours and one overnight each week.

Vacation: Presuming Plan A(2) overnights have been ongoing, parents may have two one-week periods separated by at least four weeks. Each parent shall give the other parent thirty days' written notice of his/her vacation plans and an itinerary of travel dates, destinations and places where the child or parent can be reached.

Holidays: When holidays or special occasions like Father's Day, Mother's Day and birthdays do not fall on a parent's access day, parents should consider dividing them consistent with the time blocks noted above.

Plan B: One period of three to six hours and two non-consecutive overnights each week.
Comment: Ideally a child this age should not be separated on a regular schedule from either parent for longer than three days.

Vacation: Presuming that Plan B overnights have been ongoing, Use Plan A(2) vacation plan above for this age group.

Holidays: See Plan A(2) Holidays above for this age group.

Plan C: One period of three to six hours and two consecutive overnights each week.

Vacation: Presuming that Plan C overnights have been ongoing, use Plan A(2) Vacation plan above for this age group.

Here are some popular parenting time schedules.

Parenting Time Schedules for Non-Custodial Parent

Situation #1: The children are with the non-custodial parent every-other weekend. (In this sample, Mom is the non-custodial parent.)

Sample of non-custodial parent (Mom) schedule

Sun	Mon	Tue	Wed	Thu	Fri	Sat
DAD1	DAD2	DAD3	DAD4	DAD5	MOM6	MOM7
MOM8	DAD9	DAD10	DAD11	DAD12	DAD13	DAD14

Situation #2: Dad is the non-custodial parent. The children are with Dad every other weekend from after school/work on Friday until Sunday at 6 p.m. or Monday when they return to school. Also, Dad has parenting time every Wednesday after school until bedtime or Thursday when they return to school. All other times, the child is with Mom.

Sample of non-custodial parent (Dad) schedule

Sun	Mon	Tue	Wed	Thu	Fri	Sat
MOM1	MOM2	MOM3	Time with DAD 4	MOM5	DAD6	DAD7
DAD8	MOM9	MOM10	Time with Dad11	MOM12	MOM13	MOM14

Common Joint Schedules: 50-50 Joint Residential Custody

A 5-5-2-2 Schedule

This schedule is popular when parents want the children on a set schedule during weekdays. For instance, one parent has the children every Monday and Tuesday and every other weekend Friday through Monday. The other parent has the children every Wednesday and Thursday and the alternate weekends. This schedule is helpful when a child has dance or soccer the same day every week, that way one activity does not intrude on the other parents' schedule. If five days is too long to be away from one parent, sometimes the parents provide each other an evening during the other parents' five-day parenting time, such as Wednesday from 4-7 p.m.

Sample 5-5-2-2 schedule (Week 1, Week 2 and then repeat.)

Sun	Mon	Tue	Wed	Thu	Fri	Sat
DAD1 Week 1	MOM2	MOM3	DAD4	DAD5	MOM6	MOM7
MOM8 Week 2	MOM9	MOM10	DAD11	DAD12	DAD13	DAD14

A 3-2-2-3 Schedule

This plan can be used when a child is too young to not see a parent for 5 days.

Sample 3-2-2-3 Schedule (Week 1, Week 2, Week 3 and Week 4)

Sun	Mon	Tue	Wed	Thu	Fri	Sat
DAD1 Week 1	MOM2	MOM3	MOM4	DAD5	DAD6	MOM7
MOM8 Week 2	DAD9	DAD10	DAD11	MOM12	MOM13	MOM14
DAD15 Week 3	DAD16	MOM17	MOM18	DAD19	DAD20	DAD21
MOM22 Week 4	MOM23	MOM24	DAD25	DAD26	MOM27	MOM28

Every Other Week Schedule (or Week On, Week Off Schedule)

Every other week is another popular schedule. You will need to determine when the week starts and ends and who picks up the kids where. The children are with one parent for seven days and then with the other parent seven days.

Sample of every other week schedule

Sun	Mon	Tue	Wed	Thu	Fri	Sat
MOM1	DAD2	DAD3	DAD4	DAD5	DAD6	DAD7
DAD8	MOM9	MOM10	MOM11	MOM12	MOM13	MOM14

Other Parenting Time Issues

Holidays and Summer Vacations

These should be spelled out in your parenting agreement. Here is a short sample of holidays. You need to decide drop off and pick up times and when a day starts. Most parents agree that the receiving parent picks up.

SAMPLE HOLIDAY/VACATION SCHEDULE	Even Years	Odd Years
New Year's Eve	**Mother**	**Father**
New Year's Day	**Father**	**Mother**
Easter	**Mother**	**Father**
Spring Break	**Father**	**Mother**
Memorial Day Weekend	**Mother**	**Father**
Summer Break	**Father**	**Mother**
July 4th	**Mother**	**Father**
Labor Day Weekend	**Father**	**Mother**
Fall Break	**Father**	**Mother**
Thanksgiving Day	**Mother**	**Father**
Winter Break	**Father**	**Mother**
Christmas Eve	**Father**	**Mother**
Christmas Day	**Mother**	**Father**
Hanukkah	**Mother**	**Father**
Child's Birthday	**Both parents**	**Both parents**
Mother's Birthday	**Mother**	**Mother**
Father's Birthday	**Father**	**Father**
Mother's Day	**Mother**	**Mother**
Father's Day	**Father**	**Father**

Example: For all three-day weekends: the parent who has the children over the weekend will keep them on the Monday holiday.

Summer Vacations (Uninterrupted Parenting Time)

You need to decide how long each parent can spend uninterrupted with the children during the summer. Possibilities range anywhere from one week to the entire summer, if there is a non-custodial parent (especially one who lives out of state and cannot see the children often during the year). It is a good idea to provide a deadline, such as May 1, in even-numbered years for parent number 1 to put in writing his vacation plans so there is no conflict, especially if there are work schedules, other family members, and airline tickets to consider.

Telephone Contact

It is important to recognize in writing that each parent must always allow reasonable telephone contact daily and always provide a written itinerary with emergency phone numbers, addresses, flight numbers and the like. All this should be in writing in your parenting agreement.

Parent Information Class

You will be required to go to a parenting class for your divorce. These classes focus on your children, just as you should focus on your children. They did not ask for this divorce. They love both Mom and Dad. Most likely, they do not want this divorce, nor do they have any power to stop it. They are absolutely stuck. So, please do not use your children as weapons; remember that when you criticize the other parent, you criticize half the child.

Parenting Conference Through the Courts

This meeting can be ordered by the court or requested by the parties. It is a conference with a professional to help the parents agree on a schedule and custody. It currently costs $300 per parent. The end result is a report given to the judge with all agreements by the parents in writing. The report also provides the judge with a history of the parties and facts about the family and the children. The report may also make a recommendation about a schedule and custody if the parties cannot agree. The court is free to adopt or create its own parenting agreement and custody arrangements. This conference is usually a good way for parents to negotiate with a professional who can help them. If the parents know what they want, they can make agreements on their own, without the assistance of a professional. Prior to the conference, both parties are requested to fill out an information packet to help provide the conference officer a clear picture of the family. Here are some sample questions that may be included in your information packet from your parenting conference conciliator.

PARENTING CONFERENCE QUESTIONNAIRE

Identifying Data: Parent

Your Present Name ______ Other names by which you are known ______

Date of Birth ______ Age ______ Social Security Number ______ Birth Place ______ Religion ______

Address ______ City, Zip ______

Home Phone ______ Business or Message Phone ______ e-mail address ______

Identifying Data: Children (Add attachment if needed for additional children)

1. Child's Full Name ______ Date of Birth ______ Who he/she lives with ______
   School / Day Care/Grade ______ Address, City, Zip ______ Hours of Attendance ______
2. Child's Full Name ______ Date of Birth ______ Who he/she lives with ______
   School / Day Care/Grade ______ Address, City, Zip ______ Hours of Attendance ______

INFORMATION ABOUT THE CHILDREN INVOLVED IN THE COURT ACTION

Describe the parenting-time arrangements the Court has ordered for your children:

With Father: ______

With Mother: ______

Describe your current parenting-time arrangements, if they differ from what the Court has ordered:

With Father: ______

With Mother: ______

Has legal custody been ordered by the Court? (If yes, describe)______

Physical Health:

Do any of the children have physical problems which require regular medical care and/or medications? (If yes, explain)

______

Mental Health:

Do any of the children presently have emotional problems? (If yes, explain)

______

Have any of the children been evaluated or treated by a psychiatrist, psychologist, social worker or counselor? Yes No (If yes, please complete section below)

- Child's Name ______ Presenting Problem ______
- Therapist's Name, Address, and Telephone ______ Date(s) Seen ______

INFORMATION ABOUT THE PARENTS

Residence History:

List your previous addresses for the last 5 years, beginning with the most recent.

Address	Date Moved In	Date Moved Out	Reason for Leaving

Relationship Status with other party in this case (Check all that apply)
•Never married •Never lived together •Lived together from ________ to ________

•Separated/date separated ______ •In the process of a divorce _____ •Date divorced_____

List other people who regularly spend time in your home.
Name: __________________ DOB: __________ Relation to you: __________________

Employment History:
List your employers for the last 3 years:

1. ____

Present Employer   Address   City, Zip

____

Supervisor's Name and Telephone   Type of Job

____

Date Begun   Current Work Schedule   Days Off

Legal Information:
Has either parent been charged, arrested, convicted of a crime, on parole, on probation, or otherwise been involved with law enforcement agencies?

Mother: Yes No   Father: Yes No

If yes, please give details (law enforcement agencies involved, name and telephone of probation and/or parole officer, dates of involvement)

____

Physical Health:
Do you or the other parent have any health problems? (If yes, explain)

____

Drug and Alcohol Use: (Answer questions 1 through 6, yes or no.)

1. Has either parent used illegal drugs? Mother: Yes No Father Yes No
2. Has either parent used alcohol? Mother: Yes No Father Yes No
   Frequency ______________________________
3. Does either parent currently use illegal drugs? Mother: Yes No Father Yes No
4. Does either parent currently use alcohol? Mother: Yes No Father Yes No
5. Has either parent been treated for substance abuse? Mother: Yes No Father Yes No
   (If yes, where and when did treatment take place)______________________
6. Has either parent participated in drug/alcohol testing in the past two years?
   (If yes, explain, including last test date and results) ______________________

Mental Health:
Has either parent ever been hospitalized for emotional or psychological problems?

Mother: Yes No   Father: Yes No

Dates and Place of Treatment: ______________________________

Has either parent ever seen a psychiatrist, psychologist, social worker or counselor on an outpatient basis?
(If yes, please complete section below)

Mother: Yes No   Father: Yes No

- ____

Therapist's Name   Address, City, Zip   Date(s) Seen

Are you or the other parent currently taking medication for the treatment of emotional problems? (If yes, name the medication)

____

2

Domestic Violence/Child Abuse:

1. Have any of the following occurred between you and the other parent?

Verbal confrontation?	No	Yes	Mild	Moderate	Severe
Physical confrontation?	No	Yes	Mild	Moderate	Severe
Violence to property?	No	Yes	Mild	Moderate	Severe

2. Have the police been called to protect or intervene due to a dispute between you and the other parent?
   No Yes If yes, list law enforcement agency____________________
3. Has an Order of Protection ever been issued against you or the other parent?
   No Yes If yes, which court issued the order and when? ____________________

Have you, the other parent and/or any of the children been involved with Child Protective Services? (If yes, give date and the name of the caseworker)

____

ACCESS AND PARENTING-TIME ISSUES

List ways in which the children benefit from their relationship with you.

____

List ways in which the children benefit from their relationship with the other parent.

____

Proposed Parenting-Time Arrangements:

Describe the amount of time you think the children should spend with each parent.
With Father: ____________________________________
With Mother: ____________________________________
Describe how major decisions regarding the children should be made.

____

Concerns:

List any concerns about the other parent's ability to care for the children.

1. ____________________________________
2. ____________________________________

What has prevented you and the other parent from resolving this dispute over custody and parenting time?

____

3

Sample Parenting Conference Report

Below is a portion of a sample parenting conference report that the court conciliator creates after meeting with both parties and sends to your judge:

SAMPLE

CONCILIATION SERVICES
SUPERIOR COURT OF THE STATE OF ARIZONA
MARICOPA COUNTY
http://www.superiorcourt.maricopa.gov/conciliation

PHOENIX OFFICE	SOUTHEAST OFFICE	NORTHWEST OFFICE	NORTHEAST OFFICE
201 West Jefferson Street, 3rd Floor	222 East Javelina Avenue, 1st Floor	14264 W. Tierra Buena Lane	18380 N. 40th Street
Phoenix, AZ 85003-2205	Mesa, AZ 85210-6621	Surprise, AZ 85374	Phoenix AZ 85032
Information (602) 506-3296	Information (602) 506-2300	Information (602) 372-9400	Information (602 372-7700
Fax (602) 506-7670	Fax (602) 506-3272	Fax (602) 372-9440	Fax (602) 372-7918

PARENTING CONFERENCE REPORT

Date: [redacted]

To: [redacted]

From: [redacted]

In re: [redacted]

FC#: [redacted] CS#: [redacted]

Attorney for Mother: [redacted]

Attorney for Father: [redacted]

REFERRAL AND PROCEDURE:

This case was referred to Conciliation Services by minute entry of the Court dated [redacted] for a Parenting Conference on [redacted] There is a Trial on [redacted]

The parties appeared for the Parenting Conference on [redacted] and were interviewed together for about 2 hours and 30 minutes. The Family Court case file was reviewed. Parenting Conference Questionnaires submitted by both parties were reviewed. Child Protective Services (CPS) indicated no reports on the family as of [redacted] NCIC indicated no reports on Mother. NCIC records indicated [redacted] on three charges: possession of drug paraphernalia, damage to property, and disorderly conduct. The final disposition of these charges is unknown.

BACKGROUND:

This is a paternity matter. The parties reported their relationship lasted from about October [redacted] until June [redacted], though they described their relationship as "on and off" throughout the years. The parties have two minor children: [redacted].

Father filed a Complaint for Paternity, Child Custody, Parenting Time and Child Support on August 26, [redacted]. Father filed a Petition for Temporary Orders on October 29, [redacted]. Father requested parenting time with the child, [redacted] as Father alleged Mother had prevented him from seeing [redacted] On November 25, [redacted], the Court ordered Father to have therapeutic supervised parenting time with [redacted] for a minimum of 2 hours per week. The Court ordered Father to randomly drug and alcohol test not less than once a week for an unspecified period of time. The parties filed a stipulated agreement on January 28, [redacted] regarding Father's parenting time with [redacted] The stipulation said Father would have supervised access with [redacted] two times per week and how his parenting time would be increased over time.

Father filed a Petition for Child Custody, Parenting Time and Child Support on May 10, [redacted] requesting joint legal custody of [redacted] and appropriate parenting time. Mother filed a Motion for Temporary Orders on June 29, [redacted] requesting sole custody of [redacted] and supervised parenting time that is similar to what Father has with [redacted] The Memorandum of Points and Authorities also stated there was a previous court order for Father to drug test on a random basis, but he only did it twice and the memorandum requested the Court order Father to comply with this prior order. Father filed a Response to the Motion for Temporary Orders on July 19, [redacted] Father requested joint legal custody of both children and increased parenting time with Trey and a set schedule for [redacted]

Father lives in a 5-bedroom house by himself. He works full time. Mother lives with her parents and the children. She works about 30 hours per week. The parties stated they live about 10 – 15 minutes driving distance from each other.

AREAS OF AGREEMENT:

At the time of the Parenting Conference, the parties came to a partial agreement on the parenting time plan.

The parenting time plan when Father has supervised parenting time:

- Maternal Grandfather will attempt to supervise Father's parenting time two times per month, 4 hours each time at Father's home.
- In addition, Father will continue to have supervised parenting time two times per month for two hours in a public setting.

The parenting time plan when Father begins to have unsupervised parenting time:

- The children should be in Father's care one day per week from about 10 a.m. until 6 p.m. Due to Father's work schedule, it will probably be two Saturdays per month and two Thursdays per month. Father will try to give Mother about one week notice regarding his work schedule.
- The parties will mutually decide when the children are ready to progress to overnight parenting time. Then, Father's parenting time will be alternating weekends from Friday afternoon until Sunday morning, so Mother can take the children to church.
- Father will see the children one afternoon/ evening per week. The parties will mutually decide on which day, depending on their work schedules (Father's days off vary).
- The children will be in Mother's care during all other times.

When Father's parenting time becomes unsupervised:
TRAVEL/VACATIONS:
Each parent may schedule a 1-2 week vacation period with the children. Parents will negotiate details of their vacation time at least 30 days in advance. Should either parent travel with the children out of the area, the traveling parent will inform the other parent of travel plans and provide contact information including address(es) and telephone number(s) where the traveling parent and children may be reached during the trip.
Neither parent shall travel with the children outside of Arizona without notifying the other parent.

HOLIDAY SCHEDULE: (Takes priority over the regular parenting-time schedule)
Easter: The parties will decide depending on the children's church schedule.
Mother's Day will be celebrated with Mother every year.
Memorial Day: The children will be with Mother during even-numbered years and with Father during odd-numbered years.
Father's Day will be celebrated with Father every year.

[redacted]

Page 4 of [redacted]

4th of July: The children will be with Father during odd-numbered years and with Mother during even-numbered years.

Labor Day: The children will be with Mother during even-numbered years and with Father during odd-numbered years.

Halloween: The children will be with Mother during even-numbered years and with Father during odd-numbered years.

Thanksgiving: During even-numbered years, the children will be with Mother from 8 a.m. until 2 p.m. and with Father from 2 p.m. until 8 p.m. During odd-numbered years, the children will be with Father from 8 a.m. until 2 p.m. and with Mother from 2 p.m. until 8 p.m.

Christmas Eve/ Day: The children will be with Father from 12 p.m. until 7 p.m on December 24th. The children will be with Mother from 7 p.m. on Christmas Eve and all of Christmas Day.

TELEPHONE ACCESS:

Each parent may have telephone contact with the children during the children's normal waking hours.

OTHER AREAS OF AGREEMENT:

- Mother can view Father's residence to ensure it is a safe environment for the children.
- Father will complete an anger management class.
- Transportation will be provided by both parties.
- Parents may change their parenting-time arrangements by mutual agreement.
- Each parent will inform the other parent of any change of address and/or phone number.
- Both parents agree that each will promptly inform the other of any emergency or other important event involving their children.
- Parents will consult and agree with one another regarding any extra activity that affects the children's time with the other parent.

School Records and Medical Records

Each parent, no matter the custody or parenting arrangements, has access to the minor child's school records and medical records. (See A.R.S. §25-403.06).

Mothers Unmarried to Fathers

When the mother is unmarried to the father, the mother has sole legal custody and sole physical custody, unless the parties make another arrangement or a court orders otherwise. A parent needs to file and ask for paternity (or paternity can be admitted), child custody and child support. That does not mean that an unmarried father cannot see his child without the court. The two parents can draft their own agreement and sign and date it, and it will become a court-enforceable agreement. They can also share parenting time without an agreement, but it is better to put it in writing. And, they should always have a written child support plan, usually paid through the Arizona Clearinghouse. (See Chapter 5.)

Conclusion: In closing this section on custody, we offer the following poem written by a father going through a divorce:

The Bonding

By Matthew Weissner

My son and I, we walk alone.
Through the park, midst grass and stone.
Stop to feed the ducks by the edge of a pond.
Trying to form, that so special bond.

He's so very young and alert and aware.
The light is on full, as his curiosity stares;
At all that he does, that he sees and he hears.
It's a big wide world, and he has no fears!

I want him to know always, that somebody cares.
No matter what, I will be there!
I gave him life; his love saved mine.
Our special bond will surpass all of time.

I want to know what thoughts, are on his mind.
I want to feel the needs of his heart.
I'd like to help him to seek and to find.
I need to give him one awesome start!

Along the road we'll learn and grow.
Bubble baths, make believe and nasty colds.
Bedtime "Stories That Never Grow Old."
"Dad, may I borrow the car, if I can be so bold."

Together we will forge that special bond.
Ripples cascading, rings in a pond.
Through the park, midst grass and stone;
My son and I, we walk alone.

Child Custody Questionnaire with Parenting Time and Holiday Schedule

This may help you decide the Best Interests of your child.

Child's Full Name	Date of Birth	City of Birth

Have there been any other proceedings regarding custody of your children? ______

If yes, where? ______________________

Where (at what address) does your child/ren currently live? ______________
With whom? ______________________________
For how long? ______________________________

What is your educational level? ______________________
What is your spouse's educational level? ______________________

Do you or your spouse have any children from a previous relationship? ________
If yes, list names, date of birth, and place where they live.

1. ______________________________
2. ______________________________

Do you have any specific physical or emotional health problems?
If yes, please describe:

Does your spouse have any physical or emotional health problems? __________
If yes, describe:

Do your children have any physical or emotional health problems? __________
If yes, describe:

Is any special treatment of your child required?

Any special medication?

Who is your child's doctor? ______________________
Dentist?______________________________
Who takes your child to the doctor? ______________________
Who takes your child to school/day care most days? ______________

What school/day care does your child attend? ___
Who helps with homework? ___
Who reads bedtimes stories? ___
Who takes care of bathing the children? ___
Who attends parent-teacher conferences? ___
Who prepares the child's meals? ___
Who does the grocery shopping? ___
Who does the clothes shopping? ___
Who does the dishes? ___
Who does the child's laundry? ___
Is your child involved in any activities? ___
If yes, describe:

Who goes to the games? ___
Who is the coach or teacher? ___
Is your child involved in any other type of activity, group, club, or hobby? ___
If yes, describe:

Who is your child's teacher? ___
What is your religious affiliation? ___ Your spouse's? ___
Does your child attend church with either parent? ___
Has your child expressed a preference for where he/she would like to live? ___
If yes, who? ___
Who has provided the primary care of the child since birth? ___

Do you believe that you should have primary physical custody of your child? ___

Do you believe that you and your spouse can peacefully make decisions regarding your child in the future? ___

JOINT LEGAL CUSTODY: The condition under which both parents share legal custody and neither parents' rights are superior except as specifically set forth by the court or by decision of the parents.

Can you share in making decisions jointly about: (Yes or No)
Medical issues? ___
School issues? ___
Religious issues? ___
Recreation issues? ___

JOINT PHYSICAL CUSTODY: The condition under which the physical residence of the child is shared by the parents in a manner that assures that the child has substantially equal time and contact with each parent.

It is possible to have joint legal custody and one parent have primary physical custody and the other parent has parenting time.

Please answer the following and explain in detail:

1. What do you wish for legal custody?

2. What are the child's wishes for legal custody? (Do not ask the child if you do not already know.)

3. What is the child's relationship with the parents and other family members?

4. What is the child's adjustment to home, school, and community?

5. What is the mental and physical health of everyone involved?

6. Which parent is more helpful in facilitating parenting time with the other parent?

7. Who has provided primary care of the child in the past?

8. Has either parent used coercion to obtain a custody agreement?

9. Have the parents gone to the required parenting class?

10. Has either parent filed a false report of abuse or neglect?

Physical Custody and Parenting Time Worksheet

1. Which parent will have primary physical custody of the child (with whom will the child live with primarily, more than half time)? ______________________
2. Will the parents have an approximately equal parenting time plan with the child(ren)? ___
____
3. What is address of the child's primary residence or the address the child will use for school and other information? ______________________
____
4. If there is joint physical custody, what is the day-to-day schedule for the child?

Parenting Time Calendar

	S	M	T	W	T	F	S
Week One							
Week Two							
Week Three							
Week Four							
Week Five							

5. Who will drive and pick up? ______________________
____
6. At what time? ______________________

HOLIDAY/VACATION SCHEDULE	Even Years	Odd Years
New Year's Eve		
New Year's Day		
Easter		
Spring Break		
Memorial Day Weekend		
Summer Break		
July 4th		
Labor Day Weekend		
Fall Break		
Thanksgiving Day		
Winter Break		
Christmas Eve		
Christmas Day		
Hanukkah		
Other religious holidays		
Child's birthday		
Mother's birthday		
Father's birthday		
Mother's Day		
Father's Day		

How will the parents communicate? (Via email, phone, text, etc.) ____________________
____

Do the grandparents have special time with the child? ____________________
____

Will the child go to day care or a babysitter? If yes, who? ____________________
____

Will the other parent have first right of refusal? ____________________

What last name does the child use? ____________________

Frequently Asked Questions

Do the courts favor mothers?
There is no such preference. There are many factors that the court considers, but courts do not favor mothers over fathers.

How does the court decide custody? (A.R.S. §25-403)
The court looks at the following factors:

1. The wishes of the child's parent or parents as to custody.
2. The wishes of the child as to the custodian.
3. The interaction and interrelationships of the child with the child's parent or parents, the child's siblings and any other person who may significantly affect the child's best interest.
4. The child's adjustment to home, school and community.
5. The mental and physical health of all individuals involved.
6. Which parent is more likely to allow the child frequent and meaningful continuing contact with the other parent.
7. Whether one parent, both parents or neither parent has provided primary care of the child.
8. The nature and extent of coercion or duress used by a parent in obtaining an agreement regarding custody.
9. Whether a parent has complied with Chapter 3, Article 5 of this title.
10. Whether either parent was convicted of an act of false reporting of child abuse or neglect under section 13-2907.02.

We are not yet divorced and my wife took the kids to New York.
Once the divorce is filed and served, neither parent can take the children out of state without permission of the other parent or the court.

Can I stop my spouse from dating when she has the kids?
No, as long as they are safe, there is not much you can do. You have the right to know who the children are spending time with and whether they are spending the night somewhere other than their home with the other parent. Be reasonable in these requests, but keep your children safe. You might want to know the person's birth date and Social Security number so you can run a background check on him/her. You have a right to know your children are safe.

How much do I have to pay for the kids?
It all depends; this is discussed in Chapter 5 regarding child support.

Can she schedule soccer when they are with me?
It is best if this can be negotiated. It is unknown what each judge would decide. Some believe that a parent can only schedule on their own time. This basically eliminates your children from most activities. This is probably one of the most hotly litigated issues after divorce. Think of it this way: it is not "your time;" it is your child's childhood.

My wife has the kids every other weekend, but she works and leaves them with her mother. What can I do?
You could have an agreement called a "right of first refusal." This is a common provision, which reads that if one parent who has the kids is gone for more than four hours, s/he will call the other parent and offer them the "right" to parent the kids before anyone else. If the other parent is busy, then parent number 1 can leave the kids with a responsible person of their choice. But, it often might be a good idea to allow the grandmother and the kids to bond. Did you encourage this relationship when you were still married? If so, why not continue it?

My wife has the kids every Monday and Tuesday, but she is starting school and leaves the kids with her boyfriend. Can I have parenting time with my children, instead of her boyfriend?
The right of first refusal would apply. Also, you have every right to know exactly who is taking care of your children when your spouse is not home; this includes name, address, phone number and ID information, so you can do a background check if you desire. This is not to say that you use such requests as harassment; in fact you have a similar obligation to your spouse to let her know with whom you are leaving the kids, if anyone. You both have the continuing job to make sure your children are safe.

My husband smokes pot almost daily. Should he have parenting time with the children?
Not unless it is supervised. Drug use will preclude him from having unsupervised parenting time. You should ask the court to have him drug tested at TASC (Treatment Assessment Screening Center). Their website is: www.tascaz.org. You might want to consult with an attorney, as this issue can become complicated.

My spouse has physically abused me. Can he still have custody of the kids?
Significant domestic violence is contrary to joint legal custody. This is also beyond the scope of this book. Please consult with an experienced family law attorney. (See Chapter 13.)

My 14-year-old does not like her father. Should I make her go visit him?
Do you know why she does not like to visit him? If the child is safe and his house is safe, you should do everything you can to encourage the relationship. The child may be taking on your negativity or Father may just not be a very attentive parent. Help Father be a better parent by role modeling for him and discussing this with him. Maybe they could go to counseling together. Teenagers often do not want to be with either parent. It is important, however, to provide ample time with each parent.

My ex-mother-in-law is coming for vacation. She wants to see our kids for a concert on my Saturday. I am afraid if I give in, I will always be giving in. Should I let my kids see her?
Yes, you should very seriously consider it. Do your kids want to go? Remember, while this is "your" time, it is also their childhood. Try to negotiate and get make-up time or be gracious and let it go, knowing that your former spouse will return the favor when your parents come to town. Keep your kids first. Ask yourself, would I have allowed this if I were still married?

My former spouse wants to go on a cruise to Mexico. I will not let the kids get passports. Can he get my children passports without my approval?
This can get sticky, because there are hundreds of international abductions every year. If you truly believe it is for a cruise, you might consider it. You can ask for the written itinerary and documentation showing that they are really going on the cruise. Sometimes the abduction of children comes as no surprise to the abandoned parent. You could agree to have the passports kept in a safety deposit box that requires two signatures to retrieve. If your former spouse has citizenship in another country, you might want to do research to find out about whether that country is a member of the Hague Convention and whether you could retrieve the children if they were kidnapped. You should seek legal advice if kidnapping is a real concern.

We decided our kids would be Catholic. My spouse will not take them to mass on her Sundays. Can I ask the court to make my spouse take our children to mass?
The court will generally not mandate where each parent takes the children to worship on their respective weekends. If you have a written agreement in your decree as part of your joint parenting agreement, the court may enforce it.

My son wants to go to his band banquet on Friday night, but it is my parenting time and I do not want him to go. Should I let my son go?
Is this a question you are seriously asking? If you contemplated not allowing your son to attend his band banquet then take a step back and think about your son's best interest, not yours. If you do not allow your child to go, you are forcing your son to spend time with you because it is "your" time. You should carefully consider whose needs you are thinking about. We have heard on more than one occasion that it is "not in the child's best interest" to be involved in school activities during one parent's time, but that is simply not the case. It is important that, as a parent, you stay involved in your children's lives.

How does custody affect child support?
The physical custody arrangement is one factor considered in the worksheet (see Chapter 5.) The more time you have your child, the more expensive it is.

We have not been to court yet and there are no orders. Who gets the kids right now?
It is basically a free-for-all, unless the two of you can decide. Just remember that what you do now can be reported to the court later. If you unreasonably keep the children away from one parent out of vindictiveness, that will be detrimental to your obtaining legal custody.

Can I get temporary custody?
Yes. You must file a motion asking for it, after the petition for divorce is filed or with the petition as it is being filed. The court will set a hearing date, take evidence and make a decision if you all cannot decide. You really should be able to decide on a temporary agreement. Sometimes parents try different schedules until they find one that works. Not all the children in a family have to have the same schedule.

We have a parenting schedule that we both agree with. Can we put it in writing?
Yes. You can write and sign an agreement, as can be found in the Arizona Rules of Family Law Procedure Rule 69, that will be valid in court. You can attach it to your joint parenting agreement or rewrite into your final joint parenting agreement. It is valid, even if it is not filed with the court. It is a good idea to put it in writing during the pendency of the divorce, just so you have some certainty.

My husband never really helped parent the kids, but now he wants 50/50 time with them. Is he likely to get 50/50 parenting time?
History of care giving is only one factor in determining the best interests of the children. Perhaps he never had the chance to co-parent in the past. But if he is doing a good job, the kids are happy and he is learning to be a good, involved father, congratulations to your family! Fathers often shift their work focus after a divorce so they can stay involved in their children's lives, and that is a good thing.

My husband is doing whatever I do. If I take the children for ice cream on my weekend, he does it on his next visit. When I started reading books to them at night, he started doing it on his parenting time. I bet he is just doing it to look good. What gives?
Perhaps you are modeling parenting behavior for him. He is actually learning how to be a good parent by watching you. Good for your family! Keep up the good work! Be proud of him and happy for your kids.

Will the court tell me when I can see my kids?
Only if you and your spouse cannot agree. You really do not want to turn this life-changing decision over to a stranger who will only get to know your family in an hour or so of an evidentiary hearing. Not only do you relinquish all control, but having to testify and perhaps say negative things or answer embarrassing questions can leave the family scarred and impact future interactions. There is no

need to litigate these issues unless there is a domestic violence, drug or other abuse issue, and you must have the help of the court to protect your children.

Will my kids have to go to court?
No, judges do not care to speak with children. Your children can talk to counselors and they can write reports. Also, the conciliation services may choose to interview your children as part of a parenting conference. Children over the age of 6 or 7 can usually be interviewed.

I think my spouse's behavior reflects instability and potential likelihood for harm to my children if my spouse does not undergo the proper treatment. Is there anything that I can ask the court for?
This is beyond the scope of this book, but you could ask for a Rule 63 psychological examination or a custody evaluation.

What is a parenting conference?
It is a meeting with a neutral third party who talks with both parties and then drafts a report to give to the court. It can be ordered by the court or requested by either party. (See "Parenting Conference Through the Courts," earlier in this chapter.)

Chapter Five:

CHILD SUPPORT

CHAPTER 5: CHILD SUPPORT

As this book went to publication, the child support guidelines were being changed, but had not yet been published. Please do not rely solely upon this information without first consulting our website or that of the county for updated information, as it may have changed.

This chapter will take you through the basic principles of child support and explain how it is calculated. It is important to know how much you will be ordered to pay (or receive), so that you are better able to compute your new monthly budget.

Child Support Factors to Establish Child Support

CHILD SUPPORT IS DECIDED UPON THESE BASIC FACTORS, PLUS WHATEVER ELSE EACH PARENT PAYS FOR:

- Monthly salary of each parent
- Age of children
- Parenting time
- Day care costs
- Medical insurance
- Extracurricular expenses
- Number of other children not common to the marriage

Affidavit of Financial Information

Every case with children must have a document filed called an Affidavit of Financial Information, to be filled out by both parents and notarized. Read all the fine print on this document. It requires you to attach the last three (3) years of taxes and at least six (6) months of pay stubs. (Please remember to *delete your Social Security and bank account numbers from these documents*. If you file these documents without those numbers being covered, they will become public record and you could be subjecting yourself to possible identify theft).

In the Affidavit of Financial Information, you will outline your current monthly expenses, debts and income. It is understood that these numbers will change upon dissolution (divorce), but the court's request is for the amount you are spending right now. The courts will analyze your financial position to determine how much child support you (or your spouse) should pay. We recommend that parents *omit the taxes* and supply the last three pay stubs; these can be produced without becoming part of your court file. The next page is a draft of an Affidavit of Financial Information that needs to be filled out if there are minor children in the marriage. This is a state-required form. You can find it online. (See Appendix D.)

Name: ____
Mailing Address: ____
City, State, Zip Code: ____
Daytime Phone Number: ____
Evening Phone Number: ____
Representing: ☐ Self ☐ Petitioner ☐ Respondent
State Bar Number: ____

FOR CLERK'S USE ONLY

SUPERIOR COURT OF ARIZONA IN MARICOPA COUNTY

____
Petitioner/Plaintiff

Case No. ____

ATLAS No. ____

____
Respondent

AFFIDAVIT OF FINANCIAL INFORMATION

Affidavit of ____
(Name of Person Whose Information is on this Affidavit)

IMPORTANT INFORMATION ABOUT THIS DOCUMENT

WARNING TO BOTH PARTIES: This Affidavit is an important document. You must fill out this Affidavit completely, and provide accurate information. You must provide copies of this Affidavit and all other required documents to the other party and to the judge. If you do not do this, the court may order you to pay a fine.

I have read the following document and know of my own knowledge that the facts and financial information stated below are true and correct, and that any false information may constitute perjury by me. I also understand that, if I fail to provide the required information or give misinformation, the judge may order sanctions against me, including assessment of fees for fines under Rule 31, Arizona Rules of Family Law Procedure.

____
Date

____
Signature of Person Making Affidavit

INSTRUCTIONS

1. **Complete the entire Affidavit in black ink. If the spaces provided on this form are inadequate, use separate sheets of paper to complete the answers and attach them to the Affidavit. Answer every question completely! You must complete every blank. If you do not know the answer to a question or are guessing, please state that. If a question does not apply, write "NA" for "not applicable" to indicate you read the question. Round all amounts of money to the nearest dollar.**
2. Answer the following statements **YES** or **NO**. If you mark **NO**, explain your answer on a separate piece of paper and attach the explanation to the Affidavit.

[ ] YES [ ] NO 1. I listed all sources of my income.

[ ] YES [ ] NO 2. I attached copies of my two (2) most recent pay stubs.

[ ] YES [ ] NO 3. I attached copies of my federal income tax return for the last three (3) years, and I attached my W-2 and 1099 forms from all sources of income.

DROSC13F
Use current form

Case No. ______________

1. GENERAL INFORMATION:

A. Name: ______________________________ Date of Birth: ________________

B. Current Address: ____

C. Date of Marriage: ____________________ Date of Divorce: ________________

D. Last date when you and the other party lived together: ________________

E. Full names of child(ren) common to the parties (in this case), their dates of birth:

Name	Date of Birth

F. The name, date of birth, relationship to you, and gross monthly income for each individual who lives in your household:

Name	Date of Birth	Relationship to you	Income

G. Any other person for whom you contribute support:

Name	Age	Relationship to You	Reside With You (Y/N)	Court Order to Support (Y/N)

H. Attorney's Fees paid in this matter $ __________. Source of funds ____________

2. EMPLOYMENT INFORMATION:

A. Your job/occupation/profession/title: ________________________________

Name and address of current employer: ________________________________

____

Date employment began: ________________

How often are you paid: [ ] Weekly [ ] Every other week [ ] Monthly [ ] Twice a month [ ] Other ________________________

B. If you are not working, why not? ________________________________

C. Previous employer name and address: ________________________________

____

Previous job/occupation/profession/title: ________________________________

Date previous job began: ______________ Date previous job ended: ____________

Reason you left job: ____

Gross monthly pay at previous job: $ __________

D. Total gross income from last three (3) years' tax returns (attach copies of pages 1 and 2 of your federal income tax returns for the last three (3) years):

Year ______ $ ________ Year ______ $ ________Year ______ $ ________

E. Your total gross income from January 1 of this year to the date of this Affidavit (year-to-date income): $ ______________

DROSC13F
Use current form

Case No.________________

3. YOUR EDUCATION/TRAINING: List name of school, length of time there, year of last attendance, and degree earned:

A. High School: ____________________
B. College: ____________________
C. Post-Graduate: ____________________
D. Occupational Training: ____________________

4. YOUR GROSS MONTHLY INCOME:

- List **all** income you receive from **any** source, whether private or governmental, taxable or not.
- List all income payable to you individually or payable jointly to you and your spouse.
- Use a monthly average for items that vary from month to month.
- Multiply weekly income and deductions by 4.33. Multiply biweekly income by 2.165 to arrive at the total amount for the month.

A. Gross salary/wages per month $ ________
- **Attach copies of your two most recent pay stubs.**

Rate of Pay $ ______ per [ ] hour [ ] week [ ] month [ ] year

B. Expenses paid for by your employer:
1. Automobile $ ________
2. Auto expenses, such as gas, repairs, insurance $ ________
3. Lodging $ ________
4. Other (Explain) ____________________ $ ________

C. Commissions/Bonuses $ ________
D. Tips $ ________
E. Self-employment Income (See below) $ ________
F. Social Security benefits $ ________
G. Worker's compensation and/or disability income $ ________
H. Unemployment compensation $ ________
I. Gifts/Prizes $ ________
J. Payments from prior spouse $ ________
K. Rental income (net after expenses) $ ________
L. Contributions to household living expense by others $ ________
M. Other (Explain:) ____________________ $ ________
(Include dividends, pensions, interest, trust income, annuities or royalties.)

TOTAL: $ ________

5. SELF-EMPLOYMENT INCOME (if applicable):

If you are self-employed, attach of a copy of the Schedule C for your business from your last tax return and the most recent income/expense statement from your business.

If self employed, provide the following information:

Name, address and telephone no. of business: ____________________
____
Type of business entity: ____________________
State and Date of incorporation: ____________________
Nature of your interest: ____________________
Nature of business: ____________________
Percent ownership: ____________________
Number of shares of stock: ____________________

DROSC13F
Use current form

Total issued and outstanding shares: ______________________________
Gross sales/revenue last 12 months: ______________________________

INSTRUCTIONS

Both parties must answer item 6 if either party asks for child support. These expenses include only those expenses for children who are common to the parties, which means one party is the birth/adoptive mother and the other is the birth/adoptive father of the children.

6. SCHEDULE OF ALL MONTHLY EXPENSES FOR CHILDREN:

- **DO NOT LIST** any expenses for the other party, or child(ren) who live(s) with the other party, **unless** you are paying those expenses.
- Use a monthly average for items that vary from month to month.
- If you are listing anticipated expenses, indicate this by putting an asterisk (*) next to the estimated amount.

A. HEALTH INSURANCE:

Do you have health insurance available? Yes ☐ No ☐ Are you enrolled? ________

1. Total monthly cost $ ________
2. Premium cost to insure you alone $ ________
3. Premium cost to insure child(ren) common to the parties $ ________
4. List all people covered by your insurance coverage:
   ____
   ____
5. Name of insurance company and Policy/Group Number:
   ____

B. DENTAL/VISION INSURANCE:

1. Total monthly cost $ ________
2. Premium cost to insure you alone $ ________
3. Premium cost to insure child(ren) common to the parties $ ________
4. List all people covered by your insurance coverage:
   ____
   ____
5. Name of insurance company and Policy/Group Number:
   ____

C. UNREIMBURSED MEDICAL AND DENTAL EXPENSES:

(Cost to you after, or in addition to, any insurance reimbursement)

1. Drugs and medical supplies $ ________
2. Other ______________________________ $ ________

TOTAL: $ ________

D. CHILD CARE COSTS:

1. Total monthly child care costs $ ________
   (Do not include amounts paid by D.E.S.)
2. Name(s) of child(ren) cared for and amount per child:

______________________________ $ ________
______________________________ $ ________
______________________________ $ ________

3. Name(s) and address(es) of child care provider(s):
____
____

E. EMPLOYER PRETAX PROGRAM:
Do you participate in an employer program for pretax payment of child care expenses? (Cafeteria Plan)? [ ] YES [ ] NO

F. COURT ORDERED CHILD SUPPORT:
1. Court ordered current child support for child(ren) **not common to the parties** $ ________
2. Court ordered cash medical support for child(ren) **not common to the parties** $ ________
3. Amount of any arrears payment $ ________
4. Amount per month actually paid in last 12 mos. $ ________
   - **Attach proof that you are paying**
5. Name(s) and relationship of minor child(ren) who you support or who live with you, but are **not** common to the parties.
____
____

G. COURT ORDERED SPOUSAL MAINTENANCE/SUPPORT (Alimony):
1. Court ordered spousal maintenance/support you actually pay to previous spouse: $ ________

H. EXTRAORDINARY EXPENSES :
1. For **Children** (Educational Expense/Special Needs/Other): $________
   Explain: ______________________________________
   ____
2. For **Self**: $ ________
   Explain: ______________________________________
   ____

INSTRUCTIONS
Both parties must answer items 7 and 8 if either party is requesting: • Spousal maintenance • Division of expenses • Attorneys' fees and costs • Adjustment or deviation from the child support amount • Enforcement

7. SCHEDULE OF ALL MONTHLY EXPENSES:
- Do NOT list any expenses for the other party, or children who live with the other party unless you are paying those expenses.
- Use a monthly average for items that vary from month to month.
- If you are listing anticipated expenses, indicate this by putting an asterisk (*) next to the estimated amount.

Case No. ______________

A. HOUSING EXPENSES:

1. House payment:
   a. First Mortgage $ ________
   b. Second Mortgage $ ________
   c. Homeowners Association Fee $ ________
   d. Rent $ ________
2. Repair & upkeep $ ________
3. Yard work/Pool/Pest Control $ ________
4. Insurance & taxes not included in house payment $ ________
5. Other (Explain) ______________ $ ________

TOTAL: $ ________

B. UTILITIES:

1. Water, sewer, and garbage $ ________
2. Electricity $ ________
3. Gas $ ________
4. Telephone $ ________
5. Mobile phone/pager $ ________
6. Internet Provider $ ________
7. Cable/Satellite television $ ________
8. Other (Explain:) ______________ $ ________

TOTAL: $ ________

C. FOOD:

1. Food, milk, and household supplies $ ________
2. School lunches $ ________
3. Meals outside home $ ________

TOTAL: $ ________

D. CLOTHING:

1. Clothing for you $ ________
2. Uniforms or special work clothes $ ________
3. Clothing for children living with you $ ________
4. Laundry and cleaning $ ________

TOTAL: $ ________

E. TRANSPORTATION OR AUTOMOBILE EXPENSES:

1. Car insurance $ ________
2. List all cars and individuals covered:
   ____
   ____
3. Car payment, if any $ ________
4. Car repair and maintenance $ ________
5. Gas and oil $ ________
6. Bus fare/parking fees $ ________
7. Other (explain): ______________ $ ________

TOTAL: $ ________

F. MISCELLANEOUS:

1. School and school supplies $ ________
2. School activities or fees $ ________
3. Extracurricular activities of child(ren) $ ________

Case No. ______________

4. Church/contributions $ ________
5. Newspapers, magazines and books $ ________
6. Barber and beauty shop $ ________
7. Life insurance (beneficiary: ____________________) $ ________
8. Disability insurance $ ________
9. Recreation/entertainment $ ________
10. Child(ren)'s allowance(s) $ ________
11. Union/Professional dues $ ________
12. Voluntary retirement contributions and savings deductions $ ________
13. Family gifts $ ________
14. Pet Expenses $ ________
15. Cigarettes $ ________
16. Alcohol $ ________
17. Other (explain): ____________________ $ ________

TOTAL: $ ________

8. OUTSTANDING DEBTS AND ACCOUNTS: List all debts and installment payments you currently owe, but **do not include items listed in Item 8** "Monthly Schedule of Expenses". Follow the format below. Use additional paper if necessary.

Creditor Name	Purpose of Debt	Unpaid Balance	Min. Monthly Payment	Date of Your Last Payment	Amount of Your Payment

Child Support Worksheet

The second required document is a Child Support Worksheet. Within this form, there are various boxes to input information such as your income and parenting time with the children. There are other factors that are also taken into consideration in determining this amount. The Child Support Worksheet will calculate who pays child support and how much mother or father shall pay in child support. Although you are able to access this form on the court's website, we have provided this worksheet on our website for you to download. Please be advised that the court's final determination may differ from your generated worksheet, but the worksheet should give you an idea of how much child support you will have to pay.

There are two huge factors that determine a child support obligation: each parent's gross wages and each parent's parenting time with the child. On the other hand, there are other factors that will give a parent "credit" on his or her side of the child support worksheet. These factors include whether either parent has another child from a previous marriage, has health insurance, pays spousal maintenance or child support or pays daycare expenses, among others.

Following is a copy of the short-form child support worksheet. We do not use the online form that Maricopa County provides. Like most attorneys, we use the short-form for child support calculations and provide several hypothetical cases so that you may see how child support will change when the factors change.

Examples of Child Support Calculations

Family #1

2 children: Born 1/1/06 and 1/1/96

Father's Income:	$60,000/annual
Mother's Income:	$30,000/annual
Additional children not from marriage:	Father has 1 other child
Primary Custodian:	Father
Mother's Parenting Time	125 days of parenting time
Health Insurance cost:	$200.00/month (Father pays)
Child Care cost:	$800.00/month (Father pays)

Family #1: Mother would pay $595.00 per month in child support.

Date: Jun. 5, 2010

NO. ________

Parent A ________ Petitioner

and

Parent B ________ Respondent

Child Support Worksheet
(January 1, 2005 Guidelines)

DOB:	1-1-06	1-1-96				
Age:	4.42	14.43				
Youngest Grade Estimated:			Actual Grade:			
Presumptive Termination Date:				**May 31, 2024**		

Number of Minor Children: 2 Children 12 or Over: 1

Primary Custodian Is (X): [x] Father [ ] Mother [ ] Equal

	Monthly	Annually	Hourly
Father:		60,000.00	
Mother:		30,000.00	

		Father	**Mother**
Gross Monthly Income:		$ 5,000.00	$ 2,500.00
Court Ordered Spousal Maintenance (Paid) / Received	[Mandatory]		
Court Ordered Child Support of Other Relationships (Paid)	[Mandatory]		
Custodian of F: [ ] M: [ ] Other Child(ren) Subject of Order	[Mandatory]		
Support of Other Natural or Adopted Children **Not** Ordered:	[Discretionary]		
Father's 1 Other Child Deduction Of:		(794.00)	
Mother's ___ Other Child[ren] Deduction Of:			
Adjusted Gross Income		$ 4,206.00	$ 2,500.00
Combined Adjusted Gross Income		$ 6,706.00	
Basic Child Support Obligation For [2] **Children:**		$ 1,226.00	
Additions To Child Support Obligation:			
Adjustment For 1 Child Over Age 12 at 10 %	[Discretionary]		61.30
Medical, Dental and Vision Insurance Paid By	[Mandatory]	200.00	
Monthly Childcare Costs For 1 Child Paid By:	[Discretionary]	800.00	
Less: Federal Tax Credit Allowed To Custodian of 25%		(50.00)	
Extra Education Expenses Paid By:	[Discretionary]		
Extraordinary (Gifted or Handicapped) Child Expenses Paid By:	[Discretionary]		
Total Child Support Obligation		$ 2,237.30	
Each Parent's Proportionate Percentage of Combined Income		62.72%	37.28%
Each Parent's Proportionate Share of Total Support Obligation		$ 1,403.23	$ 834.07
Parenting Time Costs Adjustment For Mother Using	[Mandatory]		
Parenting Time Table A For 125 Days At 19.5 %			(239.07)
Total Additions To Child Support Obligation From Above Paid By Each Parent		(950.00)	-
Preliminary Child Support Obligation		$ 453.23	$ 595.00
Adjustment For Essentially Equal Time With Each Parent			
Self Support Reserve Test For Mother: AGI: $ 2,500.00	[Discretionary]		
Less: Other Ordered Arrears Paid: ___ (Discretion) Less $775 = $ 1,725.00 (Maximum C.S.)			-
Child Support Obligation To Be Paid By Mother			$ 595.00

Issue Order of Assignment Against: [ ] Parent A [ ] Parent B

Family #2

2 children: Born 1/1/06 and 1/1/96

Father's Income:	$7.25/hour (minimum wage)
Mother's Income:	$36.00/hour
Primary Custodian:	Equal parenting time
Health Insurance cost:	$150.00/mo. (Mother pays)
Child Care cost:	$0.00

Family #2: Mother would pay $409.00 per month in child support.

Date: Jul. 2, 2010

NO. ______

Parent A — Petitioner

and

Parent B — Respondent

Child Support Worksheet
(January 1, 2005 Guidelines)

DOB	1-1-06	1-1-96
Age:	4.50	14.50

Youngest Grade Estimated: | Actual Grade:

Presumptive Termination Date: May 31, 2024

Number of Minor Children: 2 Children 12 or Over: 1

Primary Custodian Is (X): [ ] Father [ ] Mother [x] Equal

	Monthly	Annually	Hourly
Father:			7.25
Mother:			36.00

		Father	Mother
Gross Monthly Income:		$ 1,256.67	$ 6,240.00
Court Ordered Spousal Maintenance (Paid) / Received	[Mandatory]		
Court Ordered Child Support of Other Relationships (Paid)	[Mandatory]		
Custodian of F: [ ] M: [ ] Other Child(ren) Subject of Order	[Mandatory]		
Support of Other Natural or Adopted Children **Not** Ordered:	[Discretionary]		
Father's ___ Other Child[ren] Deduction Of:			
Mother's ___ Other Child[ren] Deduction Of:			
Adjusted Gross Income		$ 1,256.67	$ 6,240.00
Combined Adjusted Gross Income		$ 7,496.67	
Basic Child Support Obligation For [2] **Children:**		$ 1,244.00	
Additions To Child Support Obligation:			
Adjustment For 1 Child Over Age 12 at 10 %	[Discretionary]	62.20	
Medical, Dental and Vision Insurance Paid By	[Mandatory]		150.00
Monthly Childcare Costs For 1 Child Paid By:	[Discretionary]		
Less: Federal Tax Credit Allowed To Custodian of 25%			
Extra Education Expenses Paid By:	[Discretionary]		
Extraordinary (Gifted or Handicapped) Child Expenses Paid By:	[Discretionary]		
Total Child Support Obligation		$ 1,456.20	
Each Parent's Proportionate Percentage of Combined Income		16.76%	83.24%
Each Parent's Proportionate Share of Total Support Obligation		$ 244.10	$ 1,212.10
Parenting Time Costs Adjustment	[Mandatory]		
Parenting Time Table A For ____ Days At ____ %			
Total Additions To Child Support Obligation From Above Paid By Each Parent		-	(150.00)
Preliminary Child Support Obligation		$ 244.10	$ 1,062.10
Adjustment For Essentially Equal Time With Each Parent		409.00	(409.00)
Self Support Reserve Test For Mother: AGI: $ 6,240.00	[Discretionary]	653.10	653.10
Less: Other Ordered Arrears Paid: ____ (Discretion) Less $775 = $ 5,465.00 (Maximum C.S.)			
Child Support Obligation To Be Paid By **Mother**			$ 409.00

Family #3

2 children: Born 1/1/06 and 1/1/96

Father's Income:	$120,000/annual salary
Father pays spousal maintenance:	$2000.00/month
Mother's Income:	$20,000/annual salary
Mother receives spousal maintenance:	$2000.00/month
Primary Custodian:	Mother
Father's Parenting Time:	75 days of parenting time
Health Insurance cost:	$100.00/month (Father pays)
Child Care cost:	$0

Family #3: Father would pay $947.04 per month in child support.

Date: Jul. 3, 2010

NO. Family #3

Parent A
Petitioner
and

Parent B
Respondent

Child Support Worksheet
(January 1, 2005 Guidelines)

DOB:	1-1-06	1-1-96				
Age:	4.50	14.50				
Youngest Grade Estimated:		Actual Grade:				
Presumptive Termination Date:		**May 31, 2024**				

Number of Minor Children: 2 Children 12 or Over: 1

Primary Custodian Is (X): [ ] Father [x] Mother [ ] Equal

Gross Monthly Income:

	Monthly	Annually	Hourly
Father:		120,000.00	
Mother:		20,000.00	

		Father	Mother
Gross Monthly Income:		$ 10,000.00	$ 1,666.67
Court Ordered Spousal Maintenance (Paid) / Received	[Mandatory]	(2,000.00)	+ 2,000.00
Court Ordered Child Support of Other Relationships (Paid)	[Mandatory]		
Custodian of **F:** [ ] **M:** [ ] Other Child(ren) Subject of Order	[Mandatory]		
Support of Other Natural or Adopted Children **Not** Ordered:	[Discretionary]		
Father's Other Child[ren] Deduction Of:			
Mother's Other Child[ren] Deduction Of:			
Adjusted Gross Income		$ 8,000.00	$ 3,666.67
Combined Adjusted Gross Income		$ 11,666.67	
Basic Child Support Obligation For 2 **Children:**		$ 1,591.00	
Additions To Child Support Obligation:			
Adjustment For 1 Child Over Age 12 at 10 %	[Discretionary]	79.55	
Medical, Dental and Vision Insurance Paid By	[Mandatory]	100.00	
Monthly Childcare Costs For 1 Child Paid By:	[Discretionary]		
Less: Federal Tax Credit Allowed To Custodian of 25%			
Extra Education Expenses Paid By:	[Discretionary]		
Extraordinary (Gifted or Handicapped) Child Expenses Paid By:	[Discretionary]		
Total Child Support Obligation		$ 1,770.55	
Each Parent's Proportionate Percentage of Combined Income		68.57%	31.43%
Each Parent's Proportionate Share of Total Support Obligation		$ 1,214.09	$ 556.46
Parenting Time Costs Adjustment For Father Using	[Mandatory]		
Parenting Time Table A For 75 Days At 10.5 %		(167.06)	
Total Additions To Child Support Obligation From Above Paid By Each Parent		(100.00)	-
Preliminary Child Support Obligation		$ 947.04	$ 556.46
Adjustment For Essentially Equal Time With Each Parent			
Self Support Reserve Test For Father: AGI: $ 8,000.00	[Discretionary]		
Less: Other Ordered Arrears Paid: (Discretion) Less $775 = $ 7,225.00 (Maximum C.S.)		-	
Child Support Obligation To Be Paid By Father		$ 947.04	

How is Child Support Calculated?

Child support can be easily calculated under the Arizona Child Support Guidelines after several other variables have been determined. Specifically, the following information is required to calculate child support:

1. Each parent's monthly gross income

   Gross income includes: receipt of spousal maintenance, Social Security, workman's compensation, severance pay, commissions, disability benefits, unemployment benefits, retirement plans, interest, self-employment, bonuses, gifts, prizes (lottery winnings), rental income, trust income, pensions, annuities, dividends and capital gains.

2. The amount of spousal maintenance paid or received by either parent

3. The amount of court-ordered child support paid by one parent for support of children not common to the other parent

4. The cost to one parent of supporting children not common to the other parent

5. The amount of the medical insurance premium for the children

6. The child care expenses

7. The physical custody schedule

Calculation of child support never includes a new marriage partner, only the two parents of the child.

Who Pays Child Support?

Using the above-described factors, the Child Support Worksheet and the court will be able to determine which parent (if either) should pay child support. The law provides that when the court grants a custody order, it also must decide what amount of child support should be paid by each parent under the Arizona Child Support Guidelines. Joint custody does NOT mean that either parent is no longer responsible to provide for the support of the child.

How Is Child Support Paid?

Child support must be paid in money – not in clothing or gifts. It must be paid through the clearinghouse in the state of Arizona if there is a court order for support. In Arizona, most child support payments are made through the "clearinghouse," and, if possible, through wage assignment. If a parent is ordered to make child support payments through the clearinghouse, that parent shall send the payment to the clearinghouse directly, not to the other parent. The clearinghouse keeps track of all payments. If you have been ordered to make payments through the clearinghouse and you make payments directly to the other parent, those direct payments may be considered as gifts to the other parent. If that is the case, you will not be given credit that you paid child support that month and may be required to pay again to the clearinghouse.

A "wage assignment" is now required for the payment of child support, and in some cases, for the payment of spousal maintenance (alimony). An assignment requires an employer or other payor (either a person or company) of a parent who is obligated by court order to pay a certain amount of child support each month to withhold that amount from the wages or money owed to the parent (employee) and to send that amount directly to the clearinghouse. This type of assignment applies to salary, wages, commissions and any type of payments received by the parent ordered to pay support. Either the person required to pay support or the person entitled to receive it can request an assignment order (A.R.S. §25-323 and 12-2454).

Frequently Asked Questions

Agreements on child support: Can my spouse and I agree on a child support amount that is different from the statutory calculation?
The Court can permit the parties to settle on an amount of child support that is different from the statutory calculation. In order to do so, however, both parties must sign a statement indicating that they are aware of what the child support would have been had they not entered into the agreement. You must attach a Child Support Worksheet to your decree.

Income tax exemptions: Who gets the income tax exemptions for the children?
The federal and state income taxes exemptions for the children are also generally divided in proportion to the parties' incomes. In order for the paying parent to claim the children during his/her year, the parent must be current in his/her child support obligation for that year. This is determined by statute, but may be modified by agreement of both parties.

Parenting time: What if my spouse does not allow me to see my children. Do I still need to pay child support?
Yes, you still have an obligation to pay child support. You have an obligation to continue to pay child support until a court orders that you may stop. It is common for parents to want to withhold child support if the other spouse is not abiding by the court-ordered parenting time, but courts frown upon either party not following the court's orders.

When does my child support obligation end?
Child support orders apply to any child under the age of 18, or a child who is still attending high school or an equivalency program. Also, if a child is mentally or physically handicapped, the judge may order that support payments continue indefinitely, past the age of majority (18).

Out-of-state child support order: Can I enforce an out-of-state child support order in Arizona?
Yes, you can enforce the out-of-state child support order. It will be necessary for you to register the out-of-state child support order with the Arizona courts, so that Arizona has jurisdiction and you have an Arizona case number. To "register" your case means that you will need a certified copy of your domestic relations file from the other state and file it with the Arizona courts.

Do I have to pay child support if I do not have a job or lose my job?
Yes, you are under a court order to continue to pay child support. If the unfortunate circumstance occurs and a parent does not have employment, it may be necessary for that parent to request that the court modify the child support obligation to reflect the current situation.

What can I do if the obligated parent does not pay child support?
If an obligated parent does not pay child support, you may file a Petition to Enforce Child Support, Child Support Arrears and Medical Expense Reimbursement. Often, all three of those issues go together. It makes sense to include those three issues in one petition, because if the obligated parent is not paying child support, you will want to ask the court to enforce the child support order in effect. You will also want the obligated parent to pay for the months he/she did not pay, along with any medical expenses he/she did not pay. Also be advised that it is appropriate in that petition to ask for the obligated parent to pay your attorney's fees if you hire an attorney for this issue.

Can child support be modified?
Child support is modifiable if there is a change in circumstances that would result in a 15 percent change in the support amount; moreover, the support terminates upon the emancipation of the child. In Arizona, emancipation occurs at age 18 or high school graduation, whichever occurs later, but not later than age 19.

What about other child expenses that are not included in the child support worksheet?
One parent will be required to maintain health insurance for the children, and if there are any medical/dental/vision/orthodontia expenses not covered by insurance, the parties will often divide those expenses in proportion to their incomes.

Chapter Six:

PROPERTY

CHAPTER 6: PROPERTY

Personal and Real Property; Community and Separate Property

As stated earlier, all property acquired during marriage is considered community. The exceptions to that are community gifts and any property that you inherited.

How Arizona Law Sees Division of Property (A.R.S. §28-211 & 25-318)

You and your spouse may decide this for yourselves, but it is important to note that Arizona is a community property state. In accordance with Arizona Revised Statute §25-211, community property is all property acquired during the marriage by the efforts of either party through the date of service of the Petition for Dissolution. The court presumes that each spouse is entitled to 50 percent of the assets acquired during marriage. Also, the courts generally seek to *divide debt equitably* in a divorce case. This does not automatically mean that each spouse will have 50 percent of the debt assigned to them. The court will take into consideration the spouse's income, ability to pay debts and issues of waste of community property assets.

Usually, the community property is divided equally. It does not matter that one spouse contributed more than the other. The court may, in rare cases, give one spouse more than one-half because the other has destroyed, sold or given away community property or for other compelling reasons. The court may divide property by ordering it to be sold or by splitting it between the parties.

If one spouse had property prior to the marriage, but that property has increased in value during the course of the marriage, then the increase in value could be deemed community property and divided between the parties, if the increase came from labor by either spouse during the marriage or expenditure of community funds.

What Is Considered Community Property

According to Arizona Revised Statute, Section 25-211, generally, anything that a married couple accumulates during the marriage is considered community property, that is, both spouses own an undivided share of the whole. Exceptions to this general principle include those assets acquired prior to the marriage, by gift, devise (a will) or descent (inheritance). Because the Arizona courts start with a strong presumption that anything acquired during marriage is a community item, the spouse claiming a particular item is not community property has the burden of proving otherwise.

Property that is Not Divided

According to Arizona Revised Statute §25-213, "separate property" cannot be divided by the court. Separate property consists of items owned before the marriage or received as an inheritance or gift during the marriage and kept separate during the marriage. It is possible for a person to gift his or her separate property to community property—for example, by re-titling the property as community property.

Debts

Arizona Revised Statute §25-318 provides that debt incurred during the marriage is presumed to be community debt. Generally, the court divides debt equally. Debt incurred by a spouse before the marriage remains the separate debt of that spouse. The court may also order the parties to submit a debt distribution plan. This means that within thirty (30) days after receipt of a written request for information from a litigant (which includes the court name and case number), a creditor shall provide the balance and account status of any debts of either party or both spouses, identified by account number, for which the requesting spouse may be liable to the creditor.

Deferred Compensation, 401k, Retirement Benefits

The court will split these 50/50 if it was all acquired during the marriage. There is no penalty to divide and the money is not removed from the accounts. After the division, each party is subject to IRS rules for prematurely withdrawing the money. One spouse cannot create a tax liability for the other spouse. The money/account should not be withdrawn during the pending divorce.

A Qualified Domestic Relations Order may be required if you are dividing your deferred compensation, 401k or retirement benefits. If this is the case, a QDRO expert may be necessary to divide these assets. The QDRO expert will require information concerning the date of your marriage and the date of the plan to value, which is usually the date the QDRO expert actually divides the asset. You will need to contact a QDRO expert for this.

Life Insurance

Life insurance can be negotiated during the pendency of your divorce. You and your spouse can agree to divide the policy. Typically, a court will order that the life insurance policy be sold (if applicable) and the parties will split the cash amount.

Characterization of Property

The first thing to decide is the character of the property. If it is community, it can be split 50-50. If it is sole and separate, it is yours and does not need to be divided, but it must be disclosed. At the end of the divorce, you will want to divide the community property approximately equally. This includes the house, furniture, cars, boat, bank accounts, savings, stocks, investments, pensions and debts. You also need to be aware that each spouse has an obligation to disclose all property under the Rule of Family Law Procedure 49. Hiding assets will not be treated kindly by the court. Even sole and separate property must be disclosed, so the other spouse has an opportunity to determine if it really is sole and separate.

Property Worksheet

First, list all your property. It will be very helpful for you to fill this out as you get started. You need to first identify all property, regardless of whether you think it is community or sole and separate. Then, after you identify all your property, you can review the statutes and the Question and Answer section to determine how you and your spouse would like it to be divided. You can return to the worksheet and fill in how you think it should be fairly distributed. You and your spouse can each fill out a worksheet, or you can fill it out together.

The Property Worksheet: Identify ALL property.

REAL PROPERTY

Property Address	**Value of your house today. Use comps or appraisals to determine.**	**How much do you owe? (Including 1st and 2nd mortgages)**	**Net equity (Value – amount owed = net equity)**

VEHICLES

Make, Model and Year of Vehicle	**Value of vehicle (Use Kelly Blue Book and find your vehicle listed for good condition and use the suggested retail value, not the trade-in or private party value.)****	**How much is owed on the vehicle?**	**Equity of Vehicle (Value of vehicle – amount owed = vehicle equity)**

**This can be disputed but try and agree upon one method for all vehicles unless they are not all in the same condition.

BOATS, OTHER VEHICLES

Boat or other Vehicle (including recreational vehicles) (Year)	**Value of boat or vehicle**	**How much is owed on the boat or vehicle?**	**Equity of boat or Vehicle (Value – amount owed = equity)**

LIFE INSURANCE

Name of Owner	Date Purchased	Whose life is the life insurance on?	Is there any value? If yes, how much?

FURNITURE

Room	List of Items
Living Room (including couches, tables, art, chairs, televisions, DVD players)	
Dining Room (including table, chairs, rugs, art, decorations)	
Family Room (including couches, tables, art, chairs, televisions, DVD players)	
Master bedroom (including bed, dressers, art, chairs, bed stands)	
Bedroom #2 (including bed, dressers, art, chairs, bed stands)	
Bedroom #3 (including bed, dressers, art, chairs, bed stands)	
Kitchen (including appliances)	

BANK ACCOUNTS (INCLUDING CHECKING, SAVINGS, INVESTMENT ACCOUNTS)

Bank Name	Name(s) on Account	Last four digits of account number (never disclose full account numbers due to the possibility of identity theft).	Balance as of __/__/20__

DEFERRED COMPENSATION/401Ks/RETIREMENT ACCOUNTS

Bank Name	Name(s) on Account	Date account was opened	Last 4 digits on account number	Balance as of __/__/20__

WIFE'S OTHER PROPERTY (Gifts, inheritance, items owned prior to marriage, personal affects such as cameras, golf clubs, computers)

Item	Date Acquired

HUSBAND'S OTHER PROPERTY (Gifts, inheritance, items owned prior to marriage, personal effects such as cameras, golf clubs, computers)

Item	Date Acquired

Resolving Your Property Issues

The House

Is it community or sole and separate? If it is sole and separate, does the other spouse have an interest in it? Here are some questions to answer:

Whose name is on the deed? ______________________________

Did you and your spouse purchase it during the marriage? ______________

Where did the money come from for the down payment? ______________

If the house was purchased during the marriage with money from the marriage, such as money from your jobs, it most likely will be considered community property and will be divided equally.

Who, if anyone, wants to live in the home during the divorce? ____________

Do you want to sell the house, either because neither party can afford it or because neither party wants to live there? ______________________

If the House is Community Property

There are several options that you can consider:

Option 1: One spouse stays in the house and makes all the payments; the parties get the house appraised and decide the value of the house. Then the party who wants to live in the house pays the other spouse half the value of the house. This can be paid with cash in a refinance or can be "horse-traded" with other assets.

Option 2: The parties can sell the house and split the proceeds equally. The parties can split the costs of upkeep until the sale, or they can decide that one party lives there and makes all payments until the sale. Or, one spouse could move out and then combine all living expenses, with each paying half of those total expenses or each paying their prorated share, according to each party's income.

Option 3: One party stays in the house for a predetermined amount of time, such as one to two years, until a refinance must be undertaken.

There are a number of creative ways to determine the division; it is limited only by imagination and the ability to cooperate. The end goal is to split the proceeds 50-50 and not make the process more difficult than it needs to be for either party.

If the House is the Sole and Separate Property of One Spouse

If only one spouse's name is on the deed, or if one party owned the house prior to marriage, it might be considered that spouse's sole and separate property. This can become a complicated legal issue and you should seek the advice of an attorney if you have any questions.

Personal Property

Vehicles: Usually spouses have driven one vehicle and that is the one they want to keep. There may be an adjustment if one vehicle has a greater value than the other. For instance, if the truck has equity of $10,000 and the SUV has equity of $20,000, one person has $10,000 more value than the other. The truck spouse is due an additional $5,000 on his/her side of the ledger (the vehicles together equal $30,000 so each spouse should get a value of $15,000; the truck spouse only has $10,000 in value, so is due an additional $5,000).

The Furniture
Here are some ways to divide your property:

Idea #1: Using your list, have a "draft," where one party chooses, then the other, until the list has been divided.

Idea #2: Each party discusses what they want and then split the rest as above.

Idea #3: One party writes down all the community property on two separate lists. Then the other party picks which list they want.

Idea #4: The property is appraised (garage sale value) and then one party pays the other.

Idea #5: Just talk and work it out. This too, can be horse-traded with other assets if one party really wants certain property. Remember that used furniture is not that valuable; it is not worth the amount you purchased it for. One of you might want or need more furniture than the other and you could exchange it for the extra value of the vehicles. In other words, you get half the pie, but you can negotiate what pieces make up your half.

Bank Accounts, Savings Accounts and Investment Accounts

If these accounts were opened and contributed to during the marriage, they will be considered community. If one spouse had an account before marriage and did not commingle community funds, it will be sole and separate property of one spouse. If there are complications, this may be a question for an experienced family law attorney.

Property Settlement Agreement

When and How to Get Your Marital Settlement Agreement

At this point, you are probably wondering what to do with all of this information and how is it used in the divorce process. As previously discussed, it is important to know what assets you and your spouse either own together or separately and their value. It is with this information that you can begin your negotiation process with your spouse and begin drafting a Property Settlement Agreement.

A Property Settlement Agreement lays out and explains how your property will be divided. If the court ultimately decides how your property will be divided, the property division will be explained in your decree, which is public record and can be read by anyone. If, however, you negotiate and draft a Property Settlement Agreement, you can incorporate this agreement by mere reference in your divorce decree. (This means that your decree will include language referring to your Property Settlement Agreement as the explanation of the property division).

Should you write your agreement or seek the advice of an attorney? It depends on the complexity of your situation. You may consider consulting an attorney so that you understand the family law statutes and how they apply to you. If there is an impasse between you and your partner, you do not need to go to court; you can mediate (settle) your dispute with a mediator, who is preferably an experienced family law attorney.

Property Settlement Agreement Highlights

1. Timing: You must file your petition and response and wait the 60 days before filing your agreement.
2. You should take time to negotiate your agreement after you have full and complete financial disclosure.
3. Never sign an agreement without disclosure.
4. Secure promises to pay. Make sure you understand creditor rights, even if one spouse agrees to pay community debt.
5. Consider taxes for the year you are in and any part of the year you are married.
6. It must be signed and in writing to be valid, only another written document can revoke it.
7. Child support and custody are always modifiable.
8. It is best if your signatures are notarized. Keep the original(s) in a safe place.
9. Make decisions with a clear head after knowing the law and having full disclosure.

Following is a sample agreement so you know what one looks like. You can use it as a guide if you have a very simple divorce: two cars, furniture, and not much debt. For anything more complicated, you should consider consulting with an attorney.

WARNING: There are things not covered in this sample or things you might not understand. We suggest you get legal help for advice or for document drafting. These might include:

1. Spousal Support
2. Deferred compensation plans and valuation dates
3. Tax issues on spousal maintenance and how to file
4. Equalization payments
5. Security for payments of debt or money to be paid in future
6. Business Income, how to value and divide
7. Zero child support or support outside the guidelines
8. Anything you do not understand, get help!

Sample Settlement Agreement

On the next page is a sample agreement:

**The names used in this sample marital settlement agreement are fictitious and do not represent actual people.

MARITAL SETTLEMENT AGREEMENT (Case No. FN2010-000000)

THIS AGREEMENT made effective this ___ day of December, 2010, between **ALICE DODGSON** (hereinafter referred to as "Wife") and **JOHNNY DODGSON** (hereinafter referred to as "Husband"), hereinafter referred to singly as a "party" or jointly as the "parties";

WITNESETH:

A. WHEREAS, the parties were married on **March 5, 2003**;

B. WHEREAS, certain differences have arisen between the parties and a **Petition for Dissolution of Marriage without Minor Children** has been filed with the Superior Court of Maricopa County, Arizona on **September 15, 2010** bearing Superior Court Number **FN2010-000000**;

C. WHEREAS, there are no minor children;

D. WHEREAS, Wife is not now pregnant;

E. WHEREAS, the marriage of the parties is irretrievably broken an[illegible]here is [illegible] possibility of reconciliation;

F. WHEREAS, the parties have acquired certain joint, common and communi[illegible]roperty [illegible]ich they seek to divide and to make a full, complete, and final ad[illegible]tment of all ri[illegible]th[illegible]o, and the parties have incurred certain community and joint debts [illegible] obligations w[illegible] they seek to allocate responsibility therefore;

G. WHEREAS, the parties desire to enter into an [illegible]nt fo[illegible] co[illegible]te adjustment and settlement of all property rights and other righ[illegible]epende[illegible]upon a[illegible]g out of their marital relationship;

H. WHEREAS, the parties are desirous of comprom[illegible] a[illegible] settling their differences amicably and mutually declaring their rights and [illegible] of ev[illegible] sort whatsoever by entering into this settlement agreement; and

I. WHEREAS, the parties by this agre[illegible]en[illegible]end to [illegible]fect an equitable division of the community, joint and common property [illegible]quire[illegible]d obligations incurred by them during the existence of their marriage;

NOW, THEREFORE, in conside[illegible] pre[illegible]es and of the mutual covenants and agreements contained hereinafter, it is mutually a[illegible]d betw[illegible]parties as follows:

I. ADVICE OF COUNS[illegible]

Wife has had th[illegible]ice, aid and a[illegible]ance of counsel, Attorney #1 Name. Husband has had the advice, aid and assistan[illegible]l Attorn[illegible]2 Name. To the extent either of the parties did not seek appraisal of any real or [illegible]rsonal [illegible] whether community, quasi-community, joint, common or separate, the parties have b[illegible] ad[illegible]ed as to the availability of and the right to obtain such appraisals and each of the [illegible]s has know[illegible] and voluntarily waived such procedures and rights. Each of the parties understand[illegible]hat the agree[illegible]ts and obligations assumed by the other in this Marital Settlement Agreemen[illegible] ass[illegible]ith t[illegible]express understanding and agreement that they are in full satisfaction of all obligati[illegible]usba[illegible]and Wife now have or might otherwise have each towards the other.

The parties ackn[illegible]edge and agree that, except as expressly set forth in this Agreement, neither party has relied upon [illegible] warranty of the other or of any agent, employee or attorney of the other in entering into this [illegible]rital Settlement Agreement. Husband and Wife have each relied upon their independent investigators, judgments and personal assessments in reaching this agreement. The parties acknowledge and agree that this Marital Settlement Agreement has been bargained for at arm's length; that neither party has relied upon any fiduciary obligation which may have heretofore existed between the parties; and that there exists no fiduciary relationship between the parties concerning the negotiation and execution of this Agreement. Each of the parties understands the legal and practical effects of this Agreement and the provisions hereof and acknowledges that this Agreement is not the result of any fraud,

APPROVED:

duress or undue influence exercised by either party upon the other or by any other person or persons upon the parties hereto and that both parties are competent to contract and fully understand the terms and effect of this Agreement. The parties declare that they have each made a diligent and careful search of all of the real and personal property owned by the parties and each warrants, one to the other, that he and/or she has made a full and complete disclosure of all of the real and personal property owned by the community and that provision for the equitable division of this property has been made pursuant to the terms of this Agreement. If there should be community assets discovered after, then the parties shall hold that property as tenants in common.

II. LIVE SEPARATE AND APART:

The parties shall live separately from each other. Neither party will interfere with or intervene in the affairs of the other or harass, molest or annoy the other or endeavor to compel or induce the other to cohabit or dwell with him or her or compel the other to pay sums of money or to act in any way or for any purpose except as hereinafter provided.

III. IRREVOCABLE DIVISION AND NON-TAXABLE EVENT:

The divisions and transfers of real and personal property between the parties as herein provided are effective immediately and are irrevocable. The parties have agreed upon an equitable division of their community, joint, common, real and personal property, the division of which is set forth hereinafter. The parties intend the distribution of property herein to be considered a property settlement and a transfer incident to divorce and, therefore, a non-taxable event under the current federal and state tax codes, including Section 1041 of the Internal Revenue Code. Neither party shall treat the division of property provided for herein as a sale or as giving rise to gain or loss for federal income tax purposes or as entitling a party to an adjustment in the basis for income tax purposes of any item or property retained, received or transferred by this Agreement. Should either party violate the provisions of this paragraph and thereby cause tax liability to the other party, the party incurring liability shall hold the other harmless and pay all consequential liability of the other party.

IV. HUSBAND'S RELEASE OF CLAIMS:

Subject to the provisions of this Agreement, Husband hereby releases, grants, transfers, conveys, waives and quit claims any and all interest, estate or other right or cause of action which he may now or hereafter have or claim by reason of the marital relationship, premarital relationship or premarital agreement, community property theory, appellate case authority or any state or federal statute, in any or all earnings, income, profits, benefits, claims and/or property, real, personal or mixed, and wheresoever situated, previously acquired by or on behalf of Wife prior to the marriage of the parties, presently acquired by or on behalf of Wife by the terms of this Agreement and/or hereafter acquired by or on behalf of the Wife. The Husband agrees that the Wife may convey or otherwise dispose of or deal with the same as though she had never been married.

V. WIFE'S RELEASE OF CLAIMS:

Subject to the provisions of this Agreement, Wife hereby releases, grants, transfers, conveys, waives and quit claims any and all interest, estate or other right or cause of action which she may now or hereafter have or claim by reason of the marital relationship, premarital relationship or premarital agreement, community property theory, appellate case authority or any state or federal statute, in any or all earnings, income, profits, benefits, claims and/or property, real, personal or mixed, and wheresoever situated, previously acquired by or on behalf of Husband prior to the marriage of the parties, presently acquired by or on behalf of Husband by the terms of this Agreement and/or hereafter acquired by or on behalf of the Husband. The Wife agrees that the Husband may convey or otherwise dispose of or deal with the same as though he had never been married.

VI. WAIVER IN ESTATE OF OTHER PARTY:

Each provision of this Agreement shall be binding upon the estates of the respective parties, each party hereby:

APPROVED:

_________ Page 2 of 6 _________

A. Waives and releases any right or interest whether by law, dower, courtesy or otherwise in law, to or in all real or personal property which the other party may now or hereafter acquire;

B. Agrees that the estate of the other party, real and personal, shall go and belong at the death of the other party to the person or persons who have become entitled thereto as if he or she (party agreeing) had predeceased such other party;

C. Agrees that he or she will permit any Will of the other party to be probated and will allow administration upon the property of the other party to be taken out by the person or persons who would have been entitled thereto if she or he had predeceased such other party;

D. Waives any and all right to letters of administration upon the estate of the other party; and

E. Waives election and every other right granted by laws of any jurisdiction to take against any Will of the other party, whether such Will shall have been executed before or [illegible]ll be executed after the date of this Agreement.

VII. EARNINGS, INCOME AND PROPERTY HEREINAFT[illegible] SEPARATE:

Except as otherwise may be provided herein, all the earnings, i[illegible], [illegible]fits, benefits or accumulations of either party from and after the date of service and all prope[illegible]cquired h[illegible]ein and acquired in any manner hereinafter, by either party shall be and remain the sole an[illegible]arat[illegible]operty of the party so earning, receiving, accumulating or acquiring the sa[illegible]nd each of the [illegible] hereto does relinquish, waive and quit claim in favor of the other party any righ[illegible] claim of any [illegible]d or character whatsoever to such earnings, income, profits, benefits, increa[illegible]quality [illegible]umulati[illegible] and property.

VIII. EXECUTION OF DOCUMENTS:

The parties hereto agree that each will, at an[illegible]me, mak[illegible] execute [illegible] deliver all instruments, conveyances, powers of attorney, authorizations and al[illegible]r do[illegible]ments or assigns reasonably required or desirable to effectuate any conveyance or tra[illegible]er of an[illegible]d property, each to the other or for the purpose of giving full effect to this Agreeme[illegible]vided, [illegible]ver, that neither party hereto shall be required to assume liability for the payment of [illegible]ey or th[illegible]curring of any liability other than as expressly provided for in this Agreement.

IX. SOLE AND ENTIRE AGREEM[illegible]NT:

It is agreed that there is n[illegible]ontract, [illegible]l or in writing, existing between the parties hereto relative to the matters herein ment[illegible] [illegible]reements and understandings between the parties are embodied in this Agreement, tha[illegible] Agre[illegible] is entire in itself and is not a part of any other contract or agreement; th[illegible] no promises, [illegible]rranties or representations of any nature or character have been made to induce e[illegible] to enter [illegible] this Agreement and the parties hereto have agreed and acknowledged that neith[illegible] been [illegible]luenced by the other in the making or execution of this Agreement. Husband and [illegible]fe ea[illegible]y represent and warrant to the other that each has considered with particula[illegible] their res[illegible] economic circumstances as it applies to the division and disposition provided fo[illegible] this Agreem[illegible] and each is satisfied that the provisions of this Agreement are equitable, reasonabl[illegible]d fair.

X. [illegible]L [illegible] COURT, NON MERGER AND INDEPENDENT STATUS:

This Agreement s[illegible]ll be incorporated but not merged into the Consent Decree of Dissolution of Marriage entered by sai[illegible] Court in said action and shall survive as an independent contract of the parties and its validity shall [illegible] res judicata effect.

XI. SPOUSAL SUPPORT:

Husband shall pay Wife spousal maintenance for two (2) years commencing on January 1, 2011. Payments shall be made directly to Wife. Payments shall be in the amounts as follows:

1. Husband shall pay Wife $2600.00 per month.

This spousal maintenance amount is non-modifiable, except that it will terminate by death of either party or by remarriage of Wife. Spousal maintenance payments shall be taxable income to Wife and deductible to Husband.

APPROVED:

XII. PROPERTY AWARDED TO HUSBAND:

Wife shall assign, grant, confirm, convey and transfer and does hereby assign, grant, confirm, convey and transfer to the Husband as his sole and separate property, he to assume, pay and hold Wife harmless from any encumbrances thereon except as otherwise provided, all of Wife's right, title and interest in and to the property set forth as follows:

1. Ford truck
2. Individual Retirement Account with in Husband's name; and
3. $25,000.00 in his possession. There shall be no re-allocation of this or any other cash.

Husband is solely responsible for all expenses, including insurance, for the above vehicle. Each party will cooperate in transferring the certificate of title for the above-referenced vehicle within thirty (30) days of the Consent Decree being entered by the court.

XIII. PROPERTY AWARDED TO WIFE:

Husband shall assign, grant, confirm, convey and transfer and does hereby assign, grant, confirm, convey and transfer to the Wife as her sole and separate property, her to assume, pay and hold Husband harmless from any encumbrances thereon except as otherwise provided, all of Husband's right, title and interest in and to the property set forth as follows:

1. Range Rover;
2. Individual Retirement Account in Wife's name;
3. $30,000.00 in Wife's possession. There shall be no re-allocation of this or any other cash.

Wife will be solely responsible for all expenses, including insurance, for the above vehicles. Each party will cooperate in transferring the certificate of title for the above-referenced vehicles within thirty (30) days of the Consent Decree being entered by the court.

A. Real Property

Husband and Wife shall now be tenants in common for the following properties:

1. The real property located at 12[illegible] Drive, Carroll, Arizona, 85020, (hereinafter the "Carroll, Arizona residence");

B. Life Insurance

Husband will maintain this policy and will maintain Wife as a beneficiary for a benefit of $100,000 until Husband's Spousal Support obligation is paid in full. Husband shall comply with Wife's request to produce a copy of such beneficiary statement on an annual basis.

XIV. COMMUNITY BUSINESS:

Husband shall be confirmed to him as his sole and separate property Johnny D. Dodgson's cupcake business. Husband shall assume, pay and hold Wife harmless from any encumbrances or liabilities thereon except as otherwise provided all of Wife's right, title and interest in and to Johnny D. Dodgson's cupcake business. Wife expressly waives any community lien against this business.

XV. COMMUNITY OBLIGATIONS:

Husband shall assume, pay, indemnify and hold Wife harmless from the following community obligations so specified as follows:

1. Any and all credit card debt in Husband's name.

Wife shall assume, pay, indemnify, and hold Husband harmless from the following community obligations so specified as follows:

1. Any and all credit card debt in Wife's name.

Except for the obligations set forth in this Agreement elsewhere, the party incurring a debt on or after the date of service of October 1, 2010 shall pay and hold the other party harmless therefrom.

XVI. ATTORNEYS' FEES AND COSTS:

Each party shall pay his or her own attorney's fees. In the event either party is required to bring legal action against the other party to enforce any rights under this Consent Decree, the prevailing party

APPROVED:

Page 4 of 6

______ ______

shall be entitled to recover from the other all reasonable costs and expenses incurred in bringing such action including, but not limited to, reasonable attorneys' fees.

XVII. FEDERAL AND STATE INCOME TAXES:

The parties shall file separate income tax returns for tax year 2009 and thereafter; each entitled to their own refunds and responsible for their own liabilities, from which they shall indemnify and hold the other harmless. Each party shall report on their separate tax return any income earned or received by them and each shall be solely responsible for the tax treatment of any asset awarded them herein. To the extent the parties continue to jointly own any property, each shall be entitled to one-half (1/2) of any tax deduction related thereto.

XVIII. MODIFICATION IN WRITING:

A modification or waiver of any of the provisions of this Agreement shall be effective only if made in writing and executed with the same formality as this Agreement.

XIX. BINDING UPON HEIRS AND SUCCESSORS/ TIME IS OF THE ESSENCE, STRICT PERFORMANCE REQUIRED:

Except as otherwise stated herein, all of the recitals, terms, provisions and covenants of this Agreement shall apply to, be binding upon and inure to the benefit of the respective heirs, next of kin, devisees, legatees, personal representatives, executors, administrators, assigns and successors in interest of the parties. Each party waives the right of inheritance from the other and the right to act as the executor, administrator or personal representative of the estate of the other.

Time is of the essence in the performance of each and every obligation herein imposed. Husband and Wife understand and acknowledge that each intends to insist upon strict performance of each and every term, provision and payment date herein contained. No waiver or indulgence or extension of any right, privilege, breach or default under this Agreement shall be deemed a waiver of any subsequent right, privilege, breach or default.

XX. NO WAIVER BY FAILURE TO ACT:

Neither any failure nor any delay on the part of either party hereto in exercising any right hereunder shall operate as a waiver thereof; nor shall any single or partial exercise of any right hereunder preclude another for further exercise thereof for the exercise of any other right. Waiver of any breach of the Agreement shall not be deemed a waiver of any subsequent breach of the same or of any other provision of this Agreement.

XXI. GOVERNING LAW:

This Agreement shall be construed and interpreted in accordance with the laws of the state of Arizona.

XXII. EFFECTIVE DATE OF AGREEEMENT/CONSTRUCTION:

The effective date of this Agreement shall be as of the signing of the agreement. This Agreement and its Exhibits were drafted by the attorney for Husband as a matter of convenience only and shall not be construed for or against any party on that account or for any other reason.

XXIII. SEVERABILITY:

The provisions of this Agreement should be enforced to the fullest extent possible under the law and public policies applied in each jurisdiction in which enforcement is sought. If any particular provision of this Agreement or portion thereof is held to be wholly invalid or unenforceable, this Agreement shall be deemed to be amended to delete therefrom that portion thus adjudicated invalid and the deletion shall apply only with respect to the operation of said provision. Notwithstanding the foregoing, to the extent a provision of this Agreement or portion is deemed unenforceable by virtue of its scope, but may be made enforceable by limitation, each party agrees the same shall be enforceable to the fullest extent permissible under the laws and public policies applied in the jurisdiction in which enforcement is sought.

XXIV. PARAGRAPH HEADINGS:

APPROVED:

_________ Page 5 of 6 _________

The paragraph headings used herein are for convenience and reference only and are not intended to define, limit or describe the scope or intent of any provision of this Agreement.

XXV. GENDER, NUMBER AND LIMITATIONS:

This Agreement shall apply to the parties according to the context hereof and without regard to the number or gender of the words or expressions made herein and the words "include" and "including" shall mean "without limitation" regardless of the subsequent enumeration.

XXVI. SETTLEMENT DOCUMENTS:

This Agreement constitutes a settlement document and shall not constitute an admission of any fact by any party and shall not be admissible in any proceeding except a proceeding commenced to enforce any rights under this Agreement or resulting from any alleged breach of this Agreement.

XXVII. CONVEYANCE DOCUMENT:

This Agreement may be recorded by any party in any jurisdiction and in the absence of any appropriate deed, bill of sale, title, certificate or other conveyance document required or necessary to give effect to this Agreement; this Agreement may serve as and shall constitute such conveyance document. The parties hereto acknowledge that upon execution this document constitutes a conveyance of the real and personal property which is the subject of this Agreement, subject only to performance by the parties of their respective obligations under this Agreement.

XXVIII. INCORPORATION:

The recitals herein shall be considered a part of this Agreement as these covenants as if fully set forth herein and the parties hereby ratify and acknowledge each of the recitals.

XXIX. TERMINATION OF JOINT TENANCY STATUS:

The parties hereby agree that any property currently owned by the parties in joint tenancy with the right of survivorship is hereby severed and terminated in [illegible] of tenant in common status.

IN WITNESS WHEREOF the parties have signed, sealed and acknowledged this Agreement and initialed each page, a true copy of which shall constitute an original.

______________________ ______________________

ALICE DODGSON **JOHNNY DODGSON**
Petitioner Respondent

STATE OF ARIZONA)
County of Maricopa)

On this ___ day of ________, 2011 before me the undersigned authority, personally appeared **ALICE DODGSON** known to me to be the person whose name is subscribed to the foregoing instrument and who acknowledged to me that she executed the same for the purposes contained therein. In witness whereof, I have hereunto set my hand and official seal.

____
Notary Public My Commission Expires:

STATE OF ARIZONA)
County of Maricopa)

On this ___ day of ________, 2011, before me the undersigned authority, personally appeared **JOHNNY DODGSON**, known to me to be the person whose name is subscribed to the foregoing instrument and who acknowledged to me that she executed the same for the purposes contained therein. In witness whereof, I have hereunto set my hand and official seal.

____
Notary Public My Commission Expires:

APPROVED:

________ Page 6 of 6 ________

Frequently Asked Questions

How will our property be divided? (A.R.S. §28-211 and A.R.S. §25-318)
You and your spouse may decide this for yourselves, but it is important to note that Arizona is a community property state. In accordance with Arizona Revised Statute §25-211, community property is all property acquired during the marriage by the efforts of either party through the date of service of the Petition for Dissolution. The court presumes that each spouse is entitled to 50 percent of the assets acquired during marriage. Also, the courts generally seek to divide debt equitably in a divorce case. This does not automatically mean that each spouse will have 50 percent of the debt assigned to them. The court will take into consideration each spouse's income, ability to pay debts and issues of waste of community property assets.

Usually, the community property is divided equally. It does not matter that one spouse contributed more than the other. The court may, in rare cases, give one spouse more than one-half because the other has destroyed, sold or given away community property or for other compelling reasons. The court may divide property by ordering it to be sold, or by splitting it between the parties.

If one spouse had property prior to the marriage, but that property has increased in value during the course of the marriage, then the increase in value could be deemed community property and divided between the parties, if the increase came from labor by either spouse during the marriage or expenditure of community funds.

Is everything we own considered community property?
According to Arizona Revised Statute, section 25-211, generally anything that a married couple accumulates during the marriage is considered community property. That is, both spouses own an undivided share of the whole. Exceptions to this general principle include those assets acquired prior to the marriage, by gift, devise (a will) or descent (inheritance). Because the Arizona courts start with a strong presumption that anything acquired during marriage is a community item, the spouse claiming a particular item is not community property has the burden of proving otherwise.

What property is not divided?
According to Arizona Revised Statute §25-213 "separate property" cannot be divided by the court. Separate property consists of items owned before the marriage or received as an inheritance or gift during the marriage and kept separate during the marriage. It is possible for a person to gift his or her separate property to the community—for example, by re-titling the property as community property.

What about the debts?
Arizona Revised Statute §25-318 provides that debt incurred during the marriage is presumed to be community debt. Generally, the court divides debt equally. Debt incurred by a spouse before the marriage remains the separate debt of that spouse. The court may also order the parties to submit a debt distribution plan. Within thirty (30) days after receipt of a written request for information from a litigant which includes the court name and case number, a creditor shall provide the balance and account status of any debts of either party or both spouses, identified by account number, for which the requesting spouse may be liable to the creditor.

What if my spouse does not pay the community debts as ordered in the final decree? Can our creditors force me to pay?
Yes, Arizona Revised Statute §25-318 states that a creditor can collect a marital debt from either spouse, regardless of which spouse is ordered to pay the debt by the court. The innocent spouse then has the right to recover from the obligated spouse. If a party fails to comply with an order to pay debts, the court may enter orders transferring the property of that spouse to compensate the other party.

What happens when the spouses own a business together?
During the divorce process, the court will usually attempt to keep the things the way they presently are when it comes to the day-to-day operations of a family business. A business valuation expert can assess the value of the business during the pendency of the divorce matter. The court, with the input from the business valuation expert, will determine the value of the family business. The spouse that is ultimately awarded the business may be required to pay the other spouse that individual's share of the business. That amount is normally one-half of the value assigned to the family owned business. You should consult an attorney for this matter.

What if neither of us can afford the house?
This is no different than if you were together. You have the same problems and issues as if you were together (divorce just makes it more difficult). The mortgage company expects both of you to pay. If there is a deficiency judgment because of a line of credit, the creditor will look to both of you to pay, no matter what your divorce agreement says.

Decide who pays for repairs during the dissolution, who should sell and how long they have to sell. If one party agrees to buy out the other party, you need to agree when you appraise the house.

What if one party made the down payment with money earned prior to marriage, but after marriage, put the house deed in both names as joint tenants?
The house is community property and the spouse who made a down payment may have "gifted" the property to the other spouse. Some courts will award the spouse a return of the down payment and then split the net equity.

What if I paid the down payment, my spouse has lived here during our entire marriage, but her name is not on the deed?
The house most likely remains your sole and separate property, but your spouse has an equitable lien on the house for the community effort put into the house during the marriage that increased its value. You may want to consult an attorney.

My spouse and I purchased the house together, but I made her sign a disclaimer deed two years later when I refinanced the house. The house is all mine, right?
Quite possibly, but while disclaimer deeds are valid, there can be suspect issues. Disclaimer deeds make it look like you were trying to cheat your spouse out of the house. A court will want to know if she was represented by counsel and how much she understood about what she was doing. And again, there is the equitable lien issue as outlined above.

My husband will not get out of the house, and I just filed for divorce.
You will have to file a motion to ask the court for exclusive use of the home. This is discretionary with the judge, and will likely take a month or more to get a hearing; usually, this is part of a temporary orders hearing. If you both own the house, maybe you can negotiate this move. Once one person moves out, the leaving spouse should not come and go in the house without permission of the other spouse. Some judges consider the "leaving spouse" as moved out of the house until further court order.

Who pays for repairs while our house is for sale?
You can agree that the party living in it pays for everything under a certain amount, such as $100. Any other repairs are split 50-50 and can be reimbursed at the sale. It might be wise to purchase a home warranty to prevent any unexpected expenses.

Who gets the kids' furniture?
This is negotiable, but it should be a consideration if one parent has to buy all new furniture, beds, etc. for the kids in a shared custody arrangement.

What is considered my sole and separate personal property?
Anything you owned prior to marriage, property that you inherited, and usually jewelry given, gifted to you, your sports equipment, your personal electronics, clothing.

Who gets our digital camera?
If you both use it and bought it with community funds, it needs to be divided, along with other property.

Who gets the vehicles if both vehicles have debt and no equity?
Usually whoever gets the vehicle gets the debt. Remember, the lender will not honor your decree; your spouse can ruin your credit if he/she does not pay. There can still be an equitable set-off.

I inherited money when my mom died six years ago and put my husband's name on the account. Is this money community or my sole and separate money?
This might be considered gifted to him and commingled with community funds. If you can trace the amount, you can have it returned to you. A fair way to handle this is to allow you to get your lump sum deposit back. If there is an issue of commingling, such as you putting other community money into the account, it is discretionary with the judge. Let's assume that you inherited $100,000 and put it in an account and never did anything else with that account. You should be able to consider it sole and separate and it should be awarded to you.

What if my spouse does not pay the community debts as ordered in the final decree? Can our creditors force me to pay?
Yes, Arizona Revised Statute §25-318 states that a creditor can collect a marital debt from either spouse, regardless of which spouse is ordered to pay the debt by the court. The innocent spouse then has the right to recover from the obligated spouse. If a party fails to comply with an order to pay debts, the court may enter orders transferring the property of that spouse to compensate the other party.

I am getting ready to file for divorce. Can I take all the money out of our joint savings account?
No, because although the temporary injunction is not in place, you are intending to file and it is not fair to take all the money. You may take half of the money, and this should not cause any problems in case you have to explain this to a judge.

I won an award for a car accident and put it in an account in my name alone. Do I have to split it during the divorce?
No, a personal injury settlement for pain and suffering is your sole and separate property.

I won a settlement for a car accident and put it in an account with both our names on it. Do I have to split it?
If you can trace the original amount, it will most likely still be considered your sole and separate property. If it is commingled beyond recognition, you will most likely have to split it.

I had stocks before marriage, but bought more stock after marriage. Who gets the stocks?
The stocks you had prior to marriage are your sole and separate property. The stocks that you purchased with community funds are community property.

Chapter Seven:

SPOUSAL MAINTENANCE

CHAPTER 7: SPOUSAL MAINTENANCE

What is Spousal Maintenance?

Spousal maintenance (formerly known as alimony) is a monthly payment from one spouse to another, which is designed to allow for the spouse who earns less income to establish a home and living environment on his/her own. Spousal maintenance is used for an easier transition to becoming a single person in certain circumstances. Spousal maintenance will not last forever; it is designed to help a person get on his/her feet. (A questionnaire and calculation worksheet are included at the end of this chapter).

Factor One: Sufficient Property, Ability to Support Oneself, Educational Support and Marriage of Long Duration

If you answer yes to any of the following, go to Factor Two.

The first threshold question that the court must determine is whether:

1. A spouse lacks sufficient property to meet his or her reasonable needs
2. A spouse can't support him/herself by employment or must stay home with a young child
3. A spouse supported his or her spouse's education
4. The marriage was long and a spouse has little chance of employment

If one of the above threshold questions is yes, then Factor Two is analyzed.

Factor Two: Amount and Duration

If Factor One is met, then the Court considers the following:

a. Length of the marriage
b. Each party's age
c. Each party's health
d. Employment of both parties
e. The standard of living established during the marriage
f. The parties' respective resources
g. A party's deferment of career opportunities
h. Assistance in the career opportunities of the other party

Spousal Maintenance Calculation

In Arizona, there is no statutory formula for calculating spousal maintenance; however, there is an unofficial "guidelines" formula that is used by many attorneys and some judges (see questionnaire, worksheet at the end of this chapter).

Arizona judges have broad discretion in determining whether or not to award spousal maintenance and in determining the amount and duration of spousal maintenance awarded. It is best to speak directly with an attorney regarding your specific situation to get an idea of whether spousal maintenance might be awarded in your case.

Spousal Maintenance Questionnaire

(For the spouse requesting spousal maintenance)

1. How many years have you been married? ______________________

2. Are you presently employed? ______________________

If yes, where? ______________________
How long have you been employed there? ______________________
What is your rate of pay? ______________________
What education was necessary for you to acquire that position? ______________________
____

If no, where were you previously employed?
How long were you employed there? ______________________
What was your rate of pay? ______________________
What education was necessary for you to acquire that position? ______________________
____

3. List your last three (3) jobs prior to your current position:

Employer: ______________________
Dates of employment: ______________________
Rate of pay: ______________________
What education was necessary for you to acquire that position? ______________________
____

Employer: ______________________
Dates of employment: ______________________
Rate of pay: ______________________
What education was necessary for you to acquire that position? ______________________
____

Employer: ______________________
Dates of employment: ______________________
Rate of pay: ______________________
What education was necessary for you to acquire that position? ______________________
____

4. Have you been employed outside the home during the majority of your marriage? ______________________
   If no, what dates during your marriage have you not been employed outside the home? ______________________
   ____
   What did you do while not working outside the home? ______________________
   ____

5. Do you have any minor children? ____________________
If yes, how old are they? ____________________

6. Do you have any children with special needs? ____________________

7. Did you and your spouse agree for you to stop work to take care of the children? ____________________

8. What was the level of education that you had attained at the time of your marriage? ____________________

9. What is your current level of education? ____________________

10. What job skills, training, or experience did you have at the time of your marriage? ____________________

11. What job skills, training, or experience do you have now? ____________________

12. What is your usual occupation? ____________________

13. What will be your monthly income at the time of separation? ____________________

14. What will be your monthly expenses at the time of separation? (See your completed Affidavit of Financial Information (AFI).) ____________________

15. What will be the value of your half of the community property (cash, investments, retirement, house equity) at the time of separation? ____________________

16. How long would it take you to achieve the education or skills necessary to be able to individually attain the income that you need to pay your monthly expenses? ____________________

17. Did your spouse attend any special schools or training during the marriage? ____________________

18. Did you sacrifice any career opportunities in order to allow your spouse to attend school or achieve success in their occupation? ____________________

19. Do you feel you will be able to be self-sufficient after the divorce? ____________________

20. Do you anticipate any unusual expenses or circumstances in the near future that may affect your ability to become self-supporting? ______________________
____

21. Do you have any pre-marital agreement or post-marital agreement? __________
If yes, what are the details regarding spousal maintenance? ______________
____

22. Do you think you should be awarded spousal maintenance? ______________
If yes, how much? ______________________________________
For how many months or years? ________________________

23. What is your spouse's income? ________________________________

24. Other: ____
____
____

Spousal Maintenance Calculation Worksheet

If one spouse is entitled to spousal maintenance, the following is a spousal maintenance calculation as to the amount and duration to which you could be entitled:

Number of years married: ____________(A)
Husband's gross monthly income: ____________(B)
Wife's gross monthly income: ____________ (C)

Husband's gross monthly income minus (-)
Wife's gross monthly income: ____________ (D)

To determine the amount and duration of spousal maintenance, use the following formula with the above (#1-4) figures.

DURATION OF MARRIAGE: (A) years ______________

1. DURATION FACTOR: **0.015** X (A) years = _________ (E)

2. PARTIES' INCOME:

Husband/Obligor	Wife/Obligee
$(B)	$(C)

3. DIFFERENCE IN PARTIES' INCOME:
   $ (B)
   -$ (C)
   $ (D)

4. SPOUSAL MAINTENANCE
(DURATION FACTOR X DIFFERENCE OF INCOME)

(E) X $ (D) = (F)

5. DURATION (FOR HOW MANY YEARS – to be determined)
(A) Years X **0.3** = (G) years to (A) years X **0.5** = (H) years

Examples of Spousal Maintenance Calculations

As previously mentioned, the unofficial guidelines for spousal maintenance are determined with a mathematical formula. There are no guarantees of what a court will decide. Each case is very fact-specific and unique. Here are examples:

FAMILY #1

(A) Married 25 years
(B) Husband earns $140,000.00 per year ($11,666.00 per month)
(C) Wife earns $40,000.00 per year ($3333.00 per month)

(B)	–	(C)	= (D) Difference in income
$11,666.00	**–**	**$3,333.00**	**= $8,333.00**

Court used factor	x (A) years	=	(E) Duration factor
0.015	**x 25**	**=**	**0.375**

Amount

(E)	x	(D)	=	Spousal maintenance amount
0.375	**x**	**$8,333.00**	**=**	**$3,124.87**

Duration

(A) x 0.3 = Minimum duration	TO	(A) x 0.5 = Maximum duration
25 x 0.3 = 7.5 years	**TO**	**25 x 0.5 = 12.5 years**

Wife may be entitled to $3124.87 per month for 7.5 to 12.5 years.

FAMILY #2

A) Married 9 years
B) Wife earns $74,000.00 per year ($6,166.00 per month)
C) Husband earns $50,000.00 per year ($4,166.00 per month)

(B)	–	(C)	= (D) Difference in income
$6,166.00	**–**	**$4,166.00**	**= $2,000.00**

Court used factor	x (A) years	=	(E) Duration factor
0.015	**x 9**	**=**	**0.135**

Amount

(E)	x	(D)	=	Spousal maintenance amount
0.135	**x**	**$2,000.00**	**=**	**$270.00**

Duration

(A) x 0.3 = Minimum duration	TO	(A) x 0.5 = Maximum duration
9 x 0.3 = 2.7 years	**TO**	**9 x 0.5 = 4.5 years**

Husband may be entitled to $270.00 per month for 2.7 to 4.5 years.

FAMILY #3

A) Married 2 years
B) Wife earns $55,000.00 per year ($4583.00 per month)
C) Husband earns $0.00 per year ($0.00 per month)

(B)	–	(C)	= (D) Difference in income
$4,583.00	**–**	**$0.00**	**= $4,583.00**

Court used factor	x (A) years	=	(E) Duration factor
0.015	**x 2**	**=**	**0.03**

Amount

(E)	x	(D)	=	Spousal maintenance amount
0.03	**x**	**$4,583.00**	**=**	**$137.49**

Duration

(A) x 0.3 = Minimum duration	TO	(A) x 0.5 = Maximum duration
2 x 0.3 = 0.6 years	**TO**	**2 x 0.5 = 1 years**

Husband may be entitled to $137.49 for 0.6 to 1 year.

Frequently Asked Questions

How is spousal maintenance paid?
It can be paid directly from one spouse to the other. Both parties should keep very accurate records of the payments. The court may order the payments to be made through the clearinghouse, administered by the state of Arizona. They keep track of payments for you. Failure to pay is more easily handled in the court if the payments go through the clearinghouse. Be aware that there is a lag time between the time payment is made and the time it is received if you go through the state.

When does spousal maintenance end? (A.R.S. §25-327)
Spousal maintenance terminates upon the death or remarriage of the receiving spouse. This is called non-modifiable, but excludes these two situations. There will be a beginning date and an ending date for the payments if you negotiate it and if a court orders it.

Can spousal maintenance be modified?
Yes, under certain circumstances and depending upon how your decree or Property Settlement Agreement was drafted.

What if my spouse quits working in order to stop having to pay spousal maintenance?
A former spouse cannot avoid spousal maintenance or child support by voluntarily reducing or terminating his or her employment. The court has the discretion to attribute income to a spouse who voluntarily reduces his or her income and to require the paying spouse to pay spousal maintenance or child support in the former amount. The test is earning potential, not the actual earnings, if there was some kind of mischief.

What if my former spouse refuses to give me current financial information relating to support or changes in jobs? (A.R.S. §25-513)
You may send a written request by certified mail to your former spouse's employer or former employer requesting detailed information about all pay and benefits paid to your former spouse by the employer. You may also file a Petition for Order to Show Cause or Request For Expedited Hearing, requiring your spouse to provide you with the relevant information and to keep you apprised of his or her current employer's address. You should consult with an attorney.

Is spousal maintenance taxable?
Check with your accountant, but in general, spousal maintenance is taxable to receiver and tax-deductible to the payor.

Is spousal maintenance considered my salary for child support calculations?
Yes.

Can either a husband or a wife receive spousal maintenance?
Yes.

Can I waive my spousal maintenance?
Yes.

Does it matter how many children we have?
No.

Am I entitled to live the same as I did when we were married?
No. The style to which you have been accustomed is not the standard.

What if my husband had a really good job and now is unemployed?
It depends. If he cannot find employment, you may not be entitled to any spousal maintenance. You will have to investigate the reasons for the unemployment.

What if my husband has quit his job on purpose to avoid paying me?
If you can prove it, the court will consider the earning potential, not necessarily what he is actually earning. You would want to get his work records through discovery to find out if he quit, was fired, or was laid off.

Chapter Eight:

GAME-TIME

CHAPTER 8: GAME-TIME (The Documents and the Process of Divorce)

In order to file for dissolution or a legal separation there are a number of documents that need to be filled out and filed with the court. To better assist you, we have mapped out the documents you will need to file for the following types of cases:

- Dissolution without minor children (7 documents)
- Dissolution with minor children (9 documents)
- Legal Separation without minor children (6 documents)
- Legal Separation with minor children (8 documents)

Overview of Required Documents

The following is a summary of this chapter. "Required" means that the corresponding document needs to be filled out and filed with the initial petition.

Document Name	**Dissolution without minor children**	**Dissolution with minor children**	**Legal Separation without minor children**	**Legal Separation with minor children**
Family Court Cover Sheet	Required	Required	Required	Required
Sensitive Data Sheet	Required	Required	Required	Required
Summons	Required	Required	Required	Required
Preliminary Injunction	Required	Required	Required	Required
Petition	Required	Required	Required	Required
Notice of Your Rights about Health Insurance Coverage	Required	Required	Not required	Not required
Notice Regarding Creditors	Required	Required	Required	Required
Affidavit of Minor Children	Not required	Required	Not required	Required
Parent Information Class	Not required	Required	Not required	Required

Documents for Dissolution Without Minor Children

To file for dissolution of marriage without minor children the following documents need to be completed:

1. Family court cover sheet;
2. Sensitive data sheet;
3. Summons;
4. Preliminary Injunction;
5. Petition for Dissolution without Minor Children;
6. Notice of Your Rights about Health Insurance Coverage; and
7. Notice Regarding Creditors.

Documents for Dissolution With Minor Children

To file for dissolution of marriage with minor children the following documents need to be completed:

1. Family court cover sheet;
2. Sensitive data sheet;
3. Summons;
4. Preliminary Injunction;
5. Petition for Dissolution with Minor Children;
6. Notice of Your Rights about Health Insurance Coverage;
7. Notice Regarding Creditors;
8. Parent Information Class; and
9. Affidavit Regarding Minor Children.

Documents for Legal Separation Without Minor Children

To file for a legal separation without minor children the following documents need to be completed:

1. Family court cover sheet;
2. Sensitive data sheet;
3. Summons;
4. Preliminary Injunction;
5. Petition for Legal Separation without Minor Children; and
6. Notice Regarding Creditors.

Documents for Legal Separation With Minor Children

To file for a legal separation with minor children the following documents need to be completed:

1. Family court cover sheet;
2. Sensitive data sheet;
3. Summons;
4. Preliminary Injunction;
5. Petition for Dissolution with Minor Children;
6. Notice Regarding Creditors;
7. Parent Information Class; and
8. Affidavit Regarding Minor Children.

The Individual Documents

Each of these documents has a significant meaning for the courts and for you. Below is a list of the forms and their purpose.

Family Court Cover Sheet

This form helps the courts set up your file in their computer system. It should be the top form you present to the clerk when you file these forms. The clerk will want to see that all of this information is filled out, so that their court records are complete. Throughout the divorce process, the court will periodically send out minute entries or court orders to you. It is important that your personal information (especially your address) is updated with the court, so that you will receive all of these necessary documents.

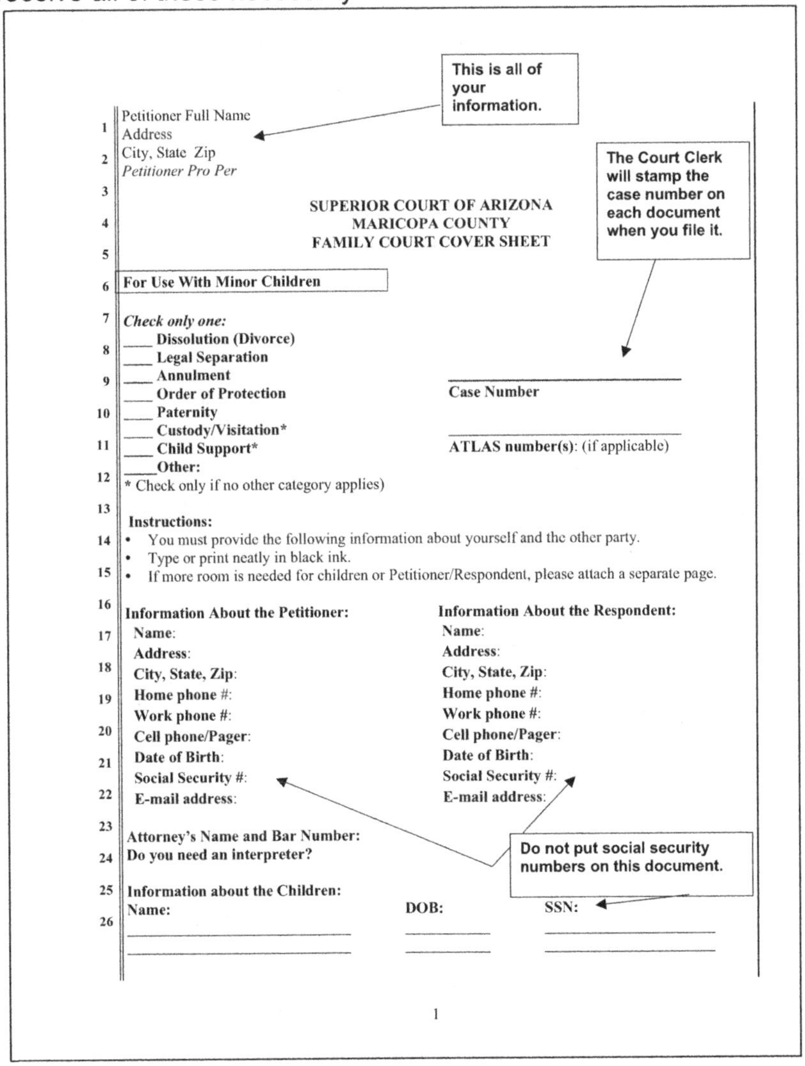

Petitioner Full Name
Address
City, State Zip
Petitioner Pro Per

SUPERIOR COURT OF ARIZONA
MARICOPA COUNTY
FAMILY COURT COVER SHEET

For Use With Minor Children

Check only one:
___ **Dissolution (Divorce)**
___ **Legal Separation**
___ **Annulment**
___ **Order of Protection**
___ **Paternity**
___ **Custody/Visitation***
___ **Child Support***
___ **Other:**
* Check only if no other category applies)

Case Number

ATLAS number(s): (if applicable)

Instructions:
- You must provide the following information about yourself and the other party.
- Type or print neatly in black ink.
- If more room is needed for children or Petitioner/Respondent, please attach a separate page.

Information About the Petitioner:
Name:
Address:
City, State, Zip:
Home phone #:
Work phone #:
Cell phone/Pager:
Date of Birth:
Social Security #:
E-mail address:

Information About the Respondent:
Name:
Address:
City, State, Zip:
Home phone #:
Work phone #:
Cell phone/Pager:
Date of Birth:
Social Security #:
E-mail address:

Attorney's Name and Bar Number:
Do you need an interpreter?

Information about the Children:

Name:	**DOB:**	**SSN:**

1

Sensitive Data Sheet

The purpose of this sensitive data sheet is to provide the court other relevant information. Please be cautioned that this information may become public record and be available for everyone to see. Do not provide complete account numbers or Social Security numbers, due to the risk of identify fraud.

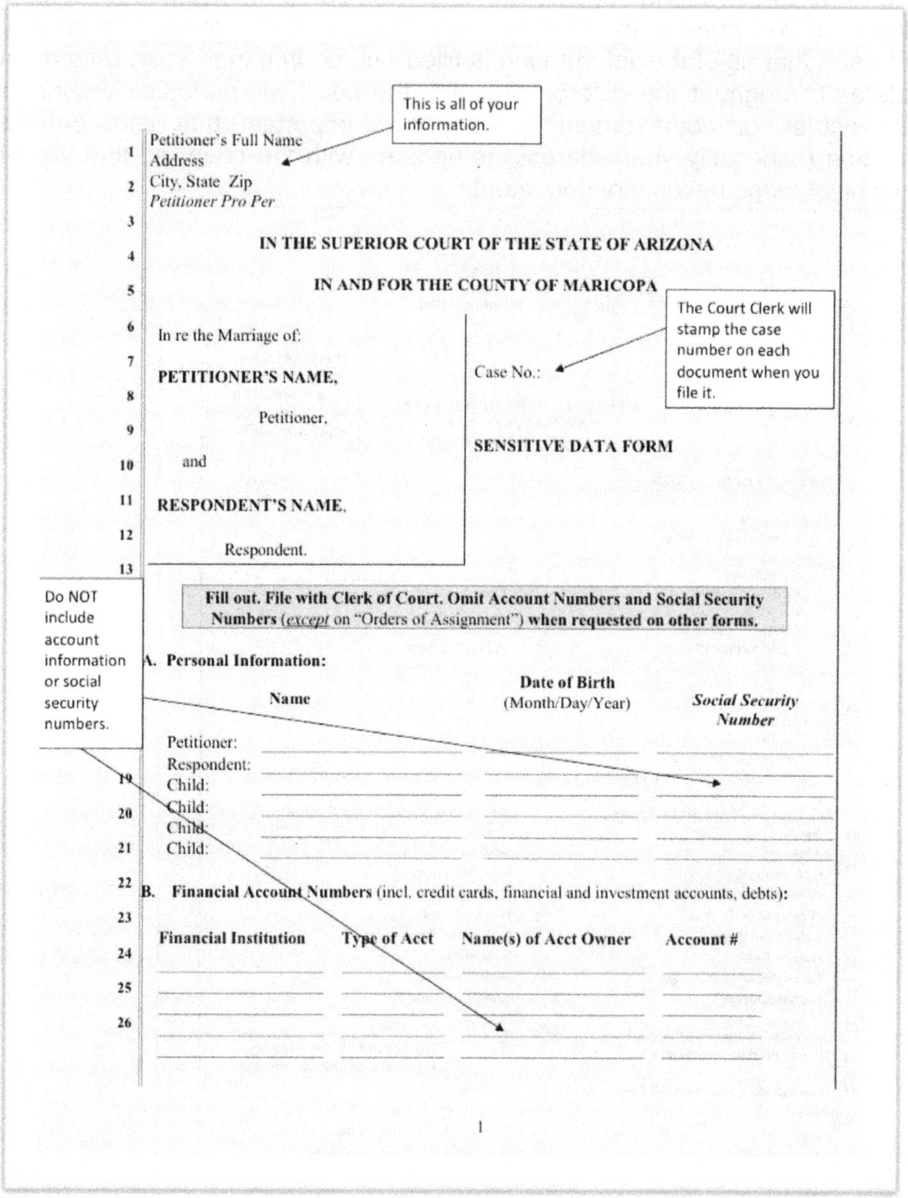

This is all of your information.

Petitioner's Full Name
Address
City, State Zip
Petitioner Pro Per

IN THE SUPERIOR COURT OF THE STATE OF ARIZONA

IN AND FOR THE COUNTY OF MARICOPA

In re the Marriage of: **PETITIONER'S NAME,** Petitioner, and **RESPONDENT'S NAME,** Respondent.	Case No.: **SENSITIVE DATA FORM**

The Court Clerk will stamp the case number on each document when you file it.

Fill out. File with Clerk of Court. Omit Account Numbers and Social Security Numbers (*except* on "Orders of Assignment") when requested on other forms.

Do NOT include account information or social security numbers.

A. Personal Information:

	Name	Date of Birth (Month/Day/Year)	*Social Security Number*
Petitioner:			
Respondent:			
Child:			
Child:			
Child:			
Child:			

B. Financial Account Numbers (incl. credit cards, financial and investment accounts, debts):

Financial Institution	Type of Acct	Name(s) of Acct Owner	Account #

1

C. Pension and Retirement Accounts (including IRAs, 401Ks):

Financial Institution	Type of Acct	Name(s) of Account Owner	Account #

D. Life Insurance Policies:

Insurance Company	Type of Policy	Name(s) of Policy Owner	Policy #

It is UNNECESSARY to provide any information in "C" and "D" at this stage.

2

Summons

The summons officially notifies the respondent that a lawsuit (divorce) has been filed against him/her and he/she is a party to the action. The summons also informs the respondent how long he/she has to answer the divorce. This document is signed by the clerk of court who, at the time of filing, will emboss the document with his official seal.

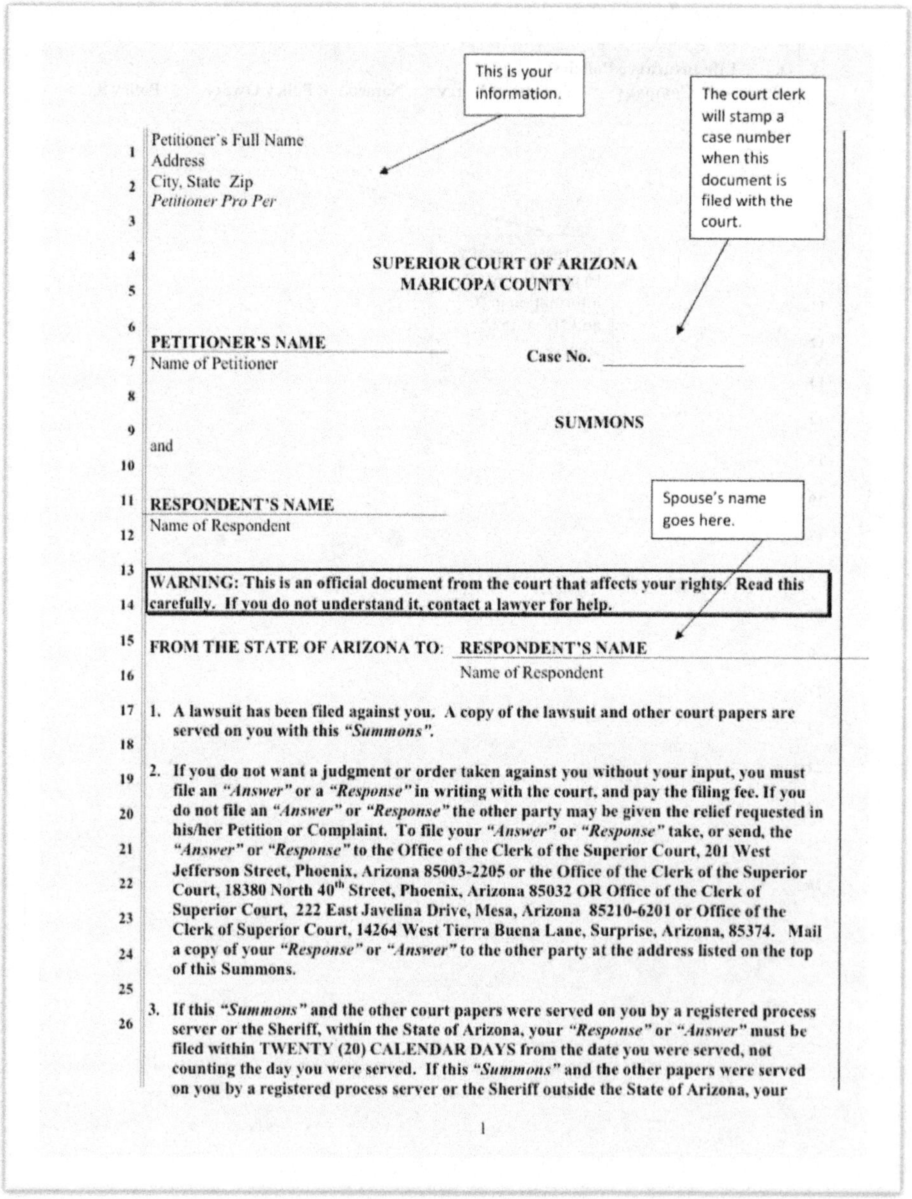

Petitioner's Full Name
Address
City, State Zip
Petitioner Pro Per

SUPERIOR COURT OF ARIZONA
MARICOPA COUNTY

PETITIONER'S NAME
Name of Petitioner

Case No. ______________

SUMMONS

and

RESPONDENT'S NAME
Name of Respondent

WARNING: This is an official document from the court that affects your rights. Read this carefully. If you do not understand it, contact a lawyer for help.

FROM THE STATE OF ARIZONA TO: RESPONDENT'S NAME
Name of Respondent

1. **A lawsuit has been filed against you. A copy of the lawsuit and other court papers are served on you with this *"Summons"*.**

2. **If you do not want a judgment or order taken against you without your input, you must file an *"Answer"* or a *"Response"* in writing with the court, and pay the filing fee. If you do not file an *"Answer"* or *"Response"* the other party may be given the relief requested in his/her Petition or Complaint. To file your *"Answer"* or *"Response"* take, or send, the *"Answer"* or *"Response"* to the Office of the Clerk of the Superior Court, 201 West Jefferson Street, Phoenix, Arizona 85003-2205 or the Office of the Clerk of the Superior Court, 18380 North 40th Street, Phoenix, Arizona 85032 OR Office of the Clerk of Superior Court, 222 East Javelina Drive, Mesa, Arizona 85210-6201 or Office of the Clerk of Superior Court, 14264 West Tierra Buena Lane, Surprise, Arizona, 85374. Mail a copy of your *"Response"* or *"Answer"* to the other party at the address listed on the top of this Summons.**

3. **If this *"Summons"* and the other court papers were served on you by a registered process server or the Sheriff, within the State of Arizona, your *"Response"* or *"Answer"* must be filed within TWENTY (20) CALENDAR DAYS from the date you were served, not counting the day you were served. If this *"Summons"* and the other papers were served on you by a registered process server or the Sheriff outside the State of Arizona, your**

1

Response must be filed within THIRTY (30) CALENDAR DAYS from the date you were served, not counting the day you were served. Service by a registered process server or the Sheriff is complete when made. Service by Publication is complete thirty (30) days after the date of the first publication.

4. **You can get a copy of the court papers filed in this case from the Petitioner at the address at the top of this paper, or from the Clerk of the Superior Court's Customer Service Center at 601 West Jackson, Phoenix, Arizona 85003 or at 222 East Javelina Drive, Mesa, Arizona 85210.**

5. **Requests for reasonable accommodation for persons with disabilities must be made to the office of the judge or commissioner assigned to the case, at least five (5) days before your scheduled court date.**

SIGNED AND SEALED this date ______________________________

MICHAEL JEANES, CLERK OF COURT

By______________________________________

Deputy Clerk

When you file this document with the court, the court clerk will sign and date this document.

Petition for Dissolution With Minor Children

This document is the most important of the nine documents initially filed. This document sets out the necessary facts of your divorce and lets the court know exactly what you are seeking in the divorce. In this petition, you are able to tell the court what kind of custody arrangement you want for the children, how you want your property divided and whether you or your spouse is entitled to child support or spousal maintenance.

This document should help you provide a good picture of what you want at the end of the divorce process. You should ask the court for *everything* that you want, even if it is not what you would settle for at the end of your dissolution. You want to request that you be awarded certain things, because if the other party does not answer the petition and you get a default (see glossary) against your spouse, your requests in that initial petition are what will be awarded to you.

The following petition is a generic, sample petition for a divorce with children. In drafting your own petition, you should be more specific than the example. Maricopa County also provides a form on their website that allows a party to be more specific. It is helpful at this stage to have consultation with an attorney or allow an attorney to draft your documents for you to ensure that you "plead" all that you need to in this petition. It is common for judges and opposing sides to refer back to your initial petition. Again, please take your time in filling out this document.

Petitioner's Full Name
Address
City, State Zip
Petitioner Pro Per

IN THE SUPERIOR COURT OF THE STATE OF ARIZONA
IN AND FOR THE COUNTY OF MARICOPA

In re the Marriage of:	)	
	)	
PETITIONER'S NAME,	)	Case No. ____________
Petitioner,	)	
	)	**PETITION FOR DISSOLUTION OF MARRIAGE WITH MINOR CHILDREN**
and,	)	
	)	
RESPONDENT'S NAME,	)	
Respondent.	)	
	)	

COMES NOW Petitioner, PETITIONER'S NAME, by and through counsel undersigned, as and for her/his PETITION FOR DISSOLUTION OF MARRIAGE WITH MINOR CHILD/CHILDREN alleges as follows:

1. Petitioner's full name is PETITIONER'S NAME (hereinafter "Wife/Husband") and she/he resides at ADDRESS, CITY, STATE, ZIP. She/he is employed/not employed. Her date of birth is MONTH, DAY, YEAR.

2. Respondent's full name is RESPONDENT'S NAME (hereinafter "Husband/Wife") and he/she resides at ADDRESS, CITY, STATE, ZIP. He/she is employed/not employed. Her date of birth is MONTH, DAY, YEAR.

3. Neither party is a member of the United States Armed Forces or Husband/Wife is a member of the United States Armed Forces.

4. Both parties/Respondent/Petitioner have/has been domiciled in the State of Arizona for more than ninety (90) days prior to the filing of this Petition.

5. The parties were married on DATE in CITY, STATE.

6. Wife is/is not now pregnant.

7. Domestic Violence has/has not occurred during this marriage.

8. The parties have NUMBER minor child/children common to the marriage, namely CHILD'S FULL NAME (hereinafter "Child") who was born on DATE OF BIRTH.

9. Mother/Father requests that the parties have joint custody/she have sole legal/Father has sole legal custody of the Child.

10. Mother/Father requests a parenting time plan of WHAT TYPE OF PARENTING PLAN.

11. The Court has jurisdiction under A.R.S. Section 25-331 to decide child custody matters because the minor Child is domiciled in the State of Arizona, and Arizona is the "home state" of the Child, as the term "home state" is defined in A.R.S. Section 8-401 et seq., and the Parental Kidnapping Prevention Act of 1980, 28 U.S.C. Section 1738A.

12. The Child/Children currently lives/live with MOTHER/FATHER/BOTH PARTIES at ADDRESS, CITY, STATE, ZIP and has/have lived with MOTHER/FATHER/BOTH PARTIES at this location for TIME PERIOD.

13. The marriage is irretrievably broken and there is no reasonable prospect of reconciliation. Conciliation proceedings have not been filed.

14. There is no agreement between the parties as to a division of the assets and liabilities of the marriage.

15. Each party has a claim to sole and separate property, which should be confirmed to that party.

16. The parties have accumulated certain community assets, which should be equitably divided.

17. The parties have accumulated certain community debts and obligations, which should be equitably divided.

18. Wife/Husband requests this Court to order/not order Husband/Wife to pay Child Support in an amount to be determined by law.

19. Wife/Husband requests an award of spousal maintenance in a sum to be determined.

20. Wife/Husband requests this Court to award a reasonable sum as and for her/his attorney's fees.

WHEREFORE, Wife/Husband requests that this Court order as follows:

1. A Decree of Dissolution of the Parties' marriage;
2. An equitable division of the assets and liabilities of the parties;
3. Child support in an amount to be determined;
4. Spousal maintenance in an amount to be determined;
5. An award of legal custody for MOTHER/FATHER/BOTH PARTIES;
6. An award of physical custody for MOTHER/FATHER/BOTH PARTIES;
6. Husband/Wife to pay to Wife/Husband her/his attorney's fees and costs incurred herein; and
7. For such other and further relief as the Court deems just and proper.

RESPECTFULLY SUBMITTED this ____ day of ________________, 2010.

____
PETITIONER'S NAME
Petitioner Pro Per

ORIGINAL filed this ____
day of ____________, 2010 with:

Clerk of Superior Court
Northeast Courthouse
18380 N. 40th St.
Phoenix, Arizona 85032

3

VERIFICATION

STATE OF ARIZONA)
)ss.
County of Maricopa)

I, PETITIONER'S NAME, being first duly sworn upon oath deposes and states as follows: I am the Petitioner in this action; I have read the PETITION FOR DISSOLUTION OF MARRIAGE WITH MINOR CHILD/CHILDREN and the related documents filed simultaneously therewith and know the contents to be true and accurate except those allegations made upon information and belief, and as to those, believe them to be true.

DATED this ____ day of ____________, 2010.

____
PETITIONER'S NAME

SUBSCRIBED AND SWORN before me this ____ day of ____________, 2010, by

____
Notary Public

My commission expires:

Notice of Your Rights About Health Insurance Coverage

This legal notice outlines how your health insurance coverage could be affected after your dissolution is final. It includes information as to whether you are included on your spouse's insurance policy, what insurance coverage applies to you and how to get it, what coverage applies to your children, preexisting conditions or exclusions from insurance coverage, and limits on rights to insurance coverage for you and your children. This document must be served on the party in a dissolution. It is not usually applicable to legal separations, but you may want to check with your insurance company.

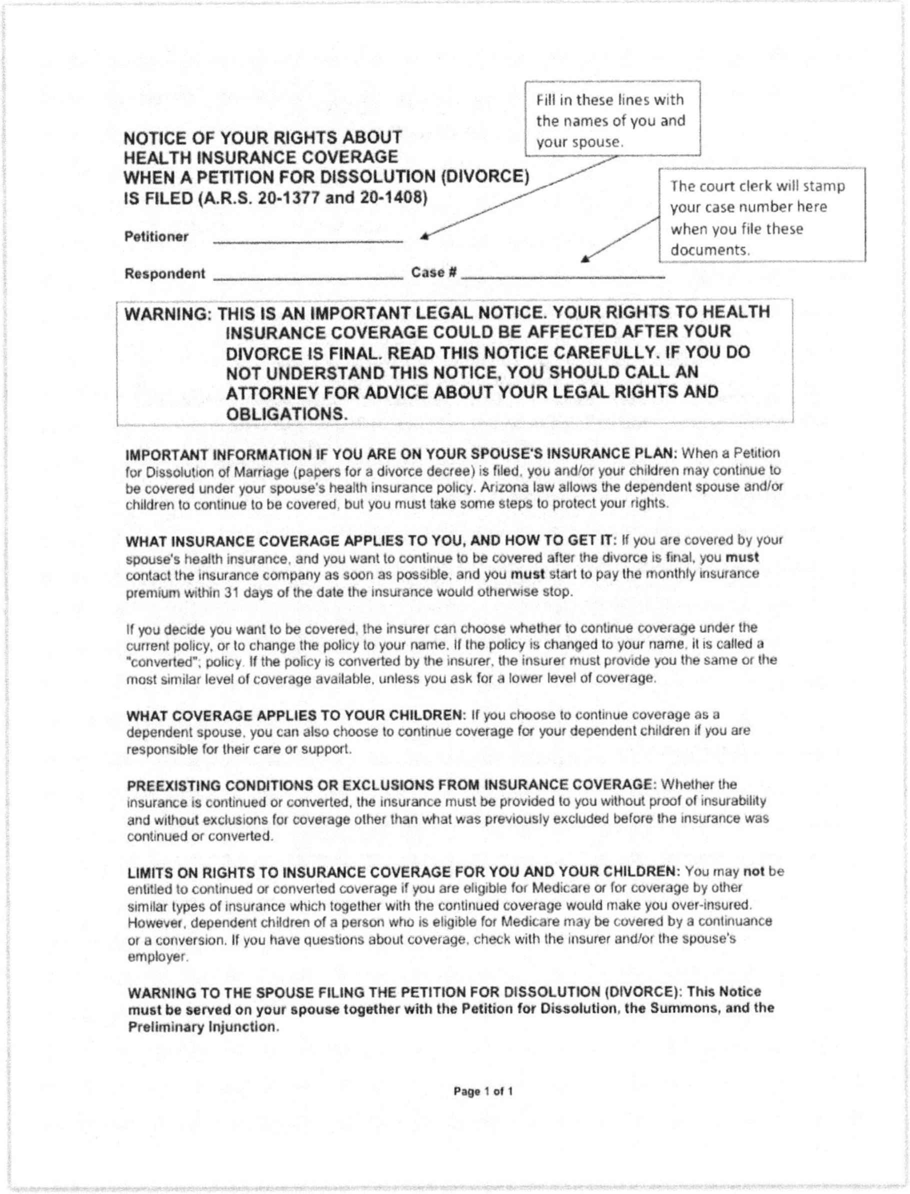

Fill in these lines with the names of you and your spouse.

The court clerk will stamp your case number here when you file these documents.

NOTICE OF YOUR RIGHTS ABOUT HEALTH INSURANCE COVERAGE WHEN A PETITION FOR DISSOLUTION (DIVORCE) IS FILED (A.R.S. 20-1377 and 20-1408)

Petitioner ____________________

Respondent ____________________ **Case #** ____________________

WARNING: THIS IS AN IMPORTANT LEGAL NOTICE. YOUR RIGHTS TO HEALTH INSURANCE COVERAGE COULD BE AFFECTED AFTER YOUR DIVORCE IS FINAL. READ THIS NOTICE CAREFULLY. IF YOU DO NOT UNDERSTAND THIS NOTICE, YOU SHOULD CALL AN ATTORNEY FOR ADVICE ABOUT YOUR LEGAL RIGHTS AND OBLIGATIONS.

IMPORTANT INFORMATION IF YOU ARE ON YOUR SPOUSE'S INSURANCE PLAN: When a Petition for Dissolution of Marriage (papers for a divorce decree) is filed, you and/or your children may continue to be covered under your spouse's health insurance policy. Arizona law allows the dependent spouse and/or children to continue to be covered, but you must take some steps to protect your rights.

WHAT INSURANCE COVERAGE APPLIES TO YOU, AND HOW TO GET IT: If you are covered by your spouse's health insurance, and you want to continue to be covered after the divorce is final, you **must** contact the insurance company as soon as possible, and you **must** start to pay the monthly insurance premium within 31 days of the date the insurance would otherwise stop.

If you decide you want to be covered, the insurer can choose whether to continue coverage under the current policy, or to change the policy to your name. If the policy is changed to your name, it is called a "converted"; policy. If the policy is converted by the insurer, the insurer must provide you the same or the most similar level of coverage available, unless you ask for a lower level of coverage.

WHAT COVERAGE APPLIES TO YOUR CHILDREN: If you choose to continue coverage as a dependent spouse, you can also choose to continue coverage for your dependent children if you are responsible for their care or support.

PREEXISTING CONDITIONS OR EXCLUSIONS FROM INSURANCE COVERAGE: Whether the insurance is continued or converted, the insurance must be provided to you without proof of insurability and without exclusions for coverage other than what was previously excluded before the insurance was continued or converted.

LIMITS ON RIGHTS TO INSURANCE COVERAGE FOR YOU AND YOUR CHILDREN: You may **not** be entitled to continued or converted coverage if you are eligible for Medicare or for coverage by other similar types of insurance which together with the continued coverage would make you over-insured. However, dependent children of a person who is eligible for Medicare may be covered by a continuance or a conversion. If you have questions about coverage, check with the insurer and/or the spouse's employer.

WARNING TO THE SPOUSE FILING THE PETITION FOR DISSOLUTION (DIVORCE): This Notice must be served on your spouse together with the Petition for Dissolution, the Summons, and the Preliminary Injunction.

Page 1 of 1

Notice Regarding Creditors

This notice is required for all actions of divorce and legal separation. This document explains that you and your spouse are responsible for community debts. It also suggests that you may want to contact your creditors to discuss the debts and the effects of your divorce or legal separation.

Your information goes here.

Petitioner's Full Name
Address
City, State Zip
Petitioner Pro Per

The court clerk will stamp your case number here when you file these documents.

SUPERIOR COURT OF ARIZONA
IN MARICOPA COUNTY

Case Number:____________________

____
Name of Petitioner

NOTICE REGARDING CREDITORS

____
Name of Respondent

Spouse's name goes here.

ARIZONA LAW REQUIRES all actions for DIVORCE or LEGAL SEPARATION to include this NOTICE and for the person filing for Divorce or Legal Separation to SERVE this NOTICE on the other party. (ARS 25-318(F).

YOU AND YOUR SPOUSE ARE RESPONSIBLE FOR COMMUNITY DEBTS. The court usually requires/orders one spouse or the other to pay certain community debts in, or through, the Decree of Dissolution or Legal Separation. A court order that does this is binding on the spouses **only, not the creditors**. You and your spouse are legally responsible for these community debts whether you are married, divorced, or legally separated. These debts are matters of contract between **both of you** and your creditors (such as banks, credit unions, credit card companies, utility companies, medical providers and retailers). On request, the court may impose a lien against the separate property of a spouse to secure payment of certain community debts.

CONTACT CREDITORS: You may want to contact your creditors to discuss the debts and the effects of your divorce/legal separation on your debts. To assist you in identifying your creditors, you may obtain a copy of your spouse's credit report by making a written request to the court for an order requiring a credit reporting agency to release the report to you. The credit report will help you identify accounts, account numbers and account balances. In addition, within thirty **(30)** days after receipt of a request from a spouse who is party to a divorce or legal separation, which includes the court and cause number of the action, creditors are required, by law, to provide information as to the balance and account status of any debts for which you or your spouse may be liable to the creditor.

WARNING: If you do not understand this notice, you should contact an attorney for advice about your legal rights and obligations.

The following page contains a sample form you *may* choose to mail to creditors to get information about debts owed by you or your spouse. It is not a required form.
DO NOT FILE THE *NEXT* PAGE WITH THE COURT.

Page 1 of 2

Preliminary Injunction

The preliminary injunction is a new set of rules that must be followed by you *and* your spouse after a spouse is served with dissolution or legal separation paperwork. These rules are explained in the Preliminary Injunction document you filed and served upon the other party. These rules are mandated for every couple going through the process of dissolution or legal separation. It is important not to violate any of these rules. See Chapter 9 for a more complete explanation of the preliminary injunction.

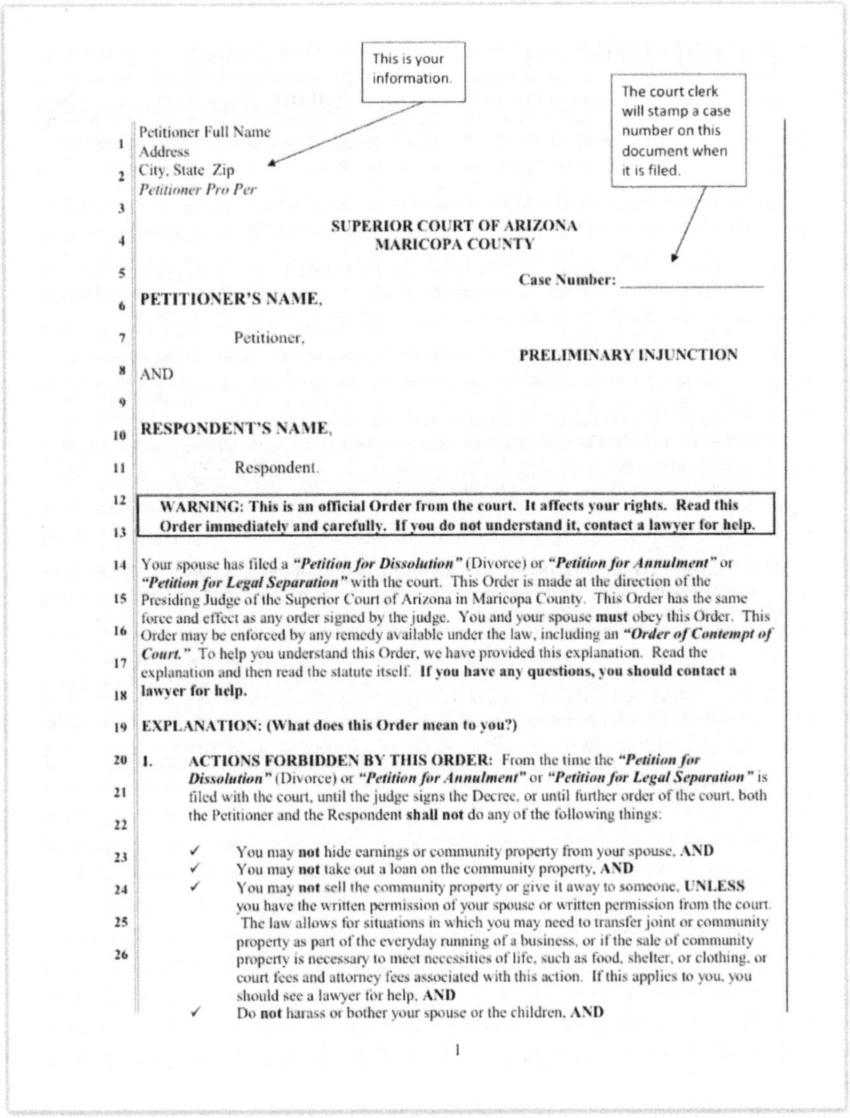

Petitioner Full Name
Address
City, State Zip
Petitioner Pro Per

SUPERIOR COURT OF ARIZONA
MARICOPA COUNTY

PETITIONER'S NAME,

Petitioner,

AND

RESPONDENT'S NAME,

Respondent.

Case Number: ______________

PRELIMINARY INJUNCTION

WARNING: This is an official Order from the court. It affects your rights. Read this Order immediately and carefully. If you do not understand it, contact a lawyer for help.

Your spouse has filed a ***"Petition for Dissolution"*** (Divorce) or ***"Petition for Annulment"*** or ***"Petition for Legal Separation"*** with the court. This Order is made at the direction of the Presiding Judge of the Superior Court of Arizona in Maricopa County. This Order has the same force and effect as any order signed by the judge. You and your spouse **must** obey this Order. This Order may be enforced by any remedy available under the law, including an ***"Order of Contempt of Court."*** To help you understand this Order, we have provided this explanation. Read the explanation and then read the statute itself. **If you have any questions, you should contact a lawyer for help.**

EXPLANATION: (What does this Order mean to you?)

1. **ACTIONS FORBIDDEN BY THIS ORDER:** From the time the ***"Petition for Dissolution"*** (Divorce) or ***"Petition for Annulment"*** or ***"Petition for Legal Separation"*** is filed with the court, until the judge signs the Decree, or until further order of the court, both the Petitioner and the Respondent **shall not** do any of the following things:

   - ✓ You may **not** hide earnings or community property from your spouse, **AND**
   - ✓ You may **not** take out a loan on the community property, **AND**
   - ✓ You may **not** sell the community property or give it away to someone, **UNLESS** you have the written permission of your spouse or written permission from the court. The law allows for situations in which you may need to transfer joint or community property as part of the everyday running of a business, or if the sale of community property is necessary to meet necessities of life, such as food, shelter, or clothing, or court fees and attorney fees associated with this action. If this applies to you, you should see a lawyer for help, **AND**
   - ✓ Do **not** harass or bother your spouse or the children, **AND**

1

- ✓ Do **not** physically abuse or threaten your spouse or the children, **AND**
- ✓ Do **not** take the minor children, common to your marriage, out of the State of Arizona for any reasons, without a written agreement between you and your spouse or a Court Order, **before** you take the minor children out of the State.
- ✓ Do **not** remove, or cause to be removed, the other party or the minor children of the parties from any existing insurance coverage, including medical, hospital, dental, automobile and disability insurance. Both parties shall maintain all insurance coverage in full force and effect.

STATUTORY REQUIREMENTS: Arizona Law, A.R.S. 25-315(A) provides:

1(a). **RESTRICTIONS ON PROPERTY OF THE MARRIAGE:** That both parties are enjoined from transferring, encumbering, concealing, selling, or otherwise disposing of any of the joint, common or community property of the parties, **except** if related to the usual course of business, the necessities of life, or court fees and reasonable attorney fees associated with an action filed under this article, without the written consent of the parties or the permission of the court.

1(b). **REQUIREMENTS OF BEHAVIOR:** That both parties are enjoined from molesting, harassing, disturbing the peace, or committing an assault or battery on, the person of the other party or any natural or adopted child of the parties.

1(c). **RESTRICTIONS ABOUT YOUR MINOR CHILDREN:** That both parties are enjoined from removing any natural or adopted minor child(ren) of the parties, then residing in Arizona, from the jurisdiction of the court without the prior written consent of the parties or the permission of the court.

1(d). **RESTRICTIONS ABOUT INSURANCE:** That both parties are enjoined from removing, or causing to be removed, the other party or the minor children of the parties from any existing insurance coverage, including medical, hospital, dental, automobile and disability insurance. Both parties shall maintain all insurance coverage in full force and effect.

2. **EFFECTIVE DATE OF THIS ORDER:** This Order is effective against the person who filed for divorce, annulment, or legal separation (the Petitioner) when the Petition was filed with the court. It is effective against the other party (the Respondent) when it is served on the other party, or on actual notice of the Order, whichever is sooner. This Order shall remain in effect until further order of the court, or the entry of a Decree of Dissolution, Annulment, or Legal Separation.

3. **ORDER TO PETITIONER:** You **must** serve a copy of this Order upon the Respondent, along with a copy of the Petition for Dissolution, Annulment or Legal Separation, the Summons, and other required court papers.

4. **WARNING:** This is an official Court Order. If you disobey this Order, the court may find you in contempt of court. You may also be arrested and prosecuted for the crime of interfering with judicial proceedings and any other crime you may have committed by disobeying this Order.

5. **LAW ENFORCEMENT:** You or your spouse may file a certified copy of this Order with your local law enforcement agency. You may obtain a certified copy from the Clerk of the Court that issues this Order. If any changes are made to this Order and you have filed a certified copy of this Order with your local law enforcement agency, you **must** notify them of the changes.

2

Petitioner:
Name:______________________________ Gender: ___ Male ___Female
Height:______________________________ Weight:__________
Driver's License No.:____________________
Date of Birth:__________

Respondent:
Name:______________________________ Gender: __ Male __ Female
Height:______________________________ Weight:______________
Driver's License No.:____________________
Date of Birth:__________

GIVEN UNDER MY HAND AND THE SEAL OF THE COURT

this _____ day of ________________________, 2010.

Clerk of the Superior Court

By:______________________________, Deputy Clerk

Do not sign or date these lines. When you file this document with the court, the court clerk will sign and date this document.

3

Parent Information Class

This form gives your spouse notice that he or she must attend a parent information class. This is a mandatory class for both parents to attend. Parents do not attend this class together and each parent is able to choose a convenient location and time to attend. Try to take this class early in your dissolution process. When you have taken the class, the instructor will give you a form to file with the court. It is important that you file it with the court; the court is then on notice that you filed it. Prior to filing, make additional copies of the form for yourself and for your spouse. You cannot get any custody without having filed this certificate.

If you are unable to take this parent information class because you are on military duty, it is possible to ask your judge if you can be exempt from taking it. There is a form, Motion to Request Exemption from Parent Information Class that you can fill out and file with the court. It is within the court's discretion whether or not to grant your request to be exempted from this requirement.

Your contact information goes here.

The court clerk will stamp your case number here when you file these documents.

Petitioner's Full Name
Address
City, State Zip
Petitioner Pro Per

SUPERIOR COURT OF ARIZONA
MARICOPA COUNTY

PETITIONER'S NAME,
Petitioner,

and

RESPONDENT'S NAME,
Respondent.

Spouse's name goes here.

Case Number: ________________

ORDER AND NOTICE TO ATTEND PARENT INFORMATION PROGRAM CLASS

READ ME. This is an Official Court Order. If you fail to obey this Order, the court may find you in Contempt of Court.

Mark an "x" next to your case type

THE COURT FINDS:

This case involves minor child(ren) and is an action for:

___ Dissolution of Marriage;
___ Legal Separation; or
___ Paternity with a Request to Determine Custody or Parenting Time or Child Support.
___ Request to Determine Custody or Parenting Time or Support

THE COURT ORDERS pursuant to ARS § 25-352:

1. ATTEND CLASS. You must attend and complete the Parent Information Program Class.

2. WITHIN 45 DAYS. Both the Petitioner and the Respondent **must** complete this class within 45 days from the date the Respondent is served with, or accepts service of, the Petition/Complaint. The Respondent **must** register for and complete the course whether or not a ***"Response"*** or ***"Answer"*** to the Petition/Complaint is filed.

3. PAY THE CLASS FEE. Each party must pay the class fee to the Program Provider, or obtain a fee deferral or waiver.

4. FILE CERTIFICATE OF COMPLETION. Both the Petitioner and the Respondent **must** each file a ***"Certificate of Completion"*** with the Clerk of the Court immediately after completing the class and prior to receiving the final judgment/order/decree in the case.

5. FAILURE TO ATTEND CLASS. If you file a Petition/Complaint or ***"Response"*** or ***"Answer"*** and do **not** complete the Parent Information Program Class, the judge **may not** sign your papers and you **may not** get the things you asked the court to give you. You may also be denied the right to seek modification and/or enforcement of the decree/judgment/order until completion of the class. If you are the party required to file a Response/Answer and choose not to file a ***"Response"*** or ***"Answer,"*** and do not complete the Parent Information Program Class, you **may be denied** the right to seek modification and/or enforcement of the decree/judgment/order until completion of the class.

Colleen McNally
Presiding Judge, Family Court Department

1

Affidavit Regarding Minor Children

In this affidavit, you are confirming who the minor children are and where they have lived during the past five (5) years. This document also asks whether there are any court cases that you have been a party to or witness to that involved the custody or parenting time of the children. The document requires you to answer whether there are any pending court cases related to the custody of the children and whether you know of any person, other than the petitioner or respondent, who has physical custody or who claims custody or parenting time rights of any of the children named in the affidavit.

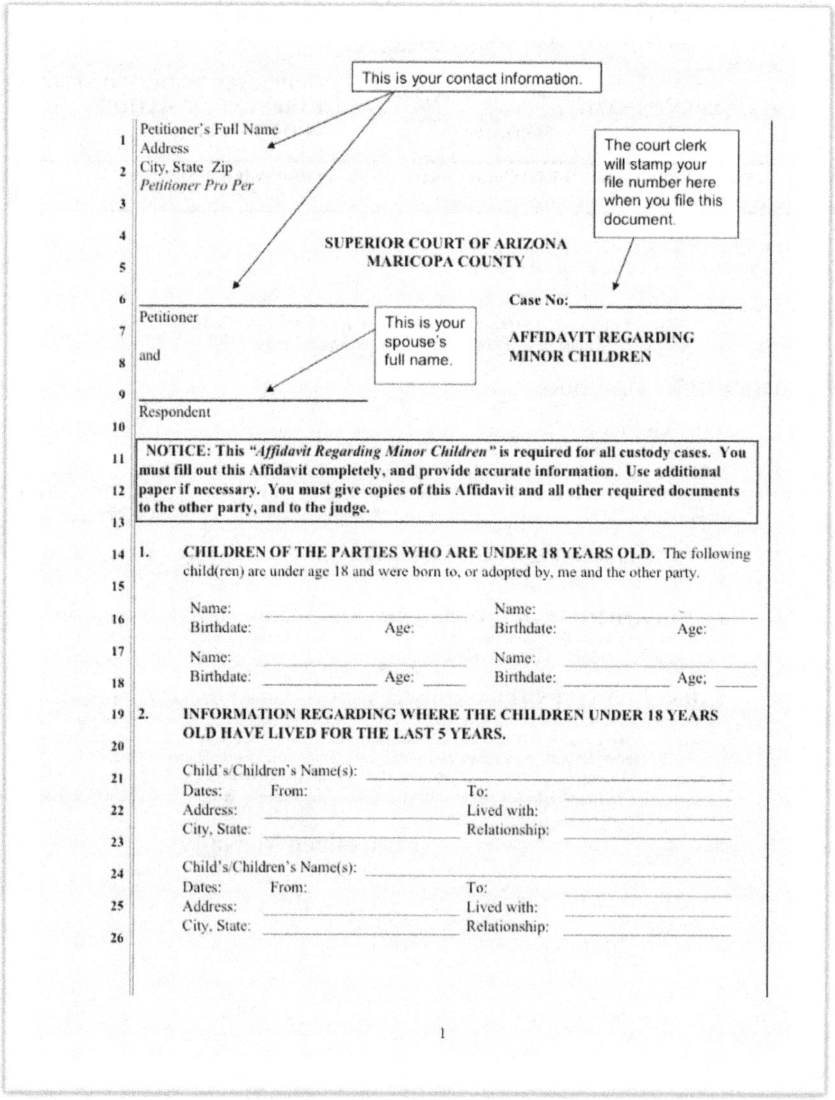

This is your contact information.

Petitioner's Full Name
Address
City, State Zip
Petitioner Pro Per

The court clerk will stamp your file number here when you file this document.

SUPERIOR COURT OF ARIZONA
MARICOPA COUNTY

______________________ **Case No:**______________

Petitioner

This is your spouse's full name.

and

AFFIDAVIT REGARDING MINOR CHILDREN

____
Respondent

NOTICE: This "*Affidavit Regarding Minor Children*" is required for all custody cases. You must fill out this Affidavit completely, and provide accurate information. Use additional paper if necessary. You must give copies of this Affidavit and all other required documents to the other party, and to the judge.

1. **CHILDREN OF THE PARTIES WHO ARE UNDER 18 YEARS OLD.** The following child(ren) are under age 18 and were born to, or adopted by, me and the other party.

Name: ____________ Name: ____________
Birthdate: ____________ Age: ____ Birthdate: ____________ Age: ____

Name: ____________ Name: ____________
Birthdate: ____________ Age: ____ Birthdate: ____________ Age: ____

2. **INFORMATION REGARDING WHERE THE CHILDREN UNDER 18 YEARS OLD HAVE LIVED FOR THE LAST 5 YEARS.**

Child's/Children's Name(s): ____________
Dates: From: ____________ To: ____________
Address: ____________ Lived with: ____________
City, State: ____________ Relationship: ____________

Child's/Children's Name(s): ____________
Dates: From: ____________ To: ____________
Address: ____________ Lived with: ____________
City, State: ____________ Relationship: ____________

1

Child's/Children's Name(s): ____
Dates: From: ____ To: ____
Address: ____ Lived with: ____
City, State: ____ Relationship: ____

Child's/Children's Name(s): ____
Dates: From: ____ To: ____
Address: ____ Lived with: ____
City, State: ____ Relationship: ____

Child's/Children's Name(s): ____
Dates: From: ____ To: ____
Address: ____ Lived with: ____
City, State: ____ Relationship: ____

Child's/Children's Name(s): ____
Dates: From: ____ To: ____
Address: ____ Lived with: ____
City, State: ____ Relationship: ____

3. **COURT CASES IN WHICH I HAVE BEEN A PARTY/WITNESS THAT INVOLVED THE CUSTODY PARENTING TIME OF THE CHILD(REN).**
(Check one box.)
☐I have or ☐I have **not** been a party/witness in court in this state or in any other state that involved the custody parenting time of the child(ren) named above. (If so, explain on separate paper; if not, go on.)

Name of each child: ____
Name of Court: ____ Court Location: ____
Court Case No.: ____ Current Status: ____
How the child was involved: ____
Summary of any Court Order: ____

4. **INFORMATION REGARDING PENDING COURT CASES RELATED TO THE CUSTODY OF THE CHILD(REN).** (Check one box.)
☐ I do have or ☐ I do not have information about a custody parenting time court case relating to any of the children named above that is pending in this state or in any other state. (If so, explain. If not, go on.)

Name of each child: ____
Name of Court: ____ Court Location: ____
Court Case No.: ____ Current Status: ____
How the child was involved: ____
Summary of any Court Order: ____

5. **CUSTODY OR PARENTING TIME CLAIMS OF ANY PERSON**. (Check one box.)
☐I do know or ☐I do not know a person other than the Petitioner or the Respondent who has physical custody or who claims custody or parenting time rights to any of the children named in this Affidavit. (If so, explain below. If not, go on.)

Name of each child: ______________________
Name of person with claim: ______________________
Address of person with claim: ______________________
Nature of the claim: ______________________

OATH OR AFFIRMATION AND VERIFICATION FOR AFFIDAVIT OF MINOR CHILD

I swear or affirm that the information on this document is true and correct under penalty of perjury.

____________________________ ____________________
Signature Date

Sworn to or Affirmed before me this: ____________ (date) by ____________________

My Commission Expires: ____________ ____________________
Deputy Clerk or Notary Public

This is the second document that you must sign and have notarized before you file it with the court clerk.

4

Steps to Filing Your Dissolution or Legal Separation Documents

1. Review your documents one last time to ensure their accuracy.
2. Sign the petition in blue ink. There are TWO places. The verification page needs a notary, as well. (Do not sign it until you are in front of a notary. Notaries are found at various locations, including law offices, banks and photocopy stores. There is sometimes a charge for this service. Usually, the bank that you bank with will do this service for free).
3. If there are minor children, sign the Affidavit of Minor Children in blue ink. This page needs a notary. (Do not sign it until you are in front of a notary).
4. Copy each document three (3) times. **Staple each individual section (such as pleadings) together.**
5. Keep each document in an individual pile. The original document should be on top, with the three copies underneath. Paperclip these four documents together.
6. If you are getting divorced with minor children, you will have nine separate piles paper-clipped together. Otherwise, you should have six or seven stacks.

Your stacks should look like this:

Stack #1: Original family court coversheet plus three copies
Stack #2: Original Sensitive Data Sheet plus three copies
Stack #3: Original Summons plus three copies
Stack #4: Original Preliminary Injunction plus three copies
Stack #5: Original petition (signed with blue ink) plus three copies
Stack #6: Original Notice of Your Rights about Health Insurance plus three copies
Stack #7: Original Notice Regarding Creditors plus three copies
Stack #8: Original Affidavit Regarding Minor Children plus three copies
Stack #9: Original parenting information class plus three copies

7. Take these documents to your nearest courthouse. Maricopa County has four different courthouses, the locations of which are in Chapter 1 of this book. Courthouses outside Maricopa County are listed in the Appendix under "courthouses." The court clerk will date stamp all of these documents. The court clerk will also assign you a case number. You must use this number when you file subsequent documents with the court. This filing date may become important, because the court uses this date as a starting date for the dissolution or legal separation.
8. Make sure you have your filing fee ready–$321.00 for initial petitions, $256.00 for responses. You can pay by cash, cashier's check or credit

card. (There is a possibility for a deferral or waiver of this fee if you are unable to pay it. Such forms are located online.)

9. The Court Clerk will keep the original copies and will date stamp your remaining copies.
10. Now, to "start the clock," you need to serve (officially give a copy) the documents on the other party. The instructions for service are below.

Simple Steps to "Serving" the Other Party

"Service" is the technical name for the other party receiving from you the documents that you have filed. Arizona courts require one party to show proof that the other person was served. In today's legal world, service does not have to be done with a process server. Instead, you can simply mail the documents to the other party, if applicable (as outlined below).

The Other Party Lives In or Out of the State of Arizona and You Know Where He or She Lives or Works

Most likely, your spouse also lives in Arizona. If this is the case, you can serve the other party as outlined below. The service methods are listed here from least to most expensive.

Option 1: Hand-delivery and an Acceptance of Service form

If you and your spouse are amicable, hand-delivery is a good option. This means that you can give the other party all six (6) or eight (8) documents (all of the documents you filed except for the Summons). If you use this method, you do not send the original Summons that you received from the court clerk when you initially filed your documents. At the same time you give the other party the papers, you should also give them an Acceptance of Service form to fill out. This form must be signed by the receiving party either in front of a notary or the court clerk. If the receiving party signs the documents in front of a notary, you should file their acceptance of service with the court after making a copy for your records.

Do not use hand-delivery and an acceptance of service form if you are a victim of domestic violence or you believe that you or your children are in danger. If this is the case, use another method of service. It is best to err on the side of being safe.

Option 2: Mail or Other Delivery Service Requiring Signature Confirmation

This option requires that you send all of your documents using certified mail, **restricted delivery.** The "restricted delivery" entails a minor fee, but ensures that the deliverer confirm that he or she is delivering personally to your spouse. When you receive this green card back in the mail, you will file this with your mailing receipt after making a copy of it for your records. This form is located online at:

http://www.superiorcourt.maricopa.gov/SuperiorCourt/Self-ServiceCenter/Forms/FamilyCourt/fc_gn2.asp. It looks like this:

(1) Person Filing: ______________________
Mailing Address: ______________________
City, State, Zip: ______________________
Telephone: ______________________
Person Filing is: ☐ SELF (No Attorney) OR ☐ Attorney
If Attorney, Bar No. ______________________

SUPERIOR COURT OF ARIZONA IN MARICOPA COUNTY

(2) ______________________
Petitioner

(2) Case Number ______________________

AFFIDAVIT OF SERVICE WITH SIGNATURE CONFIRMATION
For Family Court Cases
Arizona Rules of Family Law Procedure 41 & 42

(3) ______________________
Respondent

YOU MUST ATTACH A COPY OF A SIGNED RETURN RECEIPT FOR DELIVERED MAIL *and* A COPY OF THE RECEIPT THAT SHOWS TO WHOM AND WHERE THE DOCUMENTS WERE SENT.

I sent the family court legal documents checked or listed below to the other party in the manner indicated. The documents were signed for BY THE OTHER PARTY *ONLY* AND NO ONE ELSE. A copy of the OTHER PARTY'S SIGNATURE acknowledging receipt of delivery is attached to page 3.

Mailed to (Name): ______________________
Address: ______________________
City, State, Zip: ______________________
Date documents sent: (Month/Day/Year) ______________________
Date documents delivered: (Month/Day/Year) ______________________

Mark the box beside each document you sent to the other party. You must send each and every document listed under your type of court case unless indicated otherwise.

DIVORCE (OR ANNULMENT) **WITH CHILDREN**
☐ Petition
☐ Summons
☐ Preliminary Injunction
☐ Health Insurance Notice
☐ Parent Info. Program Notice
☐ Notice to Creditors
☐ Affidavit Regarding Minor Children

DIVORCE (OR ANNULMENT) **WITHOUT CHILDREN**
☐ Petition
☐ Summons
☐ Preliminary Injunction
☐ Health Insurance Notice
☐ Notice to Creditors

PATERNITY (to establish)
☐ Petition
☐ Summons
☐ Parent Info. Program Notice

LEGAL SEPARATION WITH CHILDREN
☐ Petition
☐ Summons
☐ Preliminary Injunction
☐ Notice to Creditors
☐ Health Insurance Notice
☐ Parent Info. Program Notice
☐ Affidavit Regarding Minor Children

LEGAL SEPARATION WITHOUT CHILDREN
☐ Petition
☐ Summons
☐ Preliminary Injunction
☐ Notice to Creditors

TEMPORARY ORDERS
☐ Motion for Temporary Order
☐ Order to Appear
Family Court Dept. Notices about:
☐ Returns/Conferences
☐ Temporary Orders
☐ Affidavit of Financial Info. *(if for spousal maintenance)*
☐ Parents Worksheet for Child Support *(if for child support)*
☐ Parenting Plan *(if for custody/parenting time)*

Page 1 of 3
DR24f
USE CURRENT VERSION

Case No. ____________

CHILD CUSTODY, PARENTING TIME, SUPPORT (to establish when paternity already *legally* established)
☐ Petition ☐ Summons ☐ Parent Info. Program Notice

CHILD SUPPORT (to establish when paternity already *legally* established)
☐ Petition ☐ Order to Appear ☐ Parents Worksheet for Child Support

MODIFY CHILD SUPPORT 15% OR MORE ("Simplified Mod")
☐ Petition to Modify
☐ Parents Worksheet for Child Support
☐ Blank Request for Hearing

MODIFY CHILD SUPPORT ("Standard Mod")
☐ Petition to Modify Child Support – Std. Process
☐ Affidavit of Financial Information
☐ Order to Appear

MODIFY SPOUSAL MAINTENANCE *OR* SPOUSAL *AND* CHILD SUPPORT ("Standard Mod")
☐ Petition to Modify Support Order
☐ Affidavit of Financial Information
☐ Order to Appear

MODIFY CUSTODY &/OR PARENTING TIME AND SUPPORT
☐ Petition to Modify
☐ Notice of Filing for Modification of Custody
☐ Parents Worksheet for Child Support
☐ Affidavit Regarding Minor Children *(only if children have not lived in Maricopa Co. whole time since last custody order)*

STOP ORDER OF ASSIGNMENT
☐ Petition to Stop Order of Assignment
☐ Blank Request for Hearing

MODIFY (Change) **ORDER OF ASSIGNMENT**
☐ Petition to Modify Order of Assignment
☐ Blank Request for Hearing

OTHER TYPE CASE (List Type): (Example: "Annulment") ____________ (Below, list name of each document you received: Example: "Petition for Annulment", "Summons", etc.)

____________	____________	____________
____________	____________	____________
____________	____________	____________
____________	____________	____________

How I sent the documents:

☐ U.S. Mail (Express or Priority Mail with Signature Confirmation, Certified or Registered Mail. **Copy of OTHER PARTY'S SIGNATURE of Receipt is attached.**

☐ Commercial Delivery Service (FEDEX, UPS, etc.) **Copy of OTHER PARTY'S SIGNATURE of Receipt is attached.**

OATH OR AFFIRMATION: By signing below, I swear or affirm under penalty of perjury that the contents of this document are true and correct to the best of my knowledge and belief.

____________ ____________
Signature of Person Sending Documents Date

Signed and Sworn to or Affirmed before me this date: ____________

(Seal/My Commission Expires) ____________
Deputy Clerk or Notary Public

DR24f
USE CURRENT VERSION

Case No. ____________________

Attach a copy/printout of the <u>other party's</u> signature acknowledging receipt of the court papers here. If using Certified Mail, tape the green signed return receipt card to this page with the signature side visible.
• **Note that the *<u>only</u>* acceptable signature is that of <u>the</u> <u>OTHER</u> <u>PARTY.</u>** • **You may specify "restricted delivery" so that no other person is permitted to sign,** • **Some delivery services *<u>do not offer</u>* restricted delivery.**

Attach a copy of the cash register receipt/mailing invoice from the Postal Service or company paid to make delivery *or* a copy of the package label that shows to whom and where the documents were sent.

Option 3: Service by a Registered Process Server

When people think of service, they generally think of a process server doing the job. With this method, you hire a process server to physically deliver those documents to your spouse. You will need to give the process server specific information as to where he or she can find your spouse. Process servers generally charge for the number of attempts it take to find your spouse. It is best to be as specific as possible and provide the process server a picture, so that he or she can identify your spouse. After the process server serves the documents on your spouse, the process server will file an affidavit of service with the court.

Option 4: Service by the Sheriff

This is usually not the most efficient way to serve the other party. First, a deposit of $200.00 is required for this method. You may ask the Sheriff's Office for a deferral or waiver of these fees. To ask the Sheriff's Office to serve your documents, you will need to fill out two (2) forms. (Both forms are on the Maricopa Superior Court website.) If you live in Maricopa County and want to serve the papers in Maricopa County, you can bring the documents to the Maricopa County Sheriff's Office, Civil Unit, 201 West Jefferson Street, First Floor, Central Court Building, Phoenix, Arizona 85003. Their telephone number is (602) 876-1840.

What if I have No Idea Where the Other Party Lives?

You qualify under this section of service if the following has been completed:

1. You have filed a petition with the accompanying documents, AND
2. You do not know where the other party is, AND
3. You have tried all reasonable ways to find your spouse, including:
    a. Mailed by certified mail to the spouse's last known address
    b. You have attempted to contact your spouse's family, friends and neighbors to retrieve an address
    c. You have contacted your spouse's place of employment
    d. You have done additional research, such as reviewing the phone book, online directories, voter registration information; and
    e. Considered hiring a professional detective or paid an online service attempt location for your spouse.
4. You are ready to testify under oath that you have tried all of these methods.

Chapter Nine:

AFTER THE COIN TOSS

CHAPTER 9: AFTER THE COIN TOSS (Before the Game Begins and the Impact of the Temporary Injunction)

Everyday courage has few witnesses. But yours is no less noble because no drum beats for you and no crowds shout your name.

~Robert Louis Stevenson

The Response

If your spouse/partner filed the action against you, you must file a responsive pleading. You have a time limit, so make sure you know what it is. If you were served in the state of Arizona, you have 20 days to respond, if you are out of state, you have 30 days. Your response should track the petition, paragraph by paragraph. You will "admit" the true things that are in the petition, such as the date of your marriage, your name, the county you live in. If you dispute some item, you respond with "deny," such as: "Denies Paragraph V as to spousal maintenance, because husband is capable of working to support himself." If you have any questions, you should consult an attorney. DO NOT IGNORE THE PETITION. You will set yourself up for a default, and that can be very dangerous. Remember to be ready to pay your responsive filing fee of $256 (at the time of this writing) when you file your response.

The "New" Rules

After a party is served with the dissolution or legal separation documents, there are new rules that must be followed by you **and** your spouse. These rules are explained in the Preliminary Injunction (A.R.S. §25-315(A)) initially filed and served upon a party. These rules are mandated for every party going through the process of dissolution or legal separation. It is crucial to follow these rules! To comply with the preliminary injunction, you shall not do any of the following:

1. Do not hide earnings or community property from your spouse.

   This injunction also applies to you when you have the intention to file for divorce or legal separation. In other words, you cannot hide money or community property from your spouse prior to filing for divorce. Throughout your divorce, all income and property must be disclosed, and it is recommended that you comply with all of the discovery rules.

2. Do not take out a loan on the community property.

3. Do not sell the community property or give it away to someone, **unless** you have written permission from your spouse or the court. There are exceptions to this rule if a party needs to transfer joint or community

property as part of the everyday running of a business, or if the sale of the community property is necessary to meet necessities of life, such as food, shelter, clothing or court fees and attorney fees associated with this action. (If this applies to you, it is recommended that you seek an attorney for help.)

4. Do not harass or bother your spouse or the children.

   While this may seem obvious, it is important to remember this part of the injunction. Feelings become strong throughout a divorce (even in amicable divorces), and it is important to be respectful, which will help the process move along more smoothly. If your spouse asks you to stop contacting him or her, please respect that request and only contact that person if absolutely necessary.

5. Do not physically abuse or threaten your spouse or the children.

   It is important to note that physical abuse or threats to your spouse or to your children during this period may have an effect on whether the court awards joint legal custody or sole legal custody to one parent. When there is significant domestic violence in a family, joint legal custody is contrary to the best interests of the children. If the court finds significant domestic violence in the family, it is more likely that the non-violent/non-abusive parent will be given sole legal custody, rather than sharing joint legal custody. Some judges do not understand the correlation between domestic violence towards a spouse and the increased likelihood that the offending parent will abuse the children. You should consider seeking the advice of an attorney if you are in this situation.

6. Do not take the minor children, common to your marriage, out of the state of Arizona for any reason without first obtaining a written agreement between you and your spouse or a court order.

   If you are concerned that your spouse may take your children out of the country and there is a chance that he or she will not return with them, make this known to the judge early on in your case and request that you maintain exclusive control over the children's passports.

7. **INSURANCE COVERAGE: Do not remove, or cause to be removed, the other party or the minor children of the parties from any existing insurance coverage, including medical, hospital, dental, automobile, and disability insurance.** Both parties shall maintain **all** insurance coverage in full force and effect. It is possible that you or your spouse loses employment upon which you rely for your insurance during this temporary injunction.

If this occurs, both parties shall attempt to gain the insurance lost. If it is economically not feasible and COBRA, for example, is too expensive for your family budget, then the court is likely to understand why you no longer have that type of insurance.

Other Issues

After the petition is served, each spouse is entitled to his or her own income. This income may be subject to child support and/or spousal maintenance that can be retroactive to the service or the separation date. Also, each party is responsible for his or her own debt incurred after that service date. Until the petition is served, all debt is presumed community. One of the ways to avoid the community debt is to prove community waste, which is beyond the scope of this book.

What Happens After the Papers are Served?

After the service of the petition other "clocks" begin ticking. For example, within forty (40) days after a party has been served with the initial documents, documentation concerning finances and property needs to be disclosed to the other party. This is mandated in Family Rule 49, which requires...

Depending upon what you request in your petition or response to dissolution or legal separation, you may be required to prove certain requests. For example, you may need to establish:

1. The birth and parentage of children
2. The acquisition of marital property
3. The existence of community debt
4. The requirement of child support
5. The need for spousal maintenance
6. The ability of the other spouse to pay support and/or maintenance
7. The fact and fairness of any settlement agreement
8. Excessive and abnormal expenditures
9. Destruction, concealment or fraudulent disposition of marital property
10. One spouse's need and the other spouse's ability to pay attorney's fees

The proof required may be in the form of witnesses, documentation, demonstrative evidence, presumptions and judicial opinions.

Early Resolution Conference or Resolution Management Conference

There are two different conferences that the court will schedule. The conference that the court schedules will be determined on whether you or your spouse is represented by counsel. If neither you nor your spouse is represented by counsel, the court will schedule an Early Resolution Conference. If either you or your spouse is represented by counsel, the court will schedule a Resolution Management Conference.

Early Resolution Conference

As previously mentioned, the court will set an Early Resolution Conference anywhere from one (1) to four (4) months from the time the papers were served. The court will set this conference at a time that will fit in with their dockets. You will receive notification in the mail. On that order, you will also have directions ordering you to fill out a Resolution Management Statement before you arrive. If your order prescribes it, you may need to file this with the court before your conference and give a copy to the other party. When your early resolution conference is scheduled, it is important that you arrive at the correct courthouse at the correct time. You do not need to bring anything with you to the conference, unless the court requests otherwise.

At this conference, you will first meet with a court representative and the other party, if there has been no domestic violence. At that time, the court representative will talk with you and determine whether you are able to settle any issues. If you and your spouse are able to come to any settlement terms, the court representative will memorialize your agreements in writing and file them with the court. Be advised that if you do not attend your scheduled early resolution conference, you will be fined $100.00. Please refer to the information that you receive from the court, because the processes and procedures are likely to change.

Resolution Management Conference

If either party is represented by an attorney, the court will set a Resolution Management Conference from one (1) to four (4) months from the date of service depending upon the court's docket. Prior to the Resolution Management Conference, both parties will receive a written notification from the court that will include the date and time for the conference. That written notification will also include requirements that must be completed prior to the conference. For example, the court will require a Resolution Management Statement. This statement outlines all of the key issues in your dissolution, including child custody and parenting issues, along with financial matters. The court will also require you and the opposing party with counsel to meet with each other for one hour in person prior to the hearing. During that period of time, the parties are encouraged to see if they can settle any issues. An example of this form is displayed below.

Example of Proposed Resolution Statement

Name: ____________________
Mailing Address: ____________________
City, State, Zip Code: ____________________
Daytime Phone Number: ____________________
Evening Phone Number: ____________________
Representing: ☐ Self ☐ Petitioner ☐ Respondent
State Bar Number: ____________________

FOR CLERK'S USE ONLY

SUPERIOR COURT OF ARIZONA IN MARICOPA COUNTY

____
Petitioner/Plaintiff

____
Respondent/Defendant

Case No. ____________________

ATLAS No. ____________________

PROPOSED RESOLUTION STATEMENT OF:
☐ **HUSBAND**
☐ **WIFE**
Date of Marriage: ____________________

I, the person signing this document (or his or her attorney), believe the issues in this case should be resolved as follows: (BE SPECIFIC.)

1. **IV-D Case:**
   ☐ I receive or have received public assistance which may include AFDC, TANF, or AHCCCS for my child(ren) or me.
   ☐ I have a case with the Division of Child Support Enforcement.

2. **Custody:** The parties have the following natural or adopted child(ren) in common. (If there are no minor or disabled children common to the parties, skip to # 3)

Child's Name	Date of Birth	Age

The child(ren) should live primarily with ☐ **Mother** ☐ **Father** and have parenting time with the other parent as follows: (check all that apply):

☐ Generally in accordance with ____________ County Guidelines for reasonable parenting time.

☐ Model Parenting Time Plan

☐ Every other weekend from ____________ (day of week) at ____ a.m./p.m. to ____________ (day of week) at ____ a.m./p.m.

DRMCR10f
Use current version

- ☐ One-half of the holidays on an alternating basis.
- ☐ For _____ weeks in the summer.
- ☐ Spring Break from school.
- ☐ Other: ____

____

____

This should be a ☐ sole custody ☐ joint custody arrangement.
☐ **Mother** ☐ **Father** ☐ **Both parents** should make decisions about the child(ren), such as schools, doctors, etc.

3. **<u>Child Support:</u>** (If there are no minor or disabled children common to the parties and were no minor or disabled children from the date the parties separated, skip to # 5.)
My position on the financial factors necessary to calculate child support under the statewide child support guidelines is as follows:

Father's Gross Monthly Income: $ ____________

Mother's Gross Monthly Income: $ ____________

- ☐ Father has _____ other child(ren) not listed above whom he is supporting who live(s) in his household.
- ☐ Father has _____ other child(ren) not listed above for whom he pays court-ordered child support in the amount of $_________per month.
- ☐ Mother has _____ other child(ren) not listed above whom she is supporting live(s) in her household.
- ☐ Mother has _____ other child(ren) not listed above for whom she pays court-ordered child support in the amount of $ __________ per month.
- ☐ Medical Insurance should be paid by [ ] Mother [ ] Father. The monthly cost for the child(ren) is $ _______.
- ☐ Dental Insurance should be paid by [ ] Mother [ ] Father.
The monthly cost for the child(ren) in this case is $ ___________
- ☐ Vision Care Insurance should be paid by [ ] Mother [ ] Father.
The monthly cost for the child(ren) in this case is $ ___________
- ☐ Neither parent has insurance which is accessible and available at a reasonable cost.
☐ **Mother** ☐ **Father** should pay cash medical support in the amount of $__________ per month.
- ☐ Monthly Child Care Costs for child(ren) in this case is $ _____________.
- ☐ Extra Education Expenses or Extraordinary Child Adjustments - I believe the court should add the following to the child support calculation (leave blank if none claimed):

Description	Monthly Amount
____	__________
____	__________

☐ Uninsured Medical/Dental/Vision Expenses should be paid:
☐ Pro rata based upon each party's income, as provided in the guidelines; or
☐ Other: ___ % paid d by Father and ___ % paid by Mother.

☐ Tax Exemptions for the child(ren) should be divided:
☐ Pro rata based upon each party's income, as provided in the guidelines; or
☐ Other: ____

4. **Past Support** should be paid by [ ] **Mother** [ ] **Father** for the period of ______________ through ____________________ in the amount of $ __________.

5. **Spousal Maintenance:** My position on spousal maintenance is:
☐ No spousal maintenance need be paid by either me or my spouse.
☐ I should pay my spouse $ _________ per month for ______ months.
☐ I should receive from my spouse $ __________ per month for _______ months.
☐ I pay spousal maintenance ordered for another marriage.

6. **Separate Property:** I believe the following property is my sole and separate property (describe):
____
____

7. **Community Liens on Separate Property:** I believe I have a community interest in the following sole and separate property of my spouse:
____
____

8. **Community Property:** I want to divide all of the community property (except tangible personal property) as follows:
Directions:
Column 1: List short description of each item of real and personal property.
Column 2: List your estimate of the fair market value of each item of property. List the loan or encumbrance amount(s) on the line directly below its value.
Column 3: List the amount of net value of each item you propose for Husband.
Column 4: List the amount of net value of each item you propose for Wife.

1. Real Property Description (real estate, land, houses, etc.)	2. Fair Market Value (Less Encumbrances)	3. Proposed for Husband	4. Proposed for Wife
a)	$		
Amount owed on this property:	-	$	$
b)			
Amount owed on this property:	-	$	$
c)			
Amount owed on this property:	-	$	$
d)			
Amount owed on this property:	-	$	$

Case No. ___________________

1. Personal Property Description (e.g. stocks, bonds, life insurance, etc.)	2. Fair Market Value (Less Encumbrances)	**3. Proposed for Husband**	**4. Proposed for Wife**
a)	$		
Amount owed on this property:	-	$	$
b)	$		
Amount owed on this property:	-	$	$
c)	$		
Amount owed on this property:	-	$	$
d)	$		
Amount owed on this property:	-	$	$

Pensions including Survivor Benefits IRAs, Roth IRAs	**2. Fair Market Value** (Less Encumbrances)	**3. Proposed for Husband**	**4. Proposed for Wife**
a)	$		
Amount owed on this property:	-	$	$
b)	$		
Amount owed on this property:	-	$	$
c)	$		
Amount owed on this property:	-	$	$

Vehicle(s)	**2. Fair Market Value** (Less Encumbrances)	**3. Proposed for Husband**	**4. Proposed for Wife**
a)	$		
Amount owed on this property:	-	$	$
b)	$		
Amount owed on this property:	-	$	$
c)	$		
Amount owed on this property:	-	$	$
Boat(s)	**2. Fair Market Value** (Less Encumbrances)	**3. Proposed for Husband**	**4. Proposed for Wife**
a)	$		
Amount owed on this property:	-	$	$
b)			
Amount owed on this property:	-	$	$

9. **Tangible Personal Property.** I believe that the value of the tangible personal property (household furniture, furnishings, jewelry etc.) in the possession of each party is as follows:

Husband has tangible personal property in his possession valued at approximately $__________

Wife has tangible personal property in her possession valued at approximately $__________

My preference to divide the tangible personal property is: (**List your order of preference, 1 – 4, with 1 being most important and 4 being the least**):

_____ Each party should keep the tangible personal property currently in his/her possession with the exception of the following items I want from my spouse:
________________________ ________________________
________________________ ________________________

_____ An equalization payment/credit should be made based upon the above values so each of us gets the same value.

_____ We should make a list of all the tangible personal property and alternately select items from the list until all the property is divided.

_____ One of us should make two (2) lists of tangible personal property both equal in value, and the other one be awarded all property on the list of his or her choice.

_____ **Other:** ____
____

10. **Debts:** The community debts should be divided as follows (complete in detail):
☐ All of the debt should be paid _____% by Husband and _____% by Wife; or
☐ Each of us should pay the following debts and amounts:

Amount To Be Paid By Husband	Amount To Be Paid By Wife	Creditor	Total Amount
$	$		$
$	$		$
$	$		$
$	$		$
$	$		$

11. **Attorney's Fees:** If the case is settled today, I want the court to order (choose one):

☐ Each of us is to pay his/her own attorney's fees and costs.

☐ My spouse should pay $ _______ of my attorney's fees and costs within _____ days.

☐ I should pay $ _______ to my spouse for attorney's fees and costs within _____days

12. **Name Change:** I want to be restored to my former name of (List full name you want restored):

____

13. **Other Issues:** Briefly state the other issues that you believe must be resolved to fully settle this case:

____
____
____
____
____
____

14. **Settlement:** I verify that the above statements are true upon my best information and belief and I am willing to settle and resolve this case based upon the information provided above. I will be prepared to show documentation to support my position at the time of the conference or hearing.

______________________ ______________________
Date Signature of ☐ Husband ☐ Wife
☐ Attorney for ☐ Husband ☐ Wife

Chapter Ten:

MEDIATION

CHAPTER 10: MEDIATION

Compromise is the best and cheapest lawyer.

~Robert Louis Stevenson

Best Law Firm provides mediation and alternative dispute resolution services to parties involved in a family law matter, such as a divorce, parenting time disputes or changes to child support.

Family law mediation is a method of resolving issues and disputes during the difficult time of divorce by talking with a mediator to resolve your disagreements. Mediation is conducted in a relaxed, comfortable office atmosphere with the mediator and the parties. Family law mediation can also be used to help persons with other legal family issues, such as separation, child custody, child support, post-decree modifications, disputes about parenting issues after a divorce, domestic partnership issues with children and property, and unmarried persons issues with children and property. There are myriad issues and problems that may confront people when they are attempting to navigate the emotional terrain of family law.

Mediation with Best Law Firm is designed to be a win-win solution for the parties involved. Parties do not require a retained attorney to represent their interests, but outside counsel is not discouraged. It is recommended that an attorney review any final legal documents before they are signed or filed with the court.

In addition to conducting the mediation, Best Law Firm can complete your family law matter by drafting all the necessary documents to be submitted to the court. We can draft a memorandum of understanding to memorialize the parties' agreements, draft the petition and supporting documents to initiate your case in the court and draft and file the consent decree, parenting plan and property settlement agreement to finalize your case.

Not Even the Winners Win in Litigation

A learned judge once said that no one wins in court. By this, he meant that the family loses control of decisions and that the expense is extreme. So, instead of spending money on two separate attorneys, mediation allows the parties to pay for one mediator to resolve all of the issues in the case. Moreover, even if the parties initially retain two separate attorneys, the court may still order the parties to attempt mediation before there is a trial. Best Law Firm welcomes parties who are represented by counsel, as well as parties who are unrepresented. Attempting mediation before courtroom litigation will save the parties time and money.

Best Law Firm can assist families throughout Arizona, including Phoenix, Mesa, Glendale, Scottsdale, Tempe, Chandler, Peoria, Gilbert, Casa Grande, Tucson, Flagstaff, Anthem, Carefree, Cave Creek, Fountain Hills, Goodyear, Apache Junction, Avondale, Queen Creek, Sun City, Surprise and all cities within Maricopa County, Yavapai County, and Pinal County.

If You Choose to Go to Court to Fight

If you choose to go to court for your case, you will be required to provide documents to the court and to the other party on strict deadlines; documents include mandatory disclosures, responses to discovery, affidavits of financial information, resolution statements, proposed findings of fact and conclusions of law and pretrial statements. Further, you may have to attend numerous court hearings, such as a resolution management conference, review hearings, return hearings, status conferences, evidentiary hearings and a trial. You are required under Rule 49 to obtain and provide copies of all pertinent documents, and the opposing party must do exactly the same. Obviously, this is time-consuming and expensive, because you are producing duplicate documents back and forth. In mediation, the parties are under the same full disclosure rules, but they can work together to produce their documents. Courts do not excuse these requirements simply because you are unrepresented.

By allowing a mediator to assist your family in resolving your issues, you can avoid court and all the other paperwork requirements for a litigated matter. You can avoid all the other steps and procedures of a litigated matter by negotiating all your issues. You must still file the initial pleadings and answer, attend the mandatory parenting class and file the required final documents, but it will be in a measured, timely fashion, one that you can choose. You never have to set foot in a courtroom once you are able to mediate all your issues.

Mediation: A step-by-step process

How Mediation Works

First, the parties must decide that they are able to discuss and consider their issues with each other through mediation. The parties may decide to initiate a free telephone consultation with one of our attorneys. Then, the parties make an appointment and come to our office. Be aware that the proceedings are confidential, and nothing can be used in a court proceeding. The success of mediation depends on the attitudes of the parties. It begins with the understanding that each party wants to mediate and resolve their dispute in a positive and calm manner. If either party has an attitude of wanting to "win" or to "hurt" the other person, mediation most likely will not work.

The process begins with an initial meeting, usually lasting one to two hours. The mediator explains her or his role of assisting the parties in resolving their issues.

Even though the mediator is an experienced family law attorney who practices law, she is not in her role as an attorney when she is a mediator. Nonetheless, her legal background helps both procedurally and substantially with the mediation process.

Issues

The mediator, in an impartial role, will help the parties define the issues, explain the legal process in the state of Arizona and then assist the parties in finding mutual agreements. The mediator's job is to keep the parties conversing about the issues and help them move toward agreements. To accomplish this, the mediator engages in conversation with the parties to identify issues and possible solutions. Throughout the conversation, the mediator may propose various settlement options.

Agreements

There is no coercion, and both parties must be in accord in order for there to be any agreements. Often, more than one conference may be needed to resolve all the issues. Family issues invoke a great deal of emotion, and sometimes people need time to think about the process and the decisions that need to be made. There is no rush about this process.

Some parties may be able to reach agreements on all issues in one session, while others may require multiple sessions. Additionally, the parties can meet together or individually with the mediator. For example, some parties may wish to sit together at a table with the mediator, while others may prefer to be in different rooms and have the mediator move between the parties, acting as a liaison between the parties. The latter approach helps minimize the emotion associated with meeting face-to-face and promotes progress on the individual issues. Each case is different, and our goal is to find an approach that will work best for your family.

The Parties Reach a Verbal Agreement

Two persons cannot divorce or legally separate unless, and until, certain paperwork is filed with the court. In Arizona, Family Law Rule 69 requires parties to have a signed, written agreement for it to be binding in court. In some cases, the parties may not need or want their agreement to be enforceable. In other situations, it is required that the agreement be filed with the court. Best Law Firm can assist the parties in completing all the required paperwork. We can also draft the necessary decree for your case or other paperwork, such as child support.

Document Drafting Service

Once the parties have reached a verbal agreement, Best Law Firm can draft a Memorandum of Understanding to memorialize the parties' agreements that complies with Family Law Rule 69. We can also draft the petition and supporting documents to initiate your case in the court, as well as draft and file the consent decree, parenting plan and property settlement agreement to finalize your case.

We can draft all your documents, from start to finish.

Advantages of Mediation

The Family

Best Interests of the Children:
Mediation is designed to help parents focus on the best interests of the children. The mediation process helps the parties remain aware that despite their differences that brought them to the mediation process, they must continue to communicate for the sake of their child. The mediation process will preserve the parties' relationship, which will benefit the child in the future years. It is also important to recognize future issues that might arise, and put a mechanism in place that will prevent future litigation.

Custom-tailored Agreements:
The relaxed atmosphere of mediation allows for creative settlements that are tailored to the parties' individualized circumstances. Mediation permits the parties, rather than the court, to control the outcome of their case. The tailored agreements typically result from both parties' determination of how they will share their children, how they will make major decisions concerning their children, who will pay child support and how much, and how to equitably divide property and debts.

The Parties' Obligations

- Desire to compromise and find a resolution
- Act in good faith
- Listen calmly to other party, even if you disagree with their statements
- Stay professional and considerate of other parties' statements
- Conduct good communication with other party and mediator
- Have an active role in the decision-making process
- Full disclosure of all debts and assets and information required in Rule 49

The Mediator's Role

- Identifies the issues with the help of the parties
- Outlines and discusses the possible solutions for each issue
- Shares experiences as a practicing family law litigation attorney
- Recognizes each parties' needs, fears and desires for the outcome
- Encourages a spirit of cooperation
- Keeps the focus on the parties' future, rather than their past
- Accepts the parties as they are and refuses to judge or control the parties

- Allows the parties to take their time and not be coerced
- Remains neutral
- Helps the parties in a professional, encouraging, courteous manner
- Emphasizes that the mediator does not represent either party nor give legal advice

Hypothetical Cases

In Arizona, family law cases generally fall into two categories: parties who are taking their family law case to court for the *first time* (also known as "pre-decree" matters, such as the initial divorce) and parties who are *returning* to court, usually to enforce or modify prior court orders (also known as "post-decree" or "post-judgment" matters, such as changing parenting time or for enforcement of support).

Divorce or Dissolution Hypothetical: David and Christina

Hypothetically, let's discuss the situation with David and Christina, who have been married for 12 years and have two children, DJ, age 10, and Eliza, age 6. David has been employed as a computer technician for most of the marriage and Christina is a teacher who has her summers off. They bought a house eight years ago and the mortgage is $1,200 per month. David moved into a small apartment three months ago. Christina also inherited $18,000 from her uncle Huck three years ago that she used to buy her car, a Volvo SUV. David has a vehicle with a loan, Christina has a retirement plan with the state of Arizona and David has almost no retirement, because they had a medical emergency three years ago for DJ's fractured leg, suffered in a ski accident. They also incurred an additional $8,000 in MasterCard debt when Christina took time off to care for DJ.

Both David and Christina have their differences and they have both decided that they need to get divorced. They are able to talk together, but they just do not agree on what they should do about custody, child support, the house and their debt. They are not even sure what custody is all about. What happens with the pension? How do they get it divided? Who pays child support and how do they pay it? Who pays for Eliza's piano lessons and summer soccer camp for both kids? Who has to pay back the MasterCard debt? Can David expect Christina to help pay rent for his apartment?

Because David and Christina have decided that they cannot each afford to pay for an attorney and they cannot afford to litigate and argue about the decisions that they have to make, they have set up a meeting at Best Law Firm. The attorney meets with David and Christina together, and they sign the mediation agreement and pay the mediation fee. After that, the real work begins. They all work together, outlining parenting and financial issues. The mediator will provide the parties with pertinent legal statutes that may apply to their issues. Remember that anything the parties say in mediation cannot be used against them in court; it is a confidential process. It is decided at the first meeting that both David and Christina need to get copies of various documents: the retirement plan, pay stubs, tax returns, credit card statements and so on. All financial documents must be disclosed, so that each party is aware of the assets and liabilities of the party under Family Law Rule 49.

At the second meeting, the parties and the mediator are able to resolve all the issues. The mediator drafts a Rule 69 agreement and the parties sign it and leave the office. The mediator then uses that agreement to draft the pertinent legal documents. For David and Christina, that includes a Joint Parenting Agreement, a Property Settlement Agreement and a Decree. David and Christina had decided to make all of these decisions before actually filing for divorce. Once the court receives the initial filings, it will be a minimum of 60 days before a judge will sign any final decree or other documents. The parties must also attend a mandatory parenting class and file the certificate with the court before their decree will be approved.

Post-Decree Hypothetical: Jackson and Jenna

Jackson and Jenna have three children, ages 8, 10 and 15. They have been divorced for four years and share joint legal custody, which allows both parents to be involved in major decisions of their children's lives. Jack has a new job in Nebraska and is going to relocate. What happens to the parenting schedule of week on and week off? What about 15-year-old Annie, who does not want to ever visit Nebraska and has a summer job at the local Dairy Queen? Does Jack have to pay more child support, and how do they figure it out?

Jack and Jenna meet with a mediation attorney at Best Law Firm, who outlines and discusses various choices and options that the parents can choose from. The mediator has experience with this particular scenario and is able to offer some creative and flexible solutions that are positive for everyone. This mediation lasts the better part of the afternoon, and the parents leave with a Rule 69 agreement that they are going to keep, but not file with the court. You might recall that a Rule 69 agreement is a written signed agreement. It was drafted for them while they were in the office, and they took it with them when they left the mediation. They decided they did not want or need to file it with the court.

Frequently Asked Questions

What is mediation?

Mediation is a negotiation method of nonbinding dispute resolution involving a neutral third party mediator who assists the parties reach a mutually agreeable resolution. Mediation is the fastest growing Alternative Dispute Resolution (ADR) method. In mediation, the parties create their own settlement terms, with the assistance of an impartial mediator.

How much does mediation cost?

On average, mediation can cost approximately 10% of the total cost in a typical litigation. The parties can share those costs any way they can agree, but the fees are usually split 50/50. At Best Law Firm, parties can pay by the hour, in a step-by-step process.

Does mediation cost less than two attorneys?
Yes. Instead of spending money on two separate attorneys, mediation allows the parties to pay for one mediator to resolve all of the issues in the case.

How will the costs be determined or divided between the parties?
The parties can decide how to divide the cost of the mediation.

What paperwork must be filed with the court to complete the mediation process?
No paperwork is required to be filed unless you are getting divorced, legally separated or want child support payments to be made through the state of Arizona Support Payment Clearinghouse.

Where does this paperwork get filed?
Best Law Firm also provides a document preparation and filing service. The paperwork agreed to in mediation can be filed with the Maricopa County Superior Court.

Can I be divorced after mediation?
You can only be divorced after the required documents are filed with the court and a judge signs a decree.

Can the mediator also act as my attorney?
No, a mediator cannot act as both your mediator and your individual attorney, because that would create a conflict of interest. If you would like an attorney to represent you individually to handle your case, you may visit our website at www.bestlawaz.com. Once an attorney becomes your mediator, he or she cannot represent either party because that would be a conflict.

What legal effects does mediation present?
Non-binding: A party in the mediation process is not bound to any outcome reached in the mediation process when they agree to mediate, sign an Agreement to Mediate or enter into the mediation process.
Binding: Mediation is binding only if an agreement is reached by both parties, it is in writing and it is signed by both parties.

How long does the average divorce take in the litigation process?
In the Phoenix area, the average divorce proceedings take 6-12 months.

Can I still have an attorney if I mediate?
Yes, retaining individual counsel is an option; however, it is not necessary. Individual attorneys may advise their clients of their legal rights throughout the mediation process and assist in reviewing agreements reached in mediation before they are signed or filed. The individual attorney may or may not choose to

attend the mediation.

If I've already filed for divorce, can we still mediate?
Yes, mediation is an option for parties even if they have already filed for divorce. Parties may decide litigation is not cost-effective, or that with the help of a third party, they can resolve their issues without the long, expensive litigation process.

When is mediation successful?
Mediation is successful when both parties are active, willing and cooperative in the mediation process. The parties must have a desire to compromise and find a resolution. In addition, the parties must act in good faith, be professional and listen to each other.

Who will prepare the mediation agreement documents?
Best Law Firm provides document preparation services, including Rule 69 agreements (Memorandum of Understanding) that memorialize the parties' agreements, the petition and supporting documents to initiate your case in the court, and draft and file consent decrees, parenting plans and property settlement agreements to finalize your case.

What if we cannot make an agreement?
If all outstanding issues cannot be resolved in the mediation process, the court will have to decide them. The mediator cannot represent either party if the mediation fails, nor can either party use any settlement negotiations as evidence in court under Arizona Rules of Evidence, Rule 408, and the family law rules.

Are there areas of family law that cannot be mediated?
Substance abuse and domestic violence are issues that are not generally suitable for mediation.

What are some helpful personal documents to bring into mediation?
All of this will be addressed at the initial meeting with the mediator. Each party is under the full disclosure requirements of the Arizona Rules of Family Law Procedure, including Rule 49.

What is special about Best Law Firm?
We care. Our attorneys have witnessed the devastation that conflict causes families. We recognize that a spirit of cooperation is a lifelong gift that families can give to themselves.

Chapter Eleven:

PLAY BALL! GOING TO COURT

CHAPTER 11: PLAY BALL! GOING TO COURT

Anger is like drinking poison and expecting the other person to die.
~Unknown

"Game on!" Just as there are certain ways to behave on a basketball court or a football field, there is protocol in the courtroom. In preparation for the "big game" (aka a hearing in front of a judge), you should be aware of certain things.

We hope that you do not have to go to court, but if you must go, you must know what you are doing. There are ways to prepare yourself so that your anxiety is reduced and you can understand the court hearings. This chapter provides information and recommendations about what you should do in the courtroom, what you should prepare before going to court and what you should wear to court. Even if you have an attorney, it is still important to know what to expect in court.

Dress the Part

You want to be taken seriously when you are in the courtroom, right? First, dress the part. When you see a judge in court, you want to present yourself so that the judge knows this is a very important matter to you. We always request that our clients show up to court looking professional.

Women should dress nicely, with either a suit or other dressy clothes. We often tell our clients to dress like they are going to church. Do not wear jeans, low-cut blouses or shorts. As for shoes, do not wear flip-flops or tennis shoes; nice sandals or heels are fine.

Men should wear a suit with a tie. While we know you may not even own a suit, your court hearings are important and you want to start out with a good impression. If you absolutely cannot get or borrow a suit, we recommend nice pants with a blazer or sport coat and tie. Again, men should not wear jeans, sweatpants, jogging suits or shorts. As for men's shoes, do not wear flip-flops, sandals or tennis shoes.

Before Heading Into the Courtroom

Most importantly, be on time! There is nothing that will annoy a judge more than tardiness. If an emergency arises and you know you will be late, we recommend that you call the court to let them know exactly what is going on.

First, know which courthouse you are assigned to. Please refer to Appendix D for a list of the four courthouses in Maricopa County and other county courthouses.

There are judges with the same last names at different courthouses. Also, make sure that you know which court personnel or judge you are going to see. If you are unsure which judge or courthouse location you are assigned, you may check your paperwork or case status at: http://www.superiorcourt.maricopa.gov/docket/FamilyCourtCases/caseSearch.asp.

When you get to the courthouse, see the directory of judges' names posted outside of their courtrooms. Once you reach the courtroom, read the signs outside the door of the court. Some judges ask that you buzz in on an intercom to let the clerk know that you have arrived. The location of the intercom is on the sign that tells you to call into the court. If you head into the courtroom prior to your scheduled time, be quiet, because there is likely another case ahead of yours. The courts are very busy these days and they try to fit many hearings into one day. This is why it is helpful if you are not distracting to the judge, the court staff or the other litigants when you enter the courtroom.

Preparing for Court

A good hockey player plays where the puck is. A great hockey player plays where the puck is going to be.

~Wayne Gretzsky

To begin, you must know why you are going into court. The best way to determine this is to read the court's "minute entry." A minute entry is the court's information and ruling memo that should be mailed to the address you have on file with the court. You are also able to find the minute entries in your case on the Internet at http://www.superiorcourt.maricopa.gov/docket/FamilyCourtCases/caseSearch.asp. The minute entry will likely request that you do certain things prior to your court date. Follow the court's instructions! For example, if the minute entry asks you to give your spouse or their counsel certain documents, do so. Whatever the court instructs you to do, do it! Another example is that prior to a resolution management conference or early resolution conference, as discussed in Chapter 9, you will be requested to fill out and file with the clerk of the court your resolution statement. Essentially, this statement is a comprehensive list as to what you would agree to in order to settle your case.

What to do with the Documents the Court Requests

As stated, the court may request that you submit certain materials to the court or the opposing side prior to your court date.
If you are required to send documents to your spouse:

1. Collect all of the documents
2. Draft a list of the documents you are providing to your spouse
3. Make a copy of all of the documents and the list for your records

4. Mail the documents and the list to your spouse or their attorney, if they are represented. You do not mail the documents to the court, but you might bring them to court with you.

If you are required to file a pleading (e.g., Resolution Management Statement) with the court:

1. Draft and fill out the requested pleading
2. Sign (and notarize if required) the pleading
3. Make three (3) copies of the pleading
4. Bring all four pleadings (the original and three copies) to the court clerk to file
5. Put one of the copies in the judge's box. If you are unsure where the judge's box is, ask at the information desk
6. Mail one copy of the pleading that you filed to your spouse or his/her counsel
7. Keep one copy of the pleading for your records

If you are required to provide documents (e.g. exhibits) to the court:

1. Collect all of the documents that the court requires
2. Draft a list of the documents you are providing to your spouse
3. Make two (2) copies of all of the documents and the list for your records (one of the copies will be given to the court, one copy will be given to your spouse or attorney and you will keep one copy)
4. Take the documents to the assigned courthouse. If you are providing exhibits, you should give them to the court clerk or put them in the judge's box. Exhibits are not filed with the court.
5. Mail the documents and the list to your spouse or his/her attorney if he/she is represented.
6. Keep one copy of the pleading for your records

When You are in the Courtroom and Your Case is Called

Courtrooms can be intimidating places if you have never been in one before. One important question you may be asking is, "Where do I sit"? Here is the rule of thumb. If you are the petitioner in your action, you sit at the "counsel table," closest to the jury box. The counsel tables are the two tables beyond the low swinging door. Obviously, if you are the respondent you sit at the counsel table furthest from the jury box. If there is not a jury box, or the judge is in the middle of the courtroom, see if there are any labels on the tables. Many judges have helped *pro per* (without attorney) litigants by labeling the tables.

Also, only you and your attorney may sit at the counsel table. It might be helpful to have friends and family attend hearings with you, but they must sit behind the railing in the "gallery." Remind your friends and family that their actions reflect upon you. Tell them to be on their best behavior. They should not speak or whisper, make noises or sighs. It is surprising what judges are able to hear up on the bench. Remind your friends that food and drinks are not appropriate for the courtroom. Turn off your cell phone and do not answer it or text message during your hearing! And, under NO circumstance should you bring your child to court or courtroom. There are very few exceptions to this rule. If a judge sees your child, the judge will immediately ask that the child be removed from the courtroom and will likely get very upset that you decided to bring your child into such an environment. This will not reflect positively on your parenting skills.

In the Courtroom

The next scenario is likely if one party or the other has an attorney and you are attending a Resolution Management Conference. Remain in your seat until the court clerk announces, "All rise." At that time, the judge enters the courtroom and tells everyone to be seated. (Every time the judge comes in or out of the courtroom, you will be requested to stand and told when to sit back down). When the judge is seated, the judge will turn on the recording system in the courtroom. This recording system and the microphone that you have at your table are extremely sensitive. It often picks up whispering. The clerk may swear in the parties before the judge enters the courtroom.

The judge will then announce your case number and your name. He or she will ask the petitioner to identify him or herself first. When this occurs, you can sit or stand, but be very polite and announce your name. The dialogue will sound something like this:

Judge: "We are here in the matter of Smith v. Smith, matter number FC2010-000000. Please state your name for the record."

Petitioner: "Good morning your honor. I am Jodi Smith and I am representing myself."

Respondent: "Good morning your honor. I am Attorney Matlock and I represent Jack Smith."

The judge will then introduce the matter and ask one party the status of your case. A typical dialogue at the Resolution Management Conference may sound something like this:

Judge: "Have any agreements been made by the parties?"

Petitioner: "Yes, your Honor. We have agreed to joint legal custody, but have not agreed on a parenting schedule yet."

Judge: "Do you agree to that, respondent?"

Respondent: "Yes, I agree to joint legal custody of our children."

Judge: "Let the record reflect that these parties have stipulated to joint legal custody of their minor children. Have you been able to reach any other agreements?"

Petitioner: "No, we have not your honor."

If there are other issues that you would like the judge to hear at this time, make sure that you tell the judge. This is your first opportunity to be heard and it is helpful to inform the court of issues in your case. For example, it may be necessary for you to inform the court that your husband moved out of the house three (3) months ago, you each have a car to drive, your husband is paying half the mortgage, your husband is providing you $350.00 per month for the two (2) children, and he sees the kids whenever he wants.

The judge will then look at your spouse to see if that is an accurate reflection of your situation. This is your time to be quiet. Do not interrupt. Take notes if you do not like something your husband says, so you can tell the judge when it is your turn again. Again, do not interrupt your spouse or the judge. This dialogue about the issues you brought up may go back and forth between you and the judge and between your spouse and the judge. Do not respond directly to your spouse; respond to the judge who asked you the question. If during this time, you and your spouse can agree to certain terms for your dissolution or legal separation, the judge will then make orders on all your agreements. The judge will dictate them to the court clerk and they will be provided in a minute entry. The minute entry may read something like this:

After discussion both parties advise the Court that they have reached partial agreement on the issues, which agreement is more fully set forth on the record and can be generally summarized as follows:

- The parties agree to permanent joint legal custody
- Mother shall be designated as the primary residential parent
- Mother shall have exclusive use of the marital residence located at Cactus Avenue
- The parties shall drive the vehicle currently in his/her possession

Petitioner and Respondent both testify that they have heard and understood the agreement as dictated in the record in open court, and that this is, in fact, their agreement.

THE COURT FINDS that the agreement entered into between the parties is not unfair, and is reasonable, and is in the best interests of the parties' minor child(ren).

IT IS ORDERED approving the agreement of the parties as a binding agreement pursuant to Rule 69, Arizona Rules of Family Law Procedure, to be included in the final Decree entered herein.

The Court finds that the minor children who are the subject of this action lived in Arizona with a parent, or a person acting as a parent, for at least six consecutive months or more prior to the commencement of this action, or at least from the time of birth of the child until this action was commenced, such that Arizona is the home state of the children vested with jurisdiction to make a child custody determination pursuant to A.R.S. § 25-1031(A)(1).

The Court finds that joint legal custody is in the best interests of the parties' minor children.

IT IS FURTHER ORDERED awarding the parties joint legal custody of their minor children,

The parties have two minor children, Mike, date of birth: September 20, 2000, and Eric, date of birth: February 28, 1997.

Mother is designated as primary residential parent and the minor children shall reside with Mother at all times except for access time specifically provided to Father.

IT IS ORDERED the parties are referred to Conciliation Services for Mediation of child custody and/or parenting-time issues, as appropriate. The parties shall comply with all instructions and directives issued by Conciliation Services.

IT IS FURTHER ORDERED that each party is directed to immediately go to Conciliation Services and complete necessary forms following this hearing. This Court has contacted Conciliation Services and set the Mediation for **September 4, 2010 at 1:30 p.m.** in Conciliation Services.

This Rule 69 agreement becomes a court order that will be very difficult to change later. Be clear on what you want and what you will agree to before you set foot into the courtroom. If you are not sure about the terms of the agreement, ask the judge before the orders are entered. After the agreements have been made, the judge will then set a trial date and ask you how much time your case will take. The court typically sets trials for one to three hours, and you will get one-half of that time to present your side of the case. If you need more time than that, you will need to ask your judge. The more time that you need for your trial will dictate when your case will be heard. It is easier for courts to schedule two-hour trials into their schedules than six-hour trials. You are likely to get your case heard more expeditiously if you ask for two hours, rather than six hours.

Before the court ends your hearing, he or she will ask if there is anything else to discuss. This is the time to ask any questions or present issues that you have. If the court does not ask this, politely inform the court that you have other issues to be heard.

After Court

The only way to overcome is to hang in. Even I'm starting to believe that.

~Dan O'Brien

After your first hearing, it is important to take a break and try to relax. Family law matters are usually full of stress that is compounded when the parties go to court. Settlement negotiations can help manage that stress. If you and your spouse are able to reach agreements, you can file a stipulated decree with the court before your actual trial date. If the court accepts your decree, your trial date will be vacated. If you file your decree within days of your trial date, be sure to call your judge's judicial assistant and let them know what you are doing, so they can clear their calendar.

A list of the judges and their office telephone numbers can be found at: http://www.superiorcourt.maricopa.gov/JudicialBiographies/judicialList.asp?title=1. Judges encourage settlement and will be pleased to know that you and your spouse were able to come to agreements on your own.

Chapter Twelve:

THE END-THE DECREE

Chapter 12: THE END—THE DECREE

If you're trying to achieve, there will be roadblocks. I've had them; everybody has had them. But obstacles don't have to stop you. If you run into a wall, don't turn around and give up. Figure out how to climb it, go through it, or work around it.

~Michael Jordan

The Decree

There are three types of decree: consent, default and judicial.

A **Consent Decree** is a decree of dissolution by consent (agreed upon) and a **Default Decree** is a decree of dissolution in which one party does not respond to the filing. If a court makes the decisions for you and your spouse, they are drafted into a decree that is neither by consent or default, but a **Judicial Decree**. A court will put all these issues into a "minute entry" and that becomes the decree. If one party has an attorney, the court will often draft the issues into a minute entry and ask one attorney to put the results into a decree.

	Consent Decree	Default Decree	(Judicial) Decree
Petitioner files documents with the Court (6-9 documents)	X	X	X
Petitioner serves the other spouse	X	X	X
No Response from spouse		X	
Petitioner files Application for Default		X	
Respondent spouse files a Response	X		X
Spouses agree to the terms of their decree	X		
Spouses cannot agree to the terms of the divorce and must have a trial			X

Consent Decree

A consent decree is the final document that the judge or commissioner signs that officially divorces a couple. That consent decree cannot be filed until the 60 days have passed since the service of the petition. Do not submit your decree to the court before the 60 days have passed, because they will return it to you; they usually will not hold it. You and your spouse have to provide your notarized signatures on the Consent Decree to indicate that you have agreed to all the terms that are in the decree. This is legally binding, so be sure you read and understand each and every sentence and the legal significance of the agreements. If you have children, you cannot get your decree signed by the judge/commissioner until you have attended the Parenting Information Class and have filed your Certificate of Attendance with the court clerk, so that it shows up in your file. If you do not understand something in your decree language, do not sign the decree until you do.

In order to prepare a consent decree, the parties need to have agreed as to all aspects of this dissolution or separation. The following issues should be determined and integrated into your decree, so that when your divorce is finalized (the decree is signed by the judge), you are completely finished and all of the issues have been discussed and explained in writing in the decree. When entering into a Consent Decree, the following issues should be decided:

1) Legal custody of children and visitation
2) Child support of children
3) Spousal maintenance
4) Attorney's fees, who pays, if either party
5) Division of all personal and real property
6) Division of retirement or pension benefits, including future benefits (may need a qualified Domestic Relations Order expert–see Chapter 6)
7) Provisions as to health insurance for children
8) Provision for children's medical care uncovered by insurance
9) Payment of debts
10) Payment of federal taxes during year of divorce and after
11) Integrated or severable provisions
12) Incorporation and merger into the decree
13) Execution of conveyances

Default Decree

A Default Decree can be obtained when only one party has been involved in the divorce proceeding. For instance, if you are the petitioner and your spouse does not answer the petition and he or she is not cooperating, you can still get divorced; you will need to file a Default Decree. Sometimes, spouses will decide that one person files and the other does not answer in order to save the answer filing fee. If you do this intentionally, you must file a Default Decree and show the court that the other side has notice of the divorce by being served with the petition and all the other papers. In a Default Decree, you can draft what you want for the division of property and for the custody of the children, but the court has the final say to make sure it is equitable, even though it is a default.

How can I get a default hearing? If service has been proper and no response was filed, you may be able to get divorced by default. See how to file for default: www.superiorcourt.maricopa.gov/SuperiorCourt/Self-ServiceCenter/Forms/FamilyCourt/fc_drdc6.asp

If you want to set a default hearing, you must complete the Application and Affidavit of Default and file it with the clerk of the court. You must be sure service of the petition was complete, and that the other party did not file a written response or answer with the court.

At the time you file the Application and Affidavit of Default with the clerk of the court, make sure you have two (2) copies of the Application and Affidavit of Default date-stamped by the clerk. You must mail or hand-deliver one copy to the other party the day that you filed the Application and Affidavit of Default with the clerk of the court. After you have given the other party a copy of the Application and Affidavit of Default, you must wait 10 court days.

If the other party still does not file a written response or answer in 10 court days, you may be able request a default hearing date.

To request a default hearing in Maricopa County, call 602-372-3332.

You will be asked the following questions before your hearing can be set:

1. **Case Number:**______________________
2. **Does your case involve children?** ☐*Yes* ☐*No*

   ✕ If Yes,

   what type of custody is asked for in the petition? ☐*Joint* ☐*Shared* ☐*Sole* ☐*N/A*

   Have you filed your Parent Information Program Certificate? ☐*Yes* ☐*No*

   Has the Respondent filed their Parent Information Program certificate? ☐*Yes* ☐*No*
3. **Do you need an interpreter?** ☐*Yes* ☐*No*

   If Yes, what language______________________
4. **For Dissolution, Legal Separation and Annulment matters only:**

   Is Spousal Maintenance/Support being requested? ☐*Yes* ☐*No*

   Has at least 64 days passed since the respondent was served? (94 days if service was by publication), *If you answer no, you must wait until the time has passed.* ☐*Yes* ☐*No*
5. **Has at least 10 working days passed since the Affidavit and Application for Default was filed?** *If you answer no, you must wait until the time has passed* ☐*Yes* ☐*No*
6. **Type of Service:**

   ☐*Acceptance* ☐*In State* ☐*Out of State*

   Date Acceptance was signed:__________________

   ☐Private Process Server/Sheriff ☐*In State* ☐*Out of State*

   ☐Registered Mail

   Date green card was signed:__________________

   ☐Publication

   Date of 1st publication______________________
7. **Date Application and Affidavit of Default was filed:**________________

What documents need to be completed to ask for a Consent Decree?

The following paperwork is required to be signed and notarized by all parties when submitting a consent decree:

- Original Consent Decree of Dissolution/Final Orders and two (2) copies
- Two (2) self-addressed stamped 9-by-12-inch envelopes

For cases with children you will also need:

- Original Parenting Plan and two (2) copies
- Original Child Support Worksheet and two (2) copies
- Original Child Support Order and two (2) copies
- Original Order of Assignment and two (2) copies
- Judgment Data Sheet
- Original Parent Information Program Certificates or conformed copies

Chapter Thirteen:

FOULS AND PENALTIES

CHAPTER 13: FOULS AND PENALTIES (Domestic Violence and Orders of Protection)

Nobody believes that domestic violence kills and nobody believes it is detrimental to children. This world has got to wake up. To me, if there is domestic violence, if the children see it or hear it, that to me is detrimental. Batterers should not have rights to children.

~Denise Brown (sister of the late Nicole Brown-Simpson)

Domestic Violence

Sadly, domestic violence has invaded homes across America. When domestic violence has seeped into a couple's relationship or the family as a whole, the members of the family must be on guard throughout the pendency of the dissolution proceedings. This is not the time to make excuses for the offending spouse; this is the time to admit the past abuse for what it was: intolerable and inexcusable. If you believe that the offending spouse will re-offend or has re-offended, it may be necessary for you to obtain an Order of Protection. The purpose of an Order of Protection is to restrain another person from committing an act of domestic violence, as defined in A.R.S.13-3601(A). To be granted an order, you must be one of the following:

- A spouse or former spouse of the defendant or a person of the opposite sex that resides or resided in the same household.
- A parent of a child of the defendant.
- Pregnant by the defendant.
- Related to the defendant or the defendant's spouse by blood or court order as a parent, grandparent, child, grandchild, brother or sister, or by marriage as a parent-in-law, grandparent-in-law, stepparent, step-grandparent, stepchild, step-grandchild, brother-in-law or sister-in-law.
- A child who resides or has resided in the same household as the defendant, and is related by blood to a former spouse of the defendant or to a person of the opposite sex who resides or who has resided in the same household as the defendant.

The clerks at any justice court will provide you with the Petition for Order of Protection. You may request that information regarding your current address, phone number and employment be kept confidential and not be disclosed to the defendant.[vi] There is also a Family Violence Center at the Maricopa County courts to help through this process.

Impact of Domestic Violence on Children

Often, families are under the misconception that if it is only the parent being battered by the offending spouse (not the children), then the abuse is confined to the abused parent. This is not the case. Domestic violence in a home with children will impact their lives forever. The following facts demonstrate the need for parents, families, communities and the courts to take domestic violence against a spouse seriously.

Children whose mothers are victims of wife battery are twice as likely to be abused themselves, as compared to those children whose mothers are not victims of abuse.[vii]

In about 43 percent of households where intimate partner violence occurs the couples have children under the age of 12.[viii]

A recent study of low-income, pre-school children in Michigan found that nearly half (46.7 percent) of the children in the study had been exposed to at least one incident of mild or severe violence in the family. Children who had been exposed to violence suffered symptoms of post-traumatic stress disorder such as bed-wetting or nightmares, and were at greater risk than their peers of having allergies, asthma, gastrointestinal problems, headaches and flu.[ix]

Battered women are not the only victims of abuse–it is estimated that anywhere between 3.3 million and 10 million children witness domestic violence annually. Research demonstrates that exposure to violence can have serious negative effects on children's development.[x]

At least 85 percent of children who live in violent homes are eyewitnesses, attempt to intervene, and/or experience the violence from behind closed doors.[xi]

When children witness violence in the home, they have been found to suffer many of the symptoms that are experienced by children who are directly abused.[xii]

In spite of evidence of violence against women and/or their children, the courts consistently ordered sole or joint custody to perpetrators in 74 percent of the cases in Maricopa County and 56 percent of the of the cases in the other counties combined.[xiii]

The Impact of Domestic Violence on Custody Determinations

Although courts should consider evidence of domestic violence at every point in custody and visitation negotiations, there is no guarantee that judges will do so.

Women often report that violence plays a significant role in divorce proceedings, specifically regarding the issues of custody, visitation and child support.[xiv]

Partner violence is a factor in anywhere from a third or a half of the cases where custody is disputed.[xv]

In disputed family court cases, somewhere between 15 percent and 25 percent show substantiating evidence of physical abuse, such as prior arrest, criminal court finding or court order.[xvi]

Many abusers appear to use the legal system to maintain contact and harass their ex-partners, at times using extensive and lengthy litigation.[xvii]

Many women compromise on their demands for resources during divorce negotiations for fear of losing custody of their children.[xviii]

In cases of domestic violence, fathers who contest custody win sole or joint custody up to 70 percent of the time.[xix]

Joint custody precludes separation between a victim and her abuser, because the parents must transfer children and have joint decision-making. This ongoing communication provides excessive, yet legally required, opportunities for the batterer to continue his abuse.[xx]

Courts seem to ignore abuse and privilege the father-child relationship despite the danger, concluding that father estrangement is more traumatic to children than paternal abuse and giving custody of the children to the abuser.[xxi]

In spite of evidence of violence against women and/or their children, the courts consistently ordered sole or joint custody to perpetrators in 74 percent of the cases in Maricopa County and 56 percent of the cases in the other counties combined.[xxii]

Orders of Protection

Orders of Protection can be issued by any court in Arizona, regardless of the location of the plaintiff and defendant. They can be issued either ex parte (with only one person present) or after a hearing. Both are good for one year after service on the defendant. Only the judge can terminate or change them.

The purpose of an Order of Protection is to restrain another person from committing an act of domestic violence, as defined in A.R.S.13-3601A. To be granted an order, you must be one of the following:

- A spouse or former spouse of the defendant or a person of the opposite sex that resides or resided in the same household.
- A parent of a child of the defendant.
- Pregnant by the defendant.
- Related to the defendant or the defendant's spouse by blood or court order as a parent, grandparent, child, grandchild, brother or sister, or by marriage as a parent-in-law, grandparent-in-law, stepparent, step-grandparent, stepchild, step-grandchild, brother-in-law or sister-in-law.
- A child who resides or has resided in the same household as the defendant, and is related by blood to a former spouse of the defendant or to a person of the opposite sex who resides or who has resided in the same household as the defendant.

To obtain an order of protection, proceed to your local courthouse. There is a video online at:
http://www.azcourts.gov/domesticviolencelaw/DomesticViolenceInformation.aspx
for you to obtain further information about filing for an Order of Protection. In the Northeast Courthouse, for example, there is a Domestic Violence Center, adjacent to the filing windows. As you enter the center, an employee will direct you to a computer to file your petition for the Order Of Protection. (You may request that information regarding your current address, phone number and employment be kept confidential and not be disclosed to the defendant.)

The petition asks you a number of questions, including your name, address, the defendant's name and address, and whether you have any children together. Most importantly, you will have the opportunity to write and explain three (3) instances when you have been the victim of domestic violence at the hands of the defendant.

Chapter Fourteen:

TIMEOUTS

CHAPTER 14: TIMEOUTS

As you walk down the fairway of life, you must smell the roses, for you only get to play one round.

~Ben Hogan

Conciliation Services

Conciliation Services is one part of the Maricopa County Superior Court. According to Maricopa County Superior Court's website, Conciliation Services provide the following:

- Conciliation counseling for parties contemplating divorce.
- Mediation of child custody and parenting time plans for families of divorce, post-divorce or paternity actions.
- Evaluation services to the court when parents are unable to agree upon a parenting plan.
- Parent Information Program, providing information to divorcing parents, or parents involved in other domestic relations actions, concerning what their children may be experiencing during this emotionally difficult period.
- High Conflict Resolution Class, designed specifically for high conflict parents.
- Premarital underage counseling for persons under the age of 16 contemplating marriage.[xxiii]

Reconciliation

At any time along the divorce or legal separation process, reconciliation may be an option. If you and your spouse decide to reconcile after dissolution documents have been filed, you can ask the court (with the signatures of both of you) to dismiss your action because you have reconciled. As you may know, there is a sixty (60) day waiting period from the time one party is served with the initial documentation until a judge will sign a decree. This period of time is a "cooling off" period. The court recognizes that reconciliation may be an option in some circumstances, and because that is the case, you can request that the court either dismiss your case or put it on the inactive calendar. Ultimately, it is up to the court to do either. If the court dismisses your case for one reason or another, you can re-file your dissolution/legal separation documents at any time. Please be advised that you will need to pay a new filing fee.

Voluntary Dismissal of Dissolution or Legal Separation

If you are the petitioner and service has not been completed, you can submit a Notice of Dismissal. If service has been completed you can file a Motion to Dismiss your divorce. If both of you agree to dismiss your divorce, you can submit a Stipulation to Dismiss your divorce. You can pick up the form from the Self Service Center or you can download the form, complete it, and return it to the court. You will need to determine which form you will need.

Non-voluntary Dismissal of Dissolution or Legal Separation

If, as a respondent, you receive a Notice of Lack of Service and Intent to Dismiss, you need to serve the other party. "Service" means that you deliver the papers to the other party through a process server or by having the other party sign a document to accept service. Your action could be dismissed without any further notice any time after if you do not take the steps listed below.

A. SERVE THE OTHER PARTY WITH THE COURT PAPERS AND FILE THE PROOF OF SERVICE. If you have served the other party, you must be sure that the proof of service has been filed with the clerk of the court at the filing counter immediately. If you need to obtain the form and instructions to serve the other party, go to one of the Self-Service Centers (see locations) or from the Self-Service Center website.
B. MOTION AND ORDER TO EXTEND TIME FOR SERVICE. You may file a motion to ask the judge for more time to serve the court papers before the court automatically dismisses your case. The order granting the extension must be SIGNED by the judge BEFORE the dismissal date indicated on the notice (download form).
C. VOLUNTARY DISMISSAL OF YOUR CASE. If you want to dismiss your case instead of waiting for the court to dismiss it, forms and instructions are available at Family Court Administration. You can also download the form and mail it to the court.

Remember that you can contact Best Law Firm at any point for advice and help with your documents.

An example of *Notice of Lack of Service and Intent to Dismiss* follows:

IN THE SUPERIOR COURT OF THE STATE OF ARIZONA
IN AND FOR THE COUNTY OF MARICOPA

Family Court Administration
201 W. Jefferson, 6th Floor
Phoenix, AZ 85003
(602) 506-1561

Case Number: [redacted]

10/21/2008

[redacted]

VS

[redacted]

NOTICE OF INTENT TO DISMISS CASE

NOTICE AND WARNING: The Court Information System indicates that at least 120 days have passed since your case was filed on 06/17/2008, and no trial, hearing, conference or Motion to Set is pending. Under these circumstances, Rule 46(B), *Arizona Rules of Family Law Procedure* allows the Court to schedule a case for dismissal for Lack of Prosecution 60 days after Notice is given to you unless appropriate actions are taken.

You are hereby notified that your case will be dismissed without prejudice on 12/22/[redacted] unless you take appropriate steps to prevent the dismissal.

- If any temporary orders have been issued in this case, THESE ORDERS WILL END WHEN YOUR CASE IS DISMISSED.
- If you do not wish to have your case dismissed for lack of prosecution, you must take one of the following actions:
  1. Have a final decree or judgment signed by a judge or commissioner prior to the dismissal date.
  2. If a response **has been** filed, you may file a proper Motion to Set prior to the dismissal date. If a response **has not** been filed, you may be able to proceed by default.
  3. If you need more time to complete your case, you may file a Motion to Extend the Dismissal Date. The judge must sign the order granting your motion prior to the dismissal date.
- The Superior Court Self Service Center has court forms and instructions you might be able to use for your court case, and also has a list of lawyers who can help you on a task-by-task basis, for a fee.

Internet:	http://www.superiorcourt.maricopa.gov/ssc/sschome.html
Downtown:	**101 W. Jefferson, East Court Building, Phoenix, AZ at the Law Library**
Mesa:	**222 E. Javelina, 1st Floor, Mesa, AZ at the Law Library**
Northwest:	**14264 W. Tierra Buena Lane, Surprise, AZ**
Northeast:	**18380 N. 40th St. Phoenix, AZ**

WARNING: THE COURT WILL DISMISS YOUR CASE without prejudice unless you do what this Notice tells you to do. "Dismiss" means there will be no court order granting or denying what you asked for in the court papers. "Without prejudice" means you can file the case again, but you might lose certain rights. If you do not understand, see a lawyer for help.

The court will NOT SEND YOU ANY MORE NOTICES about this.

NIC-Notice of Placement of the Case on Inactive Calendar and Intent to Dismiss — Report Version: (FC0748 1.0.0) — Tuesday, 21 October, 2008 — Page 1 of 1

The notice and intent to dismiss is sent to you if more that 120 days has passed from the date the petition was filed. Your case will be dismissed unless you take steps to prevent the dismissal. If temporary orders have been issued, THESE ORDERS WILL END WITH THE DISMISSAL of your action. If a paternity case has been dismissed and the parties have agreed to paternity and now have temporary orders for support, custody, etc, you may not have a final order of paternity. Temporary orders for support, custody, visitation, etc., will also end.

If you do not want your action dismissed for lack of prosecution, you must do one of the following:

1. Submit a final decree/order and have it signed by a judge or commissioner prior to the dismissal date.
2. If a response has been filed, file a proper motion to set your case for trial or conference.
3. If a response has not been filed, a proper default hearing must be scheduled by calling 602-372-3332 or online at http://ecourt.maricopa.gov/.
4. If you need more time to complete your case, you must file a motion to ask the judge for additional time. The judge must sign the order granting your motion prior to the dismissal date listed on the notice.

Uncooperative Spouses

If you have an uncooperative spouse and your divorce or legal separation is not moving along as smoothly as you think it should, it may be necessary for you to step back and allow your dissolution or legal separation to work itself through the court system. It may be better for you to spend your energy at the gym, with your children or doing something else you enjoy. This process is difficult enough, even when both spouses get along, so take some downtime and try to relax a little.

I have resolved that from this day on, I will do all the business I can honestly, have all the fun I can reasonably, do all the good I can willingly, and save my digestion by thinking pleasantly.

-Robert Louis Stevenson

Appendix A:

USEFUL ARIZONA STATUTES

APPENDIX A: USEFUL ARIZONA STATUTES (The Law)

A.R.S. §25-211. Property Acquired During Marriage as Community Property; Exceptions; Effect of Service of a Petition

A. All property acquired by either husband or wife during the marriage is the community property of the husband and wife except for property that is:

1. Acquired by gift, devise or descent.
2. Acquired after service of a petition for dissolution of marriage, legal separation or annulment if the petition results in a decree of dissolution of marriage, legal separation or annulment.

B. Notwithstanding subsection A, paragraph 2, service of a petition for dissolution of marriage, legal separation or annulment does not:

1. Alter the status of preexisting community property.
2. Change the status of community property used to acquire new property or the status of that new property as community property.
3. Alter the duties and rights of either spouse with respect to the management of community property except as prescribed pursuant to section 25-315, subsection A, paragraph 1, subdivision (a).

A.R.S. §25-213. Separate Property

A.A spouse's real and personal property that is owned by that spouse before marriage and that is acquired by that spouse during the marriage by gift, devise or descent, and the increase, rents, issues and profits of that property, is the separate property of that spouse.

B. Property that is acquired by a spouse after service of a petition for dissolution of marriage, legal separation or annulment is also the separate property of that spouse if the petition results in a decree of dissolution of marriage, legal separation or annulment.

C. Notwithstanding subsection B of this section and section 25-214, subsection C, a mortgage or deed of trust executed by a spouse who acquires the real property encumbered by that mortgage or deed of trust after service of a petition for dissolution of marriage, legal separation or annulment shall be enforceable against the real property if the petition does not result in a decree of dissolution of marriage, legal separation or annulment.

D. A contribution to an irrevocable trust that has as its principal asset life insurance on the person making the contribution is a contribution of the insured's separate property if the spouse of the insured is the primary beneficiary of the trust.

A.R.S. §25-215. Liability of Community Property and Separate Property for Community and Separate Debts

A. The separate property of a spouse shall not be liable for the separate debts or obligations of the other spouse, absent agreement of the property owner to the contrary.

B. The community property is liable for the premarital separate debts or other liabilities of a spouse, incurred after September 1, 1973 but only to the extent of the value of that spouse's contribution to the community property which would have been such spouse's separate property if single.

C. The community property is liable for a spouse's debts incurred outside of this state during the marriage which would have been community debts if incurred in this state.

D. Except as prohibited in section 25-214, either spouse may contract debts and otherwise act for the benefit of the community. In an action on such a debt or obligation the spouses shall be sued jointly and the debt or obligation shall be satisfied: first, from the community property, and second, from the separate property of the spouse contracting the debt or obligation.

A.R.S. §25-312. Dissolution of Marriage: Findings Necessary

The court shall enter a decree of dissolution of marriage if it finds each of the following:

1. That one of the parties, at the time the action was commenced, was domiciled in this state, or was stationed in this state while a member of the armed services, and that in either case the domicile or military presence has been maintained for ninety days prior to filing the petition for dissolution of marriage.
2. The conciliation provisions of section 25-381.09 and the provisions of article 5 of this chapter either do not apply or have been met.
3. The marriage is irretrievably broken or, if the marriage is a covenant marriage, any of the grounds prescribed in section 25-903.
4. To the extent it has jurisdiction to do so, the court has considered, approved and made provision for child custody, the support of any natural or adopted child common to the parties of the marriage entitled to support, the maintenance of either spouse and the disposition of property.

A.R.S. §25-313: Decree of Legal Separation: Findings Necessary

The court shall enter a decree of legal separation if it finds each of the following:

1. That one of the parties at the time the action was commenced was domiciled in this state or was stationed in this state while a member of the armed services.
2. The conciliation provisions of section 25-381.09 and the provisions of article 5 of this chapter either do not apply or have been met.
3. The marriage is irretrievably broken or one or both of the parties desire to live separate and apart or, if the marriage is a covenant marriage, any of the grounds prescribed in section 25-904.
4. The other party does not object to a decree of legal separation. If the other party objects to a decree of legal separation, on one of the parties meeting the required domicile for dissolution of marriage, the court shall direct that the pleadings be amended to seek a dissolution of the marriage.
5. To the extent it has jurisdiction to do so, the court has considered, approved or made provisions for child custody, the support of any natural or adopted child common to the parties of the marriage entitled to support, the maintenance of either spouse and the disposition of the property.

A.R.S. §25-318. Disposition of Property; Retroactivity; Notice to Creditors; Assignment of Debts; Contempt of Court

A. In a proceeding for dissolution of the marriage, or for legal separation, or in a proceeding for disposition of property following dissolution of the marriage by a court which previously lacked personal jurisdiction over the absent spouse or previously lacked jurisdiction to dispose of the property, the court shall assign each spouse's sole and separate property to such spouse. It shall also divide the community, joint tenancy and other property held in common equitably, though not necessarily in kind, without regard to marital misconduct. For the purposes of this section only, property acquired by either spouse outside this state shall be deemed to be community property if the property would have been community property if acquired in this state.

B. In dividing property, the court may consider all debts and obligations that are related to the property, including accrued or accruing taxes that would become due on the receipt, sale or other disposition of the property. The court may also consider the exempt status of particular property pursuant title 33, chapter 8.

C. This section does not prevent the court from considering all actual damages and judgments from conduct that resulted in criminal conviction of either spouse in which the other spouse or a child was the victim or excessive or abnormal expenditures, destruction, concealment or fraudulent disposition of community, joint tenancy and other property held in common.

D. The community, joint tenancy and other property held in common for which no provision is made in the decree shall be from the date of the decree held by the parties as tenants in common, each possessed of an undivided one-half interest.

E. The court may impress a lien on the separate property of either party or the marital property awarded to either party in order to secure the payment of:

1. Any interest or equity the other party has in or to the property.
2. Community debts that the court has ordered to be paid by the parties.
3. An allowance for child support or spousal maintenance, or both.
4. All actual damages and judgments from conduct that resulted in criminal conviction of either spouse in which the other spouse or a child was the victim.

F. The decree or judgment shall specifically describe by legal description any real property affected and shall specifically describe any other property affected.

G. This section applies through both prospective and retrospective operation to property without regard to the date of acquisition.

H. In all actions for the dissolution of marriage or legal separation, the court shall require the following statement in the materials provided to the petitioner and to be served on the respondent:

Notice

In your property settlement agreement or decree of dissolution or legal separation, the court may assign responsibility for certain community debts to one spouse or the other. Please be aware that a court order that does this is binding on the spouses only and does not necessarily relieve either of you from your responsibility for these community debts. These debts are matters of contract between both of you and your creditors (such as banks, credit unions, credit card issuers, finance companies, utility companies, medical providers and retailers).

Since your creditors are not parties to this court case, they are not bound by court orders or any agreements you and your spouse reach in this case. On request, the court may impose a lien against the separate property of a spouse to secure payment of debts that the court orders that spouse to pay.

You may want to contact your creditors to discuss your debts as well as the possible effects of your court case on your debts. To assist you in identifying your creditors, you may obtain a copy of your spouse's credit report by making a written request to the court for an order requiring a credit reporting agency to release the report to you. Within thirty days after receipt of a request from a spouse who is party to a dissolution of marriage or legal separation action, which includes the court and case number of the action, creditors are required by law to provide information as to the balance and account status of any debts for which the requesting spouse may be liable to the creditor. You may wish to use the following form, or one that is similar, to contact your creditors:

Creditor notification

Date: ______________________________

Creditor name and Address: __________________

Within thirty days after receipt of this notice, you are requested to provide the balance and account status of any debt identified by account number for which the requesting party may be liable to you.

Name: ______________________________

Address: ______________________ (signature)

________________________ (printed name)

I. On the written request of any party to a pending dissolution of marriage or legal separation action, the court, except for good cause shown, shall issue an order requiring any credit reporting agency to release the credit report as to the spouse of the requesting party on payment by the requesting party of any customary fee for providing the credit report.

J. On the request of either party and except for good cause shown, the court shall require the parties to submit a debt distribution plan that states the following:

1. How community creditors will be paid.
2. Whether any agreements have been entered into between the parties as to responsibility for the payment of community debts, including what, if any, collateral will secure the payment of the debt.
3. Whether the parties have entered into agreements with creditors through which a community debt will be the sole responsibility of one party.

K. The following form may be used to verify agreements with creditors:

Agreement with creditor

The parties to this agreement include ___________ and ____________ who are parties to a dissolution of marriage action filed in _______________ county superior court, Arizona, case number ___________ and ___________ who is a duly authorized representative of _________________ (creditor).

The undersigned parties agree that the debt owed by the parties to __________________ (creditor) is to be disposed of as follows (check one):

___ The debt is the joint responsibility of the parties, with payment to be made on the following terms:_______________

The balance of the debt is the sole responsibility of _______________ and the creditor releases ______________ from any further liability for that debt, with payment to be made on the following terms:

____

The debt has been paid in full as of this date.

We the undersigned acknowledge this agreement.

Dated: ______________________ **Debtor**

_______________ Creditor's representative

Subscribed and sworn to before me this _____ day of _________, _____. ______________ Notary Public

L. If the parties are not able to agree to a joint debt distribution plan pursuant to subsection J, the court may order each party to submit a proposed debt distribution plan to the court. In its orders relating to the division of property, the court shall reflect the debt distribution plan approved by the court and shall confirm that any community debts that are made the sole responsibility of one of the parties by agreement with a creditor are the sole responsibility of that party.

M. An agreement with a creditor pursuant to subsection K that assigns or otherwise modifies repayment responsibility for community debts secured by real property located in this state shall include all of the following:

1. A legal description of the real property.
2. A copy of the note and recorded security instrument, the repayment of which is to be assigned or modified by the agreement with a creditor.
3. A written and notarized acknowledgment that is executed by all parties to the debt, including the lender, and that states one of the following:

(a) The terms for the repayment of the debt remain unchanged.

(b) The terms for the repayment of the debt have been modified and, beginning on the date of the execution of the acknowledgment, the creditor has agreed that one of the debtors assumes the sole responsibility for the debt and that the other debtor is released from any further liability on the debt.

(c) The debt is paid in full and all parties to the debt are released from any further liability.

N. An agreement executed pursuant to subsection M shall be recorded by either party in the county in which the real property is located.

O. After an agreement is recorded pursuant to subsection N, either party may request that on payment of the title company's fees for the document a title company authorized to do business in this state provide the requesting party with a lien search report or other documentary evidence of liens and other agreements of record in the title to the property.

P. If a party fails to comply with an order to pay debts, the court may enter orders transferring property of that spouse to compensate the other party. If the court finds that a party is in contempt as to an order to pay community debts, the court may impose appropriate sanctions under the law. A party must bring an action to enforce an order to pay a debt pursuant to this subsection within two years after the date in which the debt should have been paid in full.

Q. Within thirty days after receipt of a written request for information from a spouse who is a party to a dissolution of marriage or legal separation action, which includes the court and case number of the action, a creditor shall provide the balance and account status of any debts of either or both spouses identified by account number for which the requesting spouse may be liable to the creditor.

R. If any part of the court's division of joint, common or community property is in the nature of child support or spousal maintenance, the court shall make specific findings of fact and supporting conclusions of law in its decree.

A.R.S. §25-319. Maintenance; Computation Factors

A. In a proceeding for dissolution of marriage or legal separation, or a proceeding for maintenance following dissolution of the marriage by a court that lacked personal jurisdiction over the absent spouse, the court may grant a maintenance order for either spouse for any of the following reasons if it finds that the spouse seeking maintenance:

1. Lacks sufficient property, including property apportioned to the spouse, to provide for that spouse's reasonable needs.
2. Is unable to be self-sufficient through appropriate employment or is the custodian of a child whose age or condition is such that the custodian should not be required to seek employment outside the home or lacks earning ability in the labor market adequate to be self-sufficient.
3. Contributed to the educational opportunities of the other spouse.
4. Had a marriage of long duration and is of an age that may preclude the possibility of gaining employment adequate to be self-sufficient.

B. The maintenance order shall be in an amount and for a period of time as the court deems just, without regard to marital misconduct, and after considering all relevant factors, including:

1. The standard of living established during the marriage.
2. The duration of the marriage.
3. The age, employment history, earning ability and physical and emotional condition of the spouse seeking maintenance.
4. The ability of the spouse from whom maintenance is sought to meet that spouse's needs while meeting those of the spouse seeking maintenance.
5. The comparative financial resources of the spouses, including their comparative earning abilities in the labor market.
6. The contribution of the spouse seeking maintenance to the earning ability of the other spouse.
7. The extent to which the spouse seeking maintenance has reduced that spouse's income or career opportunities for the benefit of the other spouse.
8. The ability of both parties after the dissolution to contribute to the future educational costs of their mutual children.
9. The financial resources of the party seeking maintenance, including marital property apportioned to that spouse, and that spouse's ability to meet that spouse's own needs independently.
10. The time necessary to acquire sufficient education or training to enable the party seeking maintenance to find appropriate employment and whether such education or training is readily available.
11. Excessive or abnormal expenditures, destruction, concealment or fraudulent disposition of community, joint tenancy and other property held in common.
12. The cost for the spouse who is seeking maintenance to obtain health insurance and the reduction in the cost of health insurance for the spouse from whom maintenance is sought if the spouse from whom maintenance is sought is able to convert family health insurance to employee health insurance after the marriage is dissolved.
13. All actual damages and judgments from conduct that results in criminal conviction of either spouse in which the other spouse or child was the victim.

C. If both parties agree, the maintenance order and a decree of dissolution of marriage or of legal separation may state that its maintenance terms shall not be modified.

D. Except as provided in subsection C of this section or section 25-317, subsection G, the court shall maintain continuing jurisdiction over the issue of maintenance for the period of time maintenance is awarded.

A.R.S. §25-320. Child Support; Factors; Methods of Payment; Additional Enforcement Provisions; Definitions

A. In a proceeding for dissolution of marriage, legal separation, maintenance or child support, the court may order either or both parents owing a duty of support to a child, born to or adopted by the parents, to pay an amount reasonable and necessary for support of the child, without regard to marital misconduct.

B. If child support has not been ordered by a child support order and if the court deems child support appropriate, the court shall direct, using a retroactive application of the child support guidelines to the date of filing a dissolution of marriage, legal separation, maintenance or child support proceeding, the amount that the parents shall pay for the past support of the child and the manner in which payment shall be paid, taking into account any amount of temporary or voluntary support that has been paid. Retroactive child support is enforceable in any manner provided by law.

C. If the parties lived apart before the date of the filing for dissolution of marriage, legal separation, maintenance or child support and if child support has not been ordered by a child support order, the court may order child support retroactively to the date of separation, but not more than three years before the date of the filing for dissolution of marriage, legal separation, maintenance or child support. The court must first consider all relevant circumstances, including the conduct or motivation of the parties in that filing and the diligence with which service of process was attempted on the obligor spouse or was frustrated by the obligor spouse. If the court determines that child support is appropriate, the court shall direct, using a retroactive application of the child support guidelines, the amount that the parents must pay for the past support of the child and the manner in which payments must be paid, taking into account any amount of temporary or voluntary support that has been paid.

D. The supreme court shall establish guidelines for determining the amount of child support. The amount resulting from the application of these guidelines is the amount of child support ordered unless a written finding is made, based on criteria approved by the supreme court, that application of the guidelines would be inappropriate or unjust in a particular case. The supreme court shall review the guidelines at least once every four years to ensure that their application results in the determination of appropriate child support amounts. The supreme court shall base the guidelines and criteria for deviation from them on all relevant factors, including:

1. The financial resources and needs of the child.
2. The financial resources and needs of the custodial parent.
3. The standard of living the child would have enjoyed had the marriage not been dissolved.
4. The physical and emotional condition of the child, and the child's educational needs.
5. The financial resources and needs of the noncustodial parent.
6. The medical support plan for the child. The plan should include the child's medical support needs, the availability of medical insurance or services provided by the Arizona health care cost containment system and whether a cash medical support order is necessary.
7. Excessive or abnormal expenditures, destruction, concealment or fraudulent disposition of community, joint tenancy and other property held in common.
8. The duration of parenting time and related expenses.

E. Even if a child is over the age of majority when a petition is filed or at the time of the final decree, the court may order support to continue past the age of majority if all of the following are true:

1. The court has considered the factors prescribed in subsection D of this section.
2. The child is severely mentally or physically disabled as demonstrated by the fact that the child is unable to live independently and be self-supporting.
3. The child's disability began before the child reached the age of majority.

F. If a child reaches the age of majority while the child is attending high school or a certified high school equivalency program, support shall continue to be provided during the period in which the child is actually attending high school or the equivalency program but only until the child reaches nineteen years of age unless the court enters an order pursuant to subsection E of this section. Notwithstanding any other law, a parent paying support for a child over the age of majority pursuant to this section is entitled to obtain all records related to the attendance of the child in the high school or equivalency program.

G. If a personal check for support payments and handling fees is rightfully dishonored by the payor bank or other drawee, the person obligated to pay support shall make any subsequent support payments and handling fees only by cash, money order, cashier's check, traveler's check or certified check. If a person required to pay support other than by personal check demonstrates full and timely payment for twenty-four consecutive months, that person may pay support by personal check if these payments are for the full amount, are timely tendered and are not rightfully dishonored by the payor bank or other

drawee.
H. Subsection G of this section does not apply to payments made by means of an assignment.
I. If after reasonable efforts to locate the obligee the clerk or support payment clearinghouse is unable to deliver payments for the period prescribed in section 25-503 due to the failure of the person to whom the support has been ordered to be paid to notify the clerk or support payment clearinghouse of a change in address, the clerk or support payment clearinghouse shall not deliver further payments and shall return the payments to the obligor consistent with the requirements of section 25-503.
J. An order for child support shall assign responsibility for providing medical insurance for the child who is the subject of the support order and shall assign responsibility for the payment of any medical costs of the child that are not covered by insurance. Each parent shall provide information to the court regarding the availability of medical insurance for the child that is accessible and available at a reasonable cost. In title IV-D cases, the parent responsible pursuant to court order for providing medical insurance for the child shall notify the child support enforcement agency in the department of economic security if medical insurance has been obtained or if the child is no longer covered under an insurance plan.
K. If the court finds that neither parent has the ability to obtain medical insurance for the child that is accessible and available at a reasonable cost, the court shall:
1. Establish a reasonable monthly cash medical support order to be paid by the obligor. If medical assistance is being provided to a child under title XIX of the social security act, cash medical support is assigned to the state pursuant to section 46-407.
2. Order one parent to provide medical insurance when it becomes accessible and available at a reasonable cost.
3. Order that medical costs in excess of the cash medical support amount shall be paid by each parent according to the percentage assigned for payment of uninsured costs.
L. If the court orders one parent to provide medical insurance the court shall also set an alternative cash medical support order to be paid by that parent if the child is not covered under an insurance plan within ninety days after entry of the order or if the child is no longer covered by insurance.
M. In title IV-D cases the superior court shall accept for filing any documents that are received through electronic transmission if the electronically reproduced document states that the copy used for the electronic transmission was certified before it was electronically transmitted.
N. The court shall presume, in the absence of contrary testimony, that a parent is capable of full-time employment at least at the applicable state or federal adult minimum wage, whichever is higher. This presumption does not apply to noncustodial parents who are under the age of eighteen and who are attending high school.
O. An order for support shall provide for an assignment pursuant to sections 25-504 and 25-323.
P. Each licensing board or agency that issues professional, recreational or occupational licenses or certificates shall record on the application the social security number of the applicant and shall enter this information in its database in order to aid the department of economic security in locating parents or their assets or to enforce child support orders. This subsection does not apply to a license that is issued pursuant to title 17 and that is not issued by an automated drawing system. If a licensing board or agency allows an applicant to use a number other than the social security number on the face of the license or certificate while the licensing board or agency keeps the social security number on file, the licensing board or agency shall advise an applicant of this fact.
Q. For the purposes of this section:
1. "Accessible" means that insurance is available in the geographic region where the child resides.
2. "Child support guidelines" means the child support guidelines that are adopted by the state supreme court pursuant to 42 United States Code sections 651 through 669B.
3. "Date of separation" means the date the married parents ceased to cohabit.
4. "Reasonable cost" means an amount that does not exceed the higher of five per cent of the gross income of the obligated parent or an income-based numeric standard that is prescribed in the child support guidelines.
5. "Support" has the same meaning prescribed in section 25-500.
6. "Support payments" means the amount of money ordered by the court to be paid for the support of the minor child or children.

A.R.S. §25-402. Definitions

In this article, unless the context otherwise requires:
1. "Joint custody" means joint legal custody or joint physical custody, or both.
2. "Joint legal custody" means the condition under which both parents share legal custody and neither parent's rights are superior, except with respect to

specified decisions as set forth by the court or the parents in the final judgment or order.
3. "Joint physical custody" means the condition under which the physical residence of the child is shared by the parents in a manner that assures that the child has substantially equal time and contact with both parents.
4. "Parenting time" means the condition under which a parent has the right to have a child physically placed with the parent and the right and responsibility to make, during that placement, routine daily decisions regarding the child's care consistent with the major decisions made by a person having legal custody.
5. "Sole custody" means the condition under which one person has legal custody.

A.R.S. §25-403. Custody; Best Interests of Child

A. The court shall determine custody, either originally or on petition for modification, in accordance with the best interests of the child. The court shall consider all relevant factors, including:
1. The wishes of the child's parent or parents as to custody.
2. The wishes of the child as to the custodian.
3. The interaction and interrelationship of the child with the child's parent or parents, the child's siblings and any other person who may significantly affect the child's best interest.
4. The child's adjustment to home, school and community.
5. The mental and physical health of all individuals involved.
6. Which parent is more likely to allow the child frequent and meaningful continuing contact with the other parent. This paragraph does not apply if the court determines that a parent is acting in good faith to protect the child from witnessing an act of domestic violence or being a victim of domestic violence or child abuse.
7. Whether one parent, both parents or neither parent has provided primary care of the child.
8. The nature and extent of coercion or duress used by a parent in obtaining an agreement regarding custody.
9. Whether a parent has complied with chapter 3, article 5 of this title.
10. Whether either parent was convicted of an act of false reporting of child abuse or neglect under section 13-2907.02.
11. Whether there has been domestic violence or child abuse as defined in section 25-403.03.
B. In a contested custody case, the court shall make specific findings on the record about all relevant factors and the reasons for which the decision is in the best interests of the child.

A.R.S. §25-403.02. Parenting Plans

A. Before an award is made granting joint custody, the parents shall submit a proposed parenting plan that includes at least the following:
1. Each parent's rights and responsibilities for the personal care of the child and for decisions in areas such as education, health care and religious training.
2. A schedule of the physical residence of the child, including holidays and school vacations.
3. A procedure by which proposed changes, disputes and alleged breaches may be mediated or resolved, which may include the use of conciliation services or private counseling.
4. A procedure for periodic review of the plan's terms by the parents.
5. A statement that the parties understand that joint custody does not necessarily mean equal parenting time.
B. If the parents are unable to agree on any element to be included in a parenting plan, the court shall determine that element. The court may determine other factors that are necessary to promote and protect the emotional and physical health of the child.

A.R.S. §25-403.03. Domestic Violence and Child Abuse

A. Notwithstanding subsection D of this section, joint custody shall not be awarded if the court makes a finding of the existence of significant domestic violence pursuant to section 13-3601 or if the court finds by a preponderance of the evidence that there has been a significant history of domestic violence.
B. The court shall consider evidence of domestic violence as being contrary to the best interests of the child. The court shall consider the safety and well-being of the child and of the victim of the act of domestic violence to be of primary importance. The court shall consider a perpetrator's history of causing or threatening to cause physical harm to another person.
C. To determine if a person has committed an act of domestic violence the court, subject to the rules of evidence, shall consider all relevant factors including the following:
1. Findings from another court of competent jurisdiction.

2. Police reports.
3. Medical reports.
4. Child protective services records.
5. Domestic violence shelter records.
6. School records.
7. Witness testimony.

D. If the court determines that a parent who is seeking custody has committed an act of domestic violence against the other parent, there is a rebuttable presumption that an award of custody to the parent who committed the act of domestic violence is contrary to the child's best interests. This presumption does not apply if both parents have committed an act of domestic violence. For the purposes of this subsection, a person commits an act of domestic violence if that person does any of the following:

1. Intentionally, knowingly or recklessly causes or attempts to cause sexual assault or serious physical injury.
2. Places a person in reasonable apprehension of imminent serious physical injury to any person.
3. Engages in a pattern of behavior for which a court may issue an ex parte order to protect the other parent who is seeking child custody or to protect the child and the child's siblings.

E. To determine if the parent has rebutted the presumption the court shall consider all of the following:

1. Whether the parent has demonstrated that being awarded sole custody or joint physical or legal custody is in the child's best interests.
2. Whether the parent has successfully completed a batterer's prevention program.
3. Whether the parent has successfully completed a program of alcohol or drug abuse counseling, if the court determines that counseling is appropriate.
4. Whether the parent has successfully completed a parenting class, if the court determines that a parenting class is appropriate.
5. If the parent is on probation, parole or community supervision, whether the parent is restrained by a protective order that was granted after a hearing.
6. Whether the parent has committed any further acts of domestic violence.

F. If the court finds that a parent has committed an act of domestic violence, that parent has the burden of proving to the court's satisfaction that parenting time will not endanger the child or significantly impair the child's emotional development. If the parent meets this burden to the court's satisfaction, the court shall place conditions on parenting time that best protect the child and the other parent from further harm. The court may:

1. Order that an exchange of the child must occur in a protected setting as specified by the court.
2. Order that an agency specified by the court must supervise parenting time. If the court allows a family or household member to supervise parenting time, the court shall establish conditions that this person must follow during parenting time.
3. Order the parent who committed the act of domestic violence to attend and complete, to the court's satisfaction, a program of intervention for perpetrators of domestic violence and any other counseling the court orders.
4. Order the parent who committed the act of domestic violence to abstain from possessing or consuming alcohol or controlled substances during parenting time and for twenty-four hours before parenting time.
5. Order the parent who committed the act of domestic violence to pay a fee to the court to defray the costs of supervised parenting time.
6. Prohibit overnight parenting time.
7. Require a bond from the parent who committed the act of domestic violence for the child's safe return.
8. Order that the address of the child and the other parent remain confidential.
9. Impose any other condition that the court determines is necessary to protect the child, the other parent and any other family or household member.

G. The court shall not order joint counseling between a victim and the perpetrator of domestic violence. The court may refer a victim to appropriate counseling and shall provide a victim with written information about available community resources related to domestic violence.

H. The court may request or order the services of the division of children and family services in the department of economic security if the court believes that a child may be the victim of child abuse or neglect as defined in section 8-201.

I. In determining whether the absence or relocation of a parent shall be weighed against that parent in determining custody or parenting time, the court may consider whether the absence or relocation was caused by an act of domestic violence by the other parent.

A.R.S. §25-500 Definitions

In this chapter, unless the context otherwise requires:

1. "Arrearage" means the total unpaid support owed, including child support, past support, spousal maintenance and interest.
2. "Business day" means a day when state offices are open for regular business.
3. "Child support guidelines" means the child support guidelines that are adopted by the state supreme

court.
4. "Child support subpoena" means a subpoena issued pursuant to section 25-520.
5. "Department" means the department of economic security.
6. "Income" means any form of payment owed to an individual, regardless of source, including wages, salaries, commissions, bonuses, workers' compensation, disability payments, payments pursuant to a pension or retirement program and interest.
7. "Obligee" means a person or agency entitled to receive support.
8. "Obligor" means a person obligated to pay support.
9. "Support" means the provision of maintenance or subsistence and includes medical insurance coverage, or cash medical support, and uncovered medical costs for the child, arrearages, interest on arrearages, past support, interest on past support and reimbursement for expended public assistance. In a title IV-D case, support includes spousal maintenance that is included in the same order that directs child support.
10. "Support payment clearinghouse" means the clearinghouse established pursuant to section 46-441.
11. "Title IV-D" means title IV-D of the social security act.

A.R.S. §25-803. Persons Who Originate Proceedings; Custody; Parenting Time; Conciliation Court

A. Proceedings to establish the maternity or paternity of a child or children and to compel support under this article may be commenced by any of the following:
1. The mother.
2. The father.
3. The guardian, conservator or best friend of a child or children born out of wedlock.
4. A public welfare official or agency of the county where the child or children reside or may be found.
5. The state pursuant to section 25-509.
B. An adult may bring an action to establish the adult's biological parent.
C. Any party to a proceeding under this article other than the state may request that custody and specific parenting time be determined as a part of the proceeding. When paternity is established the court may award custody and parenting time as provided in section 25-408. The attorney general or county attorney shall not seek or defend any ancillary matters such as custody or parenting time.
D. In any case in which paternity is established the parent with whom the child has resided for the greater part of the last six months shall have legal custody unless otherwise ordered by the court.
E. The services of the conciliation court may be used in regard to disputed matters of custody and parenting time.

A.R.S. §13-3601. Domestic Violence; Definition; Classification; Sentencing Option; Arrest and Procedure for Violation; Weapon Seizure; Notice

A. "Domestic violence" means any act which is a dangerous crime against children as defined in section 13-705 or an offense defined in section 13-1201 through 13-1204, 13-1302 through 13-1304, 13-1502 through 13-1504 or 13-1602, section 13-2810, section 13-2904, subsection A, paragraph 1, 2, 3 or 6, section 13-2916 or section 13-2921, 13-2921.01, 13-2923, 13-3019, 13-3601.02 or 13-3623, if any of the following applies:
1. The relationship between the victim and the defendant is one of marriage or former marriage or of persons residing or having resided in the same household.
2. The victim and the defendant have a child in common.
3. The victim or the defendant is pregnant by the other party.
4. The victim is related to the defendant or the defendant's spouse by blood or court order as a parent, grandparent, child, grandchild, brother or sister or by marriage as a parent-in-law, grandparent-in-law, stepparent, step-grandparent, stepchild, step-grandchild, brother-in-law or sister-in-law.
5. The victim is a child who resides or has resided in the same household as the defendant and is related by blood to a former spouse of the defendant or to a person who resides or who has resided in the same household as the defendant.
6. The relationship between the victim and the defendant is currently or was previously a romantic or sexual relationship. The following factors may be considered in determining whether the relationship between the victim and the defendant is currently or was previously a romantic or sexual relationship:
(a) The type of relationship.
(b) The length of the relationship.
(c) The frequency of the interaction between the victim and the defendant.

(d) If the relationship has terminated, the length of time since the termination.

B. A peace officer, with or without a warrant, may arrest a person if the officer has probable cause to believe that domestic violence has been committed and the officer has probable cause to believe that the person to be arrested has committed the offense, whether the offense is a felony or a misdemeanor and whether the offense was committed within or without the presence of the peace officer. In cases of domestic violence involving the infliction of physical injury or involving the discharge, use or threatening exhibition of a deadly weapon or dangerous instrument, the peace officer shall arrest a person, with or without a warrant, if the officer has probable cause to believe that the offense has been committed and the officer has probable cause to believe that the person to be arrested has committed the offense, whether the offense was committed within or without the presence of the peace officer, unless the officer has reasonable grounds to believe that the circumstances at the time are such that the victim will be protected from further injury. Failure to make an arrest does not give rise to civil liability except pursuant to section 12-820.02. In order to arrest both parties, the peace officer shall have probable cause to believe that both parties independently have committed an act of domestic violence. An act of self-defense that is justified under chapter 4 of this title is not deemed to be an act of domestic violence. The release procedures available under section 13-3883, subsection A, paragraph 4 and section 13-3903 are not applicable to arrests made pursuant to this subsection.

C. A peace officer may question the persons who are present to determine if a firearm is present on the premises. On learning or observing that a firearm is present on the premises, the peace officer may temporarily seize the firearm if the firearm is in plain view or was found pursuant to a consent to search and if the officer reasonably believes that the firearm would expose the victim or another person in the household to a risk of serious bodily injury or death. A firearm that is owned or possessed by the victim shall not be seized unless there is probable cause to believe that both parties independently have committed an act of domestic violence.

D. If a firearm is seized pursuant to subsection C of this section, the peace officer shall give the owner or possessor of the firearm a receipt for each seized firearm. The receipt shall indicate the identification or serial number or other identifying characteristic of each seized firearm. Each seized firearm shall be held for at least seventy-two hours by the law enforcement agency that seized the firearm.

E. If a firearm is seized pursuant to subsection C of this section, the victim shall be notified by a peace officer before the firearm is released from temporary custody.

F. If there is reasonable cause to believe that returning a firearm to the owner or possessor may endanger the victim, the person who reported the assault or threat or another person in the household, the prosecutor shall file a notice of intent to retain the firearm in the appropriate superior, justice or municipal court. The prosecutor shall serve notice on the owner or possessor of the firearm by certified mail. The notice shall state that the firearm will be retained for not more than six months following the date of seizure. On receipt of the notice, the owner or possessor may request a hearing for the return of the firearm, to dispute the grounds for seizure or to request an earlier return date. The court shall hold the hearing within ten days after receiving the owner's or possessor's request for a hearing. At the hearing, unless the court determines that the return of the firearm may endanger the victim, the person who reported the assault or threat or another person in the household, the court shall order the return of the firearm to the owner or possessor.

G. A peace officer is not liable for any act or omission in the good faith exercise of the officer's duties under subsections C, D, E and F of this section.

H. Each indictment, information, complaint, summons or warrant that is issued and that involves domestic violence shall state that the offense involved domestic violence and shall be designated by the letters DV. A domestic violence charge shall not be dismissed or a domestic violence conviction shall not be set aside for failure to comply with this subsection.

I. A person who is arrested pursuant to subsection B of this section may be released from custody in accordance with the Arizona rules of criminal procedure or any other applicable statute. Any order for release, with or without an appearance bond, shall include pretrial release conditions that are necessary to provide for the protection of the alleged victim and other specifically designated persons and may provide for additional conditions that the court deems appropriate, including participation in any counseling programs available to the defendant.

J. When a peace officer responds to a call alleging that domestic violence has been or may be committed, the officer shall inform in writing any alleged or potential victim of the procedures and resources available for the protection of the victim including:

1. An order of protection pursuant to section 13-3602, an injunction pursuant to section 25-315 and an injunction against harassment pursuant to section 12-1809.

2. The emergency telephone number for the local police agency.
3. Telephone numbers for emergency services in the local community.
K. A peace officer is not civilly liable for noncompliance with subsection J of this section.
L. An offense that is included in domestic violence carries the classification prescribed in the section of this title in which the offense is classified. If the defendant committed a felony offense listed in subsection A of this section against a pregnant victim and knew that the victim was pregnant or if the defendant committed a felony offense causing physical injury to a pregnant victim and knew that the victim was pregnant, section 13-709.04, subsection B applies to the sentence imposed.

M. If the defendant is found guilty of a first offense included in domestic violence, the court shall provide the following written notice to the defendant:
You have been convicted of an offense included in domestic violence. You are now on notice that:
1. If you are convicted of a second offense included in domestic violence, you may be placed on supervised probation and may be incarcerated as a condition of probation.
2. A third or subsequent charge may be filed as a felony and a conviction for that offense shall result in a term of incarceration.
N. The failure or inability of the court to provide the notice required under subsection M of this section does not preclude the use of the prior convictions for any purpose otherwise permitted.

Appendix B:

RULES OF FAMILY LAW

APPENDIX B: RULES OF FAMILY LAW

Rules of Family Law Procedures can be found online at www.supreme.state.az.us/rules/ramd-pdf/R-05-0008.pdf, but here are some of the most commonly used rules for your convenience. If you read the rules from the Internet, make sure you are reading the current year's rules, because they change from time to time, usually in January. If you have any questions about your case, you should ask an attorney.

Rule 40 (F) Service of Process, Voluntary

Rule 41 (2) Service of Process by Certified Mail

Rule 43 (D) Filing of Pleadings with the Court Clerk

Rule 44 Default Decree

Rule 45 Consent Decree

Rule 47 Temporary Orders

Rule 49 Disclosure Requirements

Rule 66 Settlement and Alternative Dispute Resolution (ADR)

Rule 67 Private Mediations, Settlement Conferences

Rule 68 Conciliation Court

Rule 69 Binding Agreements

Rule 70 Settlement

Rule 76 Resolution Management Conference (RMC)

Form 8 Consent Decree

Appendix C:

GLOSSARY OF FAMILY LAW DEFINITIONS

APPENDIX C: GLOSSARY OF FAMILY LAW DEFINITIONS

Access, Visitation, Parenting Time: Words used to describe the schedule of time that a child has with each parent.

Admissions: Statements that you agree or disagree. Usually, this comes in the form of a formal request from one party to the other.

Advanced Fee: This was formerly known as a "retainer," which is money that an attorney usually requires before beginning your case.

Affidavit: A sworn statement of fact signed by the author and witnessed by another, usually a notary.

Affidavit of Financial Information: This required document must be filed if a party wants child support or spousal maintenance. It is a court form.

Alternative Dispute Resolution (ADR): Ways to solve legal problems without a trial. Examples include mediation, resolution management conference or other settlement methods.

Annulment: In some states, it was possible to receive an "Annulment." This was a document that declared that the legal marriage never occurred in the first place.

Arrearages: Past child support or spousal maintenance payments which have not been made. A.R.S. § 25-500: The total unpaid support owed, including child support, past support, spousal maintenance and interest.

A.R.S. (Arizona Revised Statutes): This is a set of laws that governs Arizona, including Family Law. They can be found at: http://www.azleg.state.az.us/arizonarevisedstatutes.asp.

Attachment: Positive feelings of the child toward parents and other parent figures.

Best Interest of the Child: When a judge decides what would be best for the child in a custody or parenting plan issue, based on all the information. A standard by which a court determines what arrangements would be to a child's greatest benefit, often used in deciding child-custody and visitation matters and in deciding whether to approve an adoption or a guardianship. A.R.S. § 25-403: A custody determination shall be made in accordance with the best interests of the child. All relevant factors shall be considered, including: (1) the wishes of the child's parent(s) as to custody, (2) the wishes of the child as to the custodian, (3) the interaction and interrelationship of the child with the child's parent(s), the child's siblings, (4) the child's adjustment to home, school and community, (5) the mental and physical health or all individuals involved, (6) which parent is more likely to allow the child frequent and meaning continuing contact with the other parent, (7) whether one parent, both parents or neither parent has provided primary care of the child, and (8) the nature and extent of coercion or duress used by a parent in obtaining an agreement regarding custody.

Bonding: Close relationship that develops between a young child and a parent or a parent figure.

Child Custody: The care, control and maintenance of a child awarded by a court to a responsible adult. Custody involves legal custody (decision-making authority) and physical custody (care giving authority). A.R.S. §25-402(2).

Child Support: Financial support ordered to be paid by one parent to the other parent for support of a child. The amount is calculated by statutory guidelines, called Child Support Guidelines, which are calculated and reflected in a Child Support Worksheet. A.R.S. § 25-320: In a proceeding for dissolution of marriage, legal separation, maintenance or child support it may be ordered that either or both parents owing a duty of support to a child and pay an amount reasonable and necessary for support of the child, without regard to marital misconduct. When determining the amount of child support owed, income is normally the most important factor. This not only includes standard paycheck wages, but also bonuses, commission payments, overtime, disability payments, Social Security income, income from rental properties, and income from intellectual property, such as royalties. The court can also view stock option plans (which are non-retirement) as income. If one spouse is not working, the judge can still assume that this non-custodial parent is capable of obtaining a job at minimum wage for 40 hours a week.

Co-Parenting: When parents share the responsibility for raising a child, even when the parents do not live together.

Community Property: The body of law in Arizona which creates a presumption that property and debt acquired during a marriage belongs to both parties and require such property and debt to be divided equitably during a divorce. A.R.S. § 25-211: "All property acquired by either husband or wife during the marriage is the community property of the husband and wife except for property that is: (1) acquired by gift, devise or descent (2) acquired after service of a petition for dissolution..." **Community Property**: also includes pensions, benefits, stock plans, accrued vacation, deferred compensation, frequent flier miles, publishing rights, copyrights, patents, or anything else of value acquired during the marriage.

Conciliation: An alternative dispute resolution (ADR) process, whereby the parties in a divorce agree to utilize the services of a conciliator, who then meets with the parties in an attempt to resolve their differences and determine if any agreements can be made.

Conciliation Services: Services provided by Maricopa County. These details change frequently, so you should always review their website. They provide parenting conferences, mediation and early resolution conferences.

Confidentiality: Private information that cannot be shared with anyone else, except as required by law.

Consent Decree: An agreement that ends the marriage. Both parties sign and agree to the terms of the decree.

Contested Divorce: One in which your spouse is contesting your Petition for Dissolution. By contesting the petition, they will have actually filed a response with the court. The filing of the response will not prevent a future Consent Decree/Marital Settlement Agreement from being reached. In fact, the most likely scenario is that they will respond and then later work out an agreement between your attorney and theirs. This usually occurs after discovery has been concluded. If a Marital Settlement Agreement is still not reached, it is at this time that a trial will occur.

Court Appointed Attorneys for Children (Guardian ad Litum): Only rarely will a court appoint attorneys for children, but they may do so if the judge finds that the parent's position may be in conflict with the best interests of the child. Sometimes this will occur if the child is insisting on being with one parent, although a judge may feel that it conflicts with their best interest. This also helps prevent the parties from playing tug-of-war with their child.

Court Order: A written order made by a judge that must be followed.

Covenant Marriage: Special marriage designated on the marriage license. It is more difficult to get divorced if you have a covenant marriage.

Decree of Dissolution: This is the Final Judgment or Decree that will restore you and your former spouse's status of unmarried persons. They will also set out the final rulings regarding child custody, child support, property division, and other important issues regarding the termination of the marriage.

Default Judgment: A default occurs when a spouse is not responding to the Petition for Dissolution within the required amount of time (20 days if your spouse is an Arizona resident; 30 days for an out-of-state resident). Once the time limit has run out and if your spouse has failed to respond, you can then file for a Notice of Default with the court. This has the effect of asking the court to grant everything that you have asked for in your petition. Once you have filed the Notice of Default, your spouse has 10 days in which to respond. If they do not respond, then your case will be assigned to a judge to enter a Final Judgment in the form of a Decree of Dissolution. At this default hearing, you must be present at court, otherwise the judge cannot sign the decree and give you your copy.

Depositions: Court-ordered interviews that are normally conducted with both attorneys present, along with a court reporter.

Discovery Process: Discovery is the term used to describe the process by which each party is allowed to examine all possible evidence that may support their claims. In Arizona, both spouses must disclose, in writing, all legal and factual grounds for their alleged defenses and claims.

Dissolution Decree: Same as a divorce decree. The court order that dissolves a marriage and returns parties to the status of single persons and outlines the terms of the divorce, including custody, child support, spousal maintenance and division of community assets. When the parties agree to all the terms of a divorce, they can submit a Consent Decree, signed by each party, to the court for the court's approval. A.R.S. §25-312: A decree of dissolution of marriage shall be entered into if (1) one of the parties, at the time the action was commenced, was domiciled in this state, and that domicile has been maintained for ninety (90) days, (2) the conciliation provisions of § 25-381.09 and the provisions of article 5 either do not apply or have not been met, and (3) the marriage is irretrievably broken.

Dissolution of Marriage: Divorce.

Dissolution: The present day term for a divorce, meaning to dissolve the marriage.

Divorce: The legal process of dissolving a marriage.

Domestic Partnership: A non-marital relationship between two persons of the same or opposite sex who live together as a couple for a significant period of time.

Domestic Violence: Domestic violence is legally defined in Arizona in A.R.S. § 13- 3601(a) as a criminal act of physical, verbal or sexual behavior or threats or intimidation by one partner toward another. Significant domestic violence is a factor considered in determining parenting time decisions under A.R.S. § 25-403.03.

Early Resolution Conference: This is a meeting set for *pro per* clients to meet with court personnel, outside a courtroom setting, to try and resolve the divorce issues.

Emergency Temporary Orders: Can be requested by either party and normally will be heard by the court within 24 hours. These orders are normally based upon a showing of irreparable harm that may befall the children. Usually, there is a child abuse, drug abuse or mental health issue involved in these cases. Many times these orders are heard *Ex Parte* (i.e. with only one party appearing in front of the judge). At the Emergency Order's hearing, the judge will base his information upon declarations and sometimes on brief testimony.

Enforcement: The process of ordering a party to appear before the court for failing to make child support or spousal maintenance payments and requiring the party to pay arrearages.

Exchange: Pick-up and drop-off of a child between parents or other caregivers.

Exhibits: Documentary or other evidence that supports your position. Exhibits can include your Affidavit of Financial Information, bank statements, school records, etc.

Family Law Rules: The Arizona Rules of Family Law Procedure (ARFLP) are the procedure rules that guide family law litigation cases.

Family Law: The laws that relate to family relationships. They include laws about divorce, paternity, custody, parenting plans, property and debt division, child support, spousal support (alimony), and other topics. The laws are based on statutes, rules and reported court decisions.

Filing: Giving your legal papers to the clerk of the court.

Frequent and Continuing Contact: How the law refers to children having regular and ongoing contact with parents.

Full Custody: This is not a legal term defined by law in Arizona. In Arizona, the term is not used and it has no meaning. However, often this term is confused with "sole custody." (See Sole Custody.)

Grandparent Visitation: In certain situations, grandparents and great-grandparents may be entitled to visitation or parenting time with their grandchild under A.R.S. 25-409. A.R.S. § 25-409: Grandparents may be granted reasonable visitations to the child during the child's minority on a finding that the visitation rights would be in the best interests of the child.

Hague Convention: An international convention dealing with international adoption, child laundering and child trafficking.

Hearing: A scheduled appearance in court where parents and attorneys may call witnesses and introduce evidence.

Hearsay: An out-of-court statement offered to prove the truth of the matter asserted. Hearsay is allowed in family law matters, unless one party requests strict compliance with the Rules of Evidence.

Holiday Plan: A part of the parenting plan that specifies how children will spend holidays with each parent and defines each holiday, so both parents know when the holiday begins and ends.

Injunction: Order by the court to refrain from doing something.

In loco parentis: [Latin for "in the place of a parent"] When an individual acts as a guardian or caretaker of a child, taking on all or some of the responsibilities of a parent. A.R.S. § 25-415: A child custody proceeding may be commenced by a person other than a legal parent. An award of custody shall be denied unless, (1) the non-parent stands *in loco parentis* to the child, (2) it would be detrimental to the child to remain or be placed in the custody of either the child's living legal parents who seek custody, (3) an award of custody of the child has not been made within one year, unless there is reason to believe the child's current environment present dangers to the child's physical, mental, moral or emotional health, and (4) one of the legal parents is deceased, the child's legal parents are not married to each other, or there is a pending dissolution of the legal parents.

Interrogatories: Written questions that each party must answer in writing.

Irretrievably Broken/Irreconcilable Differences: These are the only grounds which are recognized for divorce in Arizona. It is not necessary to find that somebody is at fault for the dissolution. All that is required is that one party wishes to get the divorce. (See No Fault).

Joint Legal Custody: Both parents share major decision-making for their children. Neither parent can overrule the other parent, unless specifically allowed by the parenting plan or by court order. See also Legal Custody. (See A.R.S. § 25-402(2).) "The condition under which both parents share legal custody and neither parent's rights are superior…" A.R.S. § 25-402(3).

Joint Physical Custody: The child has roughly the same amount of time and contact with both parents. This does not mean the parents have joint legal custody. See also Physical Custody. (See A.R.S. § 25-402(3))

"Joint physical custody means the condition under which the physical residence of the child is shared by the parents in a manner that assures that the child has substantially equal time and contact with both parents." A.R.S. § 25-408(b): Rights of a noncustodial parent: "…both parents are entitled to custody or parenting time and both parents reside in the state, at least sixty days advance written notice shall be provided to the other parent before a parent may (1) relocate the child outside the state (2) relocate the child more than one hundred miles within the state."

Legal Custody: The right of a parent to make major decisions for the children. Major decisions may include medical care, personal appearance, religion, or education. Custody may be either joint with both parents or sole with one parent. (See A.R.S. § 25-402.)

Legal Separation: A partial or qualified divorce by which the community ends for purposes of community property, assets and debts are split, and child custody, parenting time and support is determined, but the parties remain technically married. A.R.S. § 25-313: A decree of legal separation shall be entered into if: (1) one of the parties, at the time the action was commenced, was domiciled in this state, (2) the conciliation provisions of A.R.S. § 25-381.09 and the provisions of Article 5 either do not apply or have not been met (3) the marriage is irretrievably broken or one of both of the parties desire to live separate and apart, and (4) the other party does not object to a decree of legal separation.

This can be temporary or for an unlimited period of time. It is a legal decree which is issued when the judge determines that there is an irretrievable breakdown of the marriage, or that one spouse desires to live separate and apart from the other spouse. The benefit of the legal separation is that it still leaves open the possibility of reconciliation, and it protects both spouses from the others future debts. One spouse files an objection to the legal separation, it will then be amended to a Petition for Dissolution of the marriage and the divorce process begins.

Litigate: Go to court to resolve issues.

Maiden Name Restoration: A wife's former or maiden name can be changed back upon request in the Petition for Dissolution or by pleading during the divorce.

Marital Settlement Agreement: A written document signed by both parties evidencing the agreement of the split of the parties' assets.

Maternity: A legal action that results in a court order naming the child's mother.

Mediation: A meeting with a mediator who helps the parents try to solve problems cooperatively. Mediation may occur face-to-face or separately, if necessary. Mediation is confidential. The mediator does not tell the parents what they should do or make a recommendation to the court. (See Rule of Family Law Procedure 66.B(4))

Mediator: A trained, neutral third party who helps the parents try to solve problems cooperatively through mediation.

Minute Entry: These are orders generated by the court.

Modification of Parenting Plan: Changes to the parenting plan. If agreed to, the changes can be enforced only if they are submitted to and ordered by the court. If the parties cannot agree, one party can request modification by filing a motion with the court.

Modification: Making changes to a prior agreement, court order or decree. A.R.S. § 25-411: A person shall not make a motion to modify a custody decree earlier than one year after its date, unless there is reason to believe the child's present environment may seriously endanger the child's physical, mental, moral or emotional health.

No Fault: In some states, it is required that one party be at fault for the breakup of the marriage. In Arizona, it is not necessary to have somebody to blame for the end of the marriage; therefore, Arizona is a "No Fault Divorce" state.

Non-Modifiable: This usually refers to a spousal maintenance agreement that cannot be modified. You need to be very careful with this language, because according to Arizona law, spousal maintenance ends when a party dies or the receiving spouse remarries.

Notice to Attend Parent Information Program Classes and Order: This is an official court order, and failure to obey may result in contempt of court. What this means is both you and your spouse must complete these classes within 45 days from the petition being served. Also, these classes must be completed before the judge will finalize your Decree of Dissolution.

Order of Protection: See Protective Order.

Parenting Conference: The parties and children are interviewed by a contract provider hired by the court to interview the family and write a report to the court. The fee varies and at the time of publishing, cost is $300 per person. Children are no additional cost. These are usually conducted by a psychologist.

Parenting Plan: A document that states when the child will be with each parent and how decisions will be made. The parenting plan may be developed by the parents on their own or with the help of a professional such as a mediator, an attorney or a judge.

A plan should allocate custodial responsibility and decision-making authority that serves the child's best interests and provides a mechanism for resolving any later disputes between parents. A.R.S. § 25-403.02: Before joint custody is awarded, the parents shall submit a proposed parenting plan that includes: (1) each parent's rights and responsibilities for the personal care of the child, such as education, health care and religious training, and (2) a schedule of the physical residence of the child, including holidays and school vacations.

Parenting Time: The time a child spends with each parent. This is the present-day term for visitation, during which one parent is awarded set time to have physical control and custody of a child. A.R.S. § 25-402: The condition under which a parent has the right to have a child physically placed with the parent and the right and responsibility to make, during that placement, routine daily decisions regarding the child's care, consistent with the major decisions made by a person having legal custody.

Paternity Action: This is a court proceeding brought forward to determine who is the father of a child.

Paternity: A legal action that results in a court order naming the child's father.

Pendency: The state of being pending, during the process of or in a state that is undecided.

Petition: The filing to start to the divorce.

Petitioner: The person who files the divorce or initiates the action.

Physical Custody: The actual physical residence of the child at any given time. (See and compare Joint Physical Custody and Parenting Time.)

Preliminary Injunction Order: This is the first ruling issued by the court during the dissolution proceeding. It is in effect automatically after service of the petition. This prevents you or your spouse from selling or giving property. It also prevents either you or your spouse from taking your children out of state without the prior written consent of the other spouse. You are prohibited from changing any insurance plans. Lastly, it prevents either you or your spouse from harassing or disturbing the peace of one another.

Prenuptial/Premarital Agreements: These are contracts that are entered into prior to the marriage taking place. These must be in writing and signed by both parties in order to be enforceable. The agreement has to be entered into voluntarily, and it cannot be unconscionable when executed. In addition, both spouses must be fully informed and provided with fair and reasonable disclosure of all the property and financial interests and obligations of the other spouse. In other words, all of your information must be turned over to the other spouse and their lawyer. There is an exception if your future spouse voluntarily waives the disclosure of this information and had adequate previous knowledge of your financial holdings and obligations.

Primary Residence: The parent's home where the child physically resides most of the time.

Pro per: The Latin term that courts use when referring to a party who is representing themselves. This means that the party is not represented by an attorney.

Property Settlement Agreement: This document sets forth the terms of your property agreements.

Protective Order: Refers to four types of orders (Order of Protection, Emergency Order of Protection, Injunction Against Harassment, Injunction Against Workplace Harassment) designed to prevent violence or harassment between parties. Any court in the state can issue these special orders without notice to the defendant. When the orders are set without notice, hearings must be set within 5-10 days at the request of the defendant. (See Rule 1B of the Arizona Rules of Protective Order Procedure.)

Reconciliation Request: When one party strongly believes that the marriage can be saved, they can petition the court to order marriage counseling. This order results in the dissolution proceedings being suspended for up to 120 days while the court determines whether reconciliation is possible and likely.

Redact: A form of editing that covers information that you do not want to disclose on documents.

Relocation ("Move Away" cases): When one spouse wishes to move out of the area, or out of Arizona, and they wish to take the children with them, then very specific steps need to be undertaken. The other parent must receive written notice and they have the opportunity to contest it in the court.

Request for Admissions: A written list of questions asking for very specific admissions that will save time in the preparation of the case (i.e. "Are you the father of the child?" etc.).

Request for Production of Documents: A specific request for certain documents that either side believes will be beneficial to their case.

Residency/Jurisdiction: One of the two spouses must live in Arizona for at least 90 days before the filing of a Petition for Dissolution. Residency is required in order for the court to have jurisdiction. Once the petition is filed, there is a 60-day waiting period after service of process on the other spouse before any divorce can become final. In regards to legal separation, there are no residency requirements specified, and that action can be filed at any time after one spouse establishes residency within the state of Arizona.

Resolution Management Conference: Courtroom meeting set by the court so the parties can meet the judge and discuss the case. The judge will want to meet if there are any settlements, stipulations, need for a parenting conference, conciliation, mediation or a trial date. If you do not have an attorney, you will have an Early Resolution Conference instead.

Resolution Management Statement: A court-ordered form required to be filled out and filed with the court before the management conference.

Respondent: The person who must file an answer to the divorce pleading.

Rules of Court: Court procedures are controlled by rules. Family law is controlled by the Arizona Rules of Family Law Procedure (ARFLP). The ARFLP can also be supplemented by local county rules. The ARFLP can be found at the local law library or at:
http://www.supreme.state.az.us/rules/ra md_pdf/R-05-0008.pdf.

Section or §: Specific portion of the law.

Service of Process/Summons: Once a Petition for Dissolution is filed with the court, the petitioner must have the summons and other required documents and notices served on the respondent. The best way to achieve service of process is to use a private process server. Once your spouse has been served, they must respond to the petition within 20 days, or the court may grant all relief you have requested (i.e. a Default Judgment).

Sole Custody: When only one parent has the right to make major legal decisions for the child. The sole legal custodian may not change the parenting time of the other parent without agreement. (See Legal Custody.)

Spousal Maintenance: Money paid by one married person to another for support after a divorce or legal separation. A.R.S. § 25-500: "'Support' means the provision of maintenance or subsistence and includes medical insurance coverage, or cash medical support, and uncovered medical costs for the child, arrearages, interest on arrearages, past support, interest on past support and reimbursement for expended public assistance. In a title IV-D case, support includes spousal maintenance that is included in the same order that directs child support."

Statute: A law passed by the state legislature (or adopted by initiative). Most code sections relating to family law are in Title 25 of the Arizona Revised Statutes (A.R.S.) and are available at the county law library or on the Internet at: www.azleg.state.az.us/ArizonaRevisedStatutes.asp.

Stipulation: A formal agreement of the parties. When it is written and signed by both parties and then approved by a judge, it becomes a court order.

Supervised Exchanges: Pick-up and drop-off of the child in the presence of another specified adult.

Supervised Parenting Time: Parenting time during which the parent and child must be in the presence of another specified adult.

TASC or **Treatment Assessment Screening Center**: This is an organization devoted to drug and mental health assessment. According to their website at www.tascaz.org, TASC has a state-of-the-art drugs of abuse testing laboratory onsite to provide the high-quality drug testing analyses. There are locations all over the Valley.

Temporary Orders: Orders that can be entered by the court before the divorce is final. A motion must be filed and a hearing date is set. Evidence is provided to the court in a mini trial. It normally takes a couple of months to be heard by the court.

Therapeutic Supervision: Supervision of parent-child contacts provided by a therapist.

Transition: The adjustment time for parents and the child immediately before, during and after the exchange of the child between the parents or other caregivers.

Trial: A formal hearing with witnesses and evidence. (See Hearing).

Uncontested Divorce: The type of divorce where your spouse does not file a response to the Petition for Dissolution. This can either result in a Default

Judgment, or they may have contacted you and simply entered into a Consent Decree/Marital Settlement Agreement, without any official fight or contest taking place in court.

Wage Assignment: The process whereby child support or spousal maintenance is automatically taken from your check. Your employer pays this support payment directly to the state for distribution.

Virtual Parenting: Parenting time facilitated by electronic means to supplement, but not replace, in-person parenting time. Examples include telephone calls, web cam, videoconferencing, instant messaging, online chatting, telephone texting, etc.

Visitation: This term is no longer preferred. Instead, see Access, Parenting Plan or Parenting Time.

Appendix D:

RESOURCE GUIDE

APPENDIX D: RESOURCE GUIDE

Courthouses (Superior Court)

Maricopa County

1. Maricopa Co. Superior Court: **Northeast Regional Court** Complex, 602-506-3360
   18380 N. 40th St., Phoenix 85032
   http://www.clerkofcourt.maricopa.gov/ne_court.asp

2. Maricopa County Superior Court: **Northwest Court** Complex, 602-506-3360
   14264 W. Tierra Buena Lane, Surprise 85374
   http://www.clerkofcourt.maricopa.gov/northwest_loc.asp

3. Maricopa Co. Superior Court: **Downtown Phoenix Court** Complex, 602-506-3204
   101/201 W. Jefferson, Phoenix 85003-2205
   http://www.superiorcourt.maricopa.gov/courtinformation/locations/index.asp

4. Maricopa Co. Superior Court: **Southeast Regional Court** Complex, 602-506-3360
   222 E. Javelina Ave., Mesa 85210-6201
   http://www.clerkofcourt.maricopa.gov/se_court.asp

5. Maricopa County Superior Court: **Old Courthouse**
   125 W. Washington, Phoenix 85003

6. Maricopa County Superior Court: **West Court**
   111 S. Third Ave., Phoenix 85003-2243

Other Counties

Apache County Superior Court, 928-337-7550
P.O. Box 365, St. Johns 85936
http://www.apacheclerk.net or http://www.co.apache.az.us

Cochise County Superior Court, 520-432-8601
P.O. Drawer CK, Bisbee 85603
http://www.cochise.az.gov

Coconino County Superior Court, 928-679-7600
200 N. San Francisco, Flagstaff 86001
http://www.coconino.az.gov

Gila County Superior Court, 928-402-8866
1400 E. Ash, Globe 85501
http://supreme.state.az.us/gilasc

Graham County Superior Court, 928-428-3100
800 Main St., Safford 85546
http://www.graham.az.gov

Greenlee County Superior Court, 928-865-4242
P.O. Box 1027, Clifton 85533
http://www.co.greenlee.az.us/

La Paz County Superior Court, 928-669-6134
1316 S. Kofa Ave., Suite 607, Parker 85344-5724
http://www.co.la-paz.az.us/

Mohave County Superior Court, 928-753-0790
401 Spring St., Kingman 86401
http://www.mohavecourts.com/

Navajo County Superior Court, 928-524-4000
100 East Carter Dr., South Highway 77
P.O. Box 668 Holbrook 86025
http://www.navajocountyaz.gov/

Pima County Superior Court, 520-740-3200
110 W. Congress St., Tucson 85701-1317
http://www.cosc.pima.gov

Pinal County Superior Court, 520-866-5400
971 Jason Lopez Circle, Building A, Florence 85132
http://www.pinalcountyaz.gov/Departments/JudicialBranch/Home.aspx

Santa Cruz County Superior Court, 520-375-7700
2150 N. Congress Dr., Nogales 85621
http://www.co.santa-cruz.az.us/clerk/index.html

Yavapai County Superior Court, 928-771-3100
120 S. Cortez St., Prescott 86303
http://www.co.yavapai.az.us/clerksupct.aspx

Yuma County Superior Court, 928-373-1010
198 S. Main St., Yuma 85364
http://www.yumacountyaz.gov/

Law Resources

7. Maricopa County Superior Court: **Law Library**
   http://www.superiorcourt.maricopa.gov/lawlibrary/

8. Arizona **Rules of Family Law** Procedure
   http://www.azcourts.gov/rules/recentamendments/morerules/ArizonaRulesofFamilyLawProcedure.aspx

Support Services

9. Maricopa County **Family Support Center**, 602-506-3762
   http://www.familysupportcenter.com/

10. State of Arizona Supreme Court: **Self-Service Center**, 602-506-7353
www.azcourts.gov/Default.aspx?alias=www.azcourts.gov/SelfService

11. Arizona Department of **Economic Security**
http://www.azdes.gov/

12. Ariz. Dept. of Econ. Security **Child Support Enforcement**, 602-252-4045
http://www.azdes.gov/dcse/

13. Maricopa County Superior Court: **Conciliation Services**
http://www.superiorcourt.maricopa.gov/SuperiorCourt/FamilyCourt/Services/ConciliationServices/index.asp

14. Maricopa County Superior Court: **Case Information**
http://www.superiorcourt.maricopa.gov/docket/index.asp

15. Maricopa County Superior Court: **Guide for Parents** Living Apart
http://www.azcourts.gov/Portals/31/ParentingTime/PPWguidelines.pdf and Planning for Parenting Time: Arizona's **Guide for Parents** Living Apart(2009)
http://www.azcourts.gov/familylaw/ChildrenFamilyIssues.aspx

16. Model **Parenting Time Plans** for Parent/Child Access (2001)
http://www.superiorcourt.maricopa.gov/sscDocs/pdf/drv10h.pdf

17. Maricopa County Superior Court: **Divorce/Parenting Issues**
http://www.azcourts.gov/familylaw/DivorceParentingIssues.aspx

18. Maricopa County Superior Court: **Counseling Resources**, 602-263-8856
www.superiorcourt.maricopa.gov/superiorcourt/familycourt/resources.asp

19. **Catholic Social Service** of Central and Northern Arizona, 928-774-9125
http://www4.nau.edu/csw/Directory/catholic.html

Violence and Family Services

20. Chrysalis **Shelter for Victims of Domestic Violence**, Inc., 602-955-9059
http://www.noabuse.org/

21. **Jewish Family and Children's Service**, 602-279-7655
http://www.jfcsaz.org/

22. **Native American Community Health** Center, Inc., 602-279-5262
http://www.nativehealthphoenix.com/

23. Organization for **Non-Violence Education**, 623-934-0696
http://www.oneincusa.org/

24. Sojourner Center: **Domestic Violence Shelter**, 602-244-0089
http://www.sojournercenter.org/go2/index.php

25. **Child Crisis Center**, 480-969-2308
http://www.childcrisis.org/

26. Crisis Nursery, Inc.: **Child Abuse Shelter**, 602-273-7363
http://www.crisisnurseryphx.org/nursery/

27. West Valley Child Crisis Center: **Foster and Adoption Services** 623-848-8863
http://www.wvccc.org/

Appendix E:

END NOTES

APPENDIX E: END NOTES

[i] A.R.S. §25-312 outlines the Arizona requirements for divorce.
[ii] Domicile means a party's residence, but a temporary absence necessitated by business, occupation, or military service does not defeat residence. (36 A.L.R.2d at 763 (1954).) Page 105 in Practice Guide.
[iii] *From an article titled "After the Split" in the August 16, 1998 edition of The Kansas City Star MoneyWise section, written by staffer Gene Meyer, quoted by Diane Sollee on the Coalition for Marriage, Family and Couples Education,LLC (CMFCE) listserv*
[iv] Moore, Marsha K., "Interest of the Child," http://www.familyfriendpoems.com/family/poetry.asp?poem=1402, 2006.
[v] Best Interest Of The Child, Divorce Poems
http://www.familyfriendpoems.com/family/poetry.asp?poem=1402#ixzz0uucg91jg
[vi] http://www.azcadv.org/domestic-violence-info/domestic-violence-fa/definitions-of-domes/top.
[vii] (US Department of Health and Human Services, Administration for Children and Families, Fact Sheet, April 2000)
[viii] (Bureau of Justice Statistics Report. *Intimate Partner Violence*, United States Department of Justice, May 2000. NCJ 178247)
[ix] (Sandra Graham-Bermann & Julie Seng, *Violence Exposure and Traumatic Stress Symptoms as Additional Predictors of Health Problems in High-Risk Children*, 146 J. of Pediatrics 309 (2005).
[x] Sharmila Lawrence, National Center for Children in Poverty, Domestic Violence and Welfare Policy: *Research Findings That Can Inform Policies on Marriage and Child Well-Being* 5 (2002).
[xi] (American Bar Association, Judicial Subcommittee of the American Bar Association's Commission on Domestic Violence, Judicial Checklist)
[xii] US Department of Health and Human Services, Administration for Children and Families, Domestic Violence Fact Sheet, 1998)
[xiii] ("Battered Mothers' Testimony Project: A Human Rights Approach to Child Custody and Domestic Violence," Arizona Coalition Against Domestic Violence, June 2003.)
[xiv] (Bergen, Issues in Intimate Violence, Sage Publications, 1998)
[xv] (Johnson, MP (2005) Apples and oranges in child custody disputes: Intimate terrorism vs. situational couple violence. Journal of Child Custody. 2(4) 43-52.)
[xvi] (Kernic, M.A., Monary-Ernsdorff, D.J., Koespell, J.K., & Holt, V.L. 92005). Children in the crossfire: Child custody determinations among couples with a history of intimate partner violence. Violence against Women, 11, 991-1021) et al. 2005)
[xvii] (Saunders, D. (2007, October). Child custody and visitation decisions in domestic violence cases: Legal trends, risk factors, and safety concerns. Harrisburg, PA: VAWnet, a project of the National Resource Center on Domestic Violence/Pennsylvania Coalition Against Domestic Violence. Retrieved 05/26/2009, from: http://www.vawnet.org)
[xviii] (Bergen, Issues in Intimate Violence, Sage Publications, 1998)
[xix] (Zorza, Joan. "Batterer Manipulation and Retaliation: Denial & Complicity in the Family Courts." 4 Feminista, (2001) <www.feminista.com/v4n7/zorza.html> (4/24/03)
[xx] (Brown, Molly A. *Child Custody in Cases Involving Domestic Violence: Is it really in the "Best Interest" of Children to Have unrestricted Contact With Their Mother's Abusers?* Journal of the Missouri Bar, November-December 2001)
[xxi] (Jaffe, Peter, Ph.D. "Impact of Domestic Violence on Children and Families in Divorce." Expose: The Failure of Family Courts to Protect Children From Abuse in Custody Disputes – A Resource Book for Lawmakers, Judges, Attorneys, and Mental Health Professionals, los Gatos: Our Children Our Future Charitable Foundation, 1999, 135.)
[xxii] http://www.azcadv.org/domestic-violence-info/domestic-violence-fa/facts-and-statistics/domesticviolenceandcustody/top .("Battered Mothers' Testimony Project: A Human Rights Approach to Child Custody and Domestic Violence," Arizona Coalition Against Domestic Violence, June 2003.
[xxiii] http://www.superiorcourt.maricopa.gov/SuperiorCourt/FamilyCourt/Services/ConciliationServices/

Made in the USA
Monee, IL
06 November 2026

67375738R00136